The Price Reporters

Every consumer in a modern economy is indirectly exposed to the work of a price reporting agency (PRA) each time they fill up their car, take a flight or switch on a light, and yet the general public is completely unaware of the existence of PRAs. Firms like Platts, Argus, ICIS and OPIS, which are referenced every day by commodity traders and which influence billions of dollars of trade, are totally unfamiliar to consumers.

The Price Reporters: A Guide to PRAs and Commodity Benchmarks brings the mysterious world of price reporting out of the shadows for the first time, providing a comprehensive guide to the agencies that set the world's commodity prices. This book explains the importance of PRAs to the global commodities industry, highlighting why PRAs affect every consumer around the world. It introduces the individual PRAs, their history and the current state of play in the industry, and also presents the challenges that the PRA industry is facing now and in the future, in particular how regulation might impact on the PRAs, their relationships with commodity exchanges, and their likely direction.

This is the first-ever guide to PRAs and is destined to become the standard reference work for anyone with an interest in commodity prices and the firms that set them.

Owain Johnson is Managing Director for Energy Research & Product Development at CME Group. He previously served as Managing Director of the Dubai Mercantile Exchange. He has worked for a number of pricing and media companies and has a degree from Cambridge University.

The Price Reporters

A Guide to PRAs and
Commodity Benchmarks

Owain Johnson

Routledge
Taylor & Francis Group

LONDON AND NEW YORK

First published 2018
by Routledge
2 Park Square, Milton Park, Abingdon, Oxon OX14 4RN

and by Routledge
711 Third Avenue, New York, NY 10017

Routledge is an imprint of the Taylor & Francis Group, an informa business

British Library Cataloguing-in-Publication Data
A catalogue record for this book is available from the British Library

Library of Congress Cataloging-in-Publication Data
Names: Johnson, Owain, author. Title: The price reporters : a guide to
PRAs and commodity benchmarks / Owain Johnson. Description: Abingdon,
Oxon ; New York, NY : Routledge, 2018. | Includes bibliographical references
and index. Identifiers: LCCN 2017015118 | ISBN 9781138721555 (hardback) |
ISBN 9781138721562 (pbk.) | ISBN 9781315194271 (ebook) Subjects: LCSH:
Prices. | Price indexes. | Commodity exchanges. Classification: LCC HB221
.J54 2018 | DDC 338.5/2—dc23 LC record available at https://lccn.loc.gov/
2017015118

ISBN: 978-1-138-72155-5 (hbk)
ISBN: 978-1-138-72156-2 (pbk)
ISBN: 978-1-315-19427-1 (ebk)

Typeset in Bembo
by Fish Books Ltd.

Contents

Tables

Acknowledgements

A big thank you to all my current and previous colleagues and customers in the commodities, pricing and derivatives industries for sharing their knowledge and insights with me over the years. It's been an interesting journey.

Preparing this book was a great excuse to get in touch with a large number of people – some old friends and some new. My gratitude for their advice in specific areas goes to Peter Caddy, Raju Daswani, Bassam Fattouh, Christopher Flook, Charles Fryer, James Gooder, Brodie Govan, Julien Hall, Kathy Hall, Patrick Heren, Gavin Lee, David Lehman, Siobhan Lismore-Scott, John Mathias, Jorge Montepeque, Peter Stewart, Matthew Stone, Richard Stevens and Paul Young.

Particular thanks are due to Michelle Zhang for her help with Chinese-language translation and with navigating the Chinese price reporting agencies.

I am also very grateful to those people that made great contributions but preferred to remain anonymous.

Every reader of the manuscript made valuable suggestions that improved the content. Of course, any errors or omissions that remain in the text or tables are entirely my responsibility.

Thanks also to the team at Routledge who have been understanding when work and family life had to take precedence.

Finally, a very special thanks to my wonderful family who have been very patient with me when I was distracted by my strange obsession with commodity pricing methodologies, German-language benchmark providers and the history of polymer assessments.

1 PRAs and the commodity markets they serve

Introducing the PRAs

Every energy user is indirectly exposed to the work of a price reporting agency (PRA) each time they fill up their car, take a flight or switch on a light. And yet the general public is completely unaware of the existence of PRAs. Firms like Platts, Argus, ICIS and OPIS, which are referenced every day by commodity traders and which influence billions of dollars of trade, are totally unfamiliar to consumers.

Even specialists who have spent their whole working lives in the commodity industry do not pay much attention to the role of PRAs the vast majority of the time, or at least until they violently disagree with something a PRA publishes or with its pricing methodology. Commodity traders reference PRA prices in their trades and place great reliance on their ability to assess prices fairly and accurately, but relatively few could explain why their market uses one PRA rather than another or exactly how PRAs reach their price assessments.

If even the professionals that depend so heavily on PRAs can get a little hazy regarding the finer details, it is not surprising that the general public has so little awareness of the key role played by PRAs in the modern economy.

There are over 100 agencies of various types that produce commodity benchmarks around the world today and they employ over 10,000 staff between them. These price reporters generate well over 100,000 assessments of commodity prices every week, with the largest PRAs assessing thousands of prices every day across a vast range of commodity markets.

Energy companies and to a lesser extent firms in the metals and agricultural industry rely upon these independent price assessments published by PRAs to manage their businesses. Trading in the energy markets would be paralyzed if the PRAs ever took a day off work. The PRAs are an integral part of the modern commodity business and therefore of the global economy.

PRAs have traditionally considered themselves to be media firms or publishers rather than providers of financial data. As such, it is only in the last few years that regulators have begun to examine the work of PRAs and look at how their assessment processes shape market behaviour and, ultimately, affect consumer prices.

The PRAs are slowly coming out of their relative obscurity into the light. Their work deserves to be better known. PRAs play a crucial role in the development of new markets and they help to promote trade in even the most developed markets by providing independent price references that everyone can agree upon. Price reporters in traditionally opaque markets like commodities do not have an easy time of it, but without their work many important markets would experience a reduction in transparency that would have knock-on effects on confidence, activity levels and, ultimately, on the cost of everyday goods and services.

Historical development

Most PRAs were founded by a single charismatic figure who decided to set up an information service after encountering a lack of transparency in a commodity market with which he or she was intimately familiar. Many of these founders were larger-than-life characters and they came from very disparate backgrounds: John Newbery was a key figure in British children's literature as well as publishing *The Public Ledger*; John Williams founded *The Iron Age* after fleeing a failed uprising in Ireland; high-school dropout Warren Platt was on the spot in Ohio for the break-up of Standard Oil; Humphrey Hinshelwood founded ICIS after a spell as a music critic and theatre director; while Jan Nasmyth of Argus was a former British commando officer.

The first PRAs mostly started as mailed or faxed newssheets prepared by small teams of specialist commodity journalists. Publishing price assessments was an important element of their reports but was not necessarily the dominant business driver that it is today. Most started as journalistic enterprises and so provided news about market developments and company activities as well as analysis of price trends. This information was generally sold to customers on an annual subscription basis. Many PRAs have not moved far from their original business model, except that they generally now have websites and email their reports rather than posting them.

With time, other more ambitious PRAs expanded their coverage outside their original specialism into other commodity markets or into other regions of the world. Some have moved well beyond their humble beginnings to become billion-dollar diversified companies or profitable business units within giant corporations. But, whatever their size, all successful PRAs still share one characteristic: they are closely entwined with the commodity markets that they cover. Without a deep understanding of their chosen commodities, PRAs would become irrelevant and disappear.

Introducing the commodity markets

Commodities are defined as unprocessed or partially processed goods, such as grain, metals or crude oil. The markets for commodities are simply immense. Every minute of the day minerals are being mined, crops are being harvested and oil and gas is being produced. Every single country on earth imports or exports commodities: while Saudi Arabia will export crude oil and import rice, Thailand will do the opposite. Every single individual on the planet who is living above subsistence level is affected in multiple ways by international commodity prices, through the food they eat, the clothes they wear or the energy they consume.

This is why commodity prices matter. Changes in commodity prices can reshape the world. In recent years, rises in the price of agricultural products led in part to the upheavals of the Arab Spring, while dramatic movements in the price of crude oil – the king of commodities – have been responsible for changes of government and various ups and downs in diplomatic and military alliances. Sharp falls in oil prices in the late 1980s and 1990s led to regime change in Algeria and have been cited as a partial cause for the break-up of the Soviet Union, Iraq's invasion of Kuwait, and the decline of the social-democratic consensus in Venezuela. Research by academic Jeff Colgan even suggested that between a quarter and a half of all international conflicts since 1973 have been related to oil and the oil price.[1]

Supply and demand

Commodity prices are largely determined by supply and demand. In its simplest form, if the soybean crop is smaller than expected while demand is stable, then soybean prices will rise. And if oil-producing nations pump more oil than the world needs at that moment, then oil prices will fall. But in real life the markets are more complicated. For instance, governments may intervene in the price of commodities; changes in the foreign exchange markets affect commodity prices; while future expectations regarding supply and demand can influence prices now, even when the current supply–demand situation is quite different.

If we acknowledge the huge importance of commodity prices and the complexity of the factors that determine them, then it follows that accurate information about prices and the factors that generated them must be essential. How then does the world agree on what is the price of certain commodities? After all, there is no obligation on a Vietnamese farming cooperative to disclose the price at which it sold its coffee crop to a Swiss-based trading house. In fact, many traders make absolute secrecy about price one of the conditions of their deals.

In some countries, certain commodity prices are fixed by governments and there is no room for debate, although this is the exception rather than the rule. Other commodities are traded in public exchanges that make price information available either in real-time or with a small delay. But exchanges are primarily interested in listing commodities that trade very frequently and which are relatively transparent. This leaves a huge information gap for smaller or more niche commodities and this is precisely the gap that has been filled by the price-reporting agencies.

One very brief definition of PRAs could therefore be that they are firms that "report the price of commodities that are difficult to assess". No one would subscribe to a PRA if they just had a general interest in the prices of the most transparent commodities. After all, every newspaper with a business page carries data on the trends in the price of major commodities like WTI crude oil or French wheat.

A subscriber to a PRA service is looking for much more detailed information and is prepared to pay a premium price for the data.

Some subscribers may be looking for much greater detail about the major exchange-traded commodities. A newspaper report can tell anyone where Brent crude oil traded yesterday but only a PRA can provide information about the likely trading level of, for example, a North Sea crude oil cargo delivered into a southern Chinese port in four months' time. But in the main, though, PRA subscribers are looking for information about the hundreds of commodity markets that never feature in the newspapers or on business television shows. European jet fuel, Black Sea wheat, Australian iron ore and Brazilian ethanol are all major markets of global significance, but detailed information about their trading activity and price levels is hard to obtain. Information about these less commonly discussed markets is very valuable to commodity traders. This is the profitable niche that the PRAs occupy.

What do PRAs do?

Commodity markets are clearly hugely significant and PRAs are equally clearly important to those markets. But what exactly is the precise role of a PRA?

Anyone who has worked at one of these firms and has tried to explain their job to a loved one will understand how elusive a simple explanation can be. The working definition that we will use is that: "PRAs are firms that assess the fair price of commodities and report these values to a wider audience that then uses those assessments of price either for information purposes or else as the basis for physical or financial transactions."

In order to be clear about what this definition means, we will break it down into its constituent parts.

PRAs assess the fair price of commodities

The first part of our definition was that PRAs assess the fair price of commodities. We have seen why the price of commodities matters so much to us all and we have also seen how difficult it might be to obtain information about commodity prices. The skill of the PRA is to obtain hard-to-find information about opaque commodity markets. As we will see in the next chapter, often the more difficult the information is to find, the higher its value to subscribers.

Even when there is a lot of information about what is happening in a particular market, the data can be confusing. Natural buyers of commodities usually want lower prices and so they will tend to pass on information that shows the market is oversupplied and that prices are weak. In contrast, natural sellers will constantly be reporting high-priced deals, shortages of material and frantic demand from buyers. Meanwhile, speculative commodity traders will flip between one side and the other depending on their position on any given day or week.

The skill of the PRA is to steer a path through these conflicting sources in order to reach an assessment of where the market really values a particular commodity. This requires a well-designed methodology for assessing prices. Assessments can be made in a number of ways and each PRA will make use of different methods depending on its preferences and on the market that it is covering. There will, however, always be some structure involved in the assessment process and this is typically provided nowadays in the form of written explanation of procedures and methodology.

There are many ways for price reporters to learn about how the market they cover is functioning. One traditional method of assessing prices is for the price reporter to talk to as many market participants as possible and to then make an editorial judgment call. More recently, new developments in technology have allowed price reporters to make use of trading screens to assess the fair value of commodities.

The key word in the phrase above from the definition is "fair". In order to assess prices fairly and not to favour either buyers or sellers, the PRA needs a robust methodology and good engagement with a range of market sources. Any PRA that consistently assesses the market in favour of one side or the other will soon lose credibility. The most valuable asset for any PRA is its reputation: any perception that its assessments are biased would make it difficult for its business to survive.

Reporting values to a wider audience

Once the PRA has found out what is happening in the market and has hopefully reached a fair assessment of the price of a commodity, the PRA needs to spread the word. PRAs derive their revenue from reporting "these values to a wider audience" of paying subscribers. In the early days of PRAs, their reports would have been in the form of a printed sheet of prices, news and market commentary that was sent to subscribers. Technology has evolved: subscribers to a PRA's services will now typically receive price updates by email or SMS, or else the PRA's pricing data will flow into their company's systems and appear automatically on their desktop.

The PRA has to strike a balance between ensuring its prices are accessible to as wide an audience of subscribers as possible, while also ensuring that its intellectual property is respected. PRAs cannot give away their information for a low price, like a newspaper does, because they rely on subscription revenue rather than advertising to cover their costs. It is a balancing act: PRAs want to charge a premium for their services that guarantees their profitability but at the same time they want to become the most widely referenced price in the market they are covering and so they generally cannot afford to price their services at too high a premium to their competitors.

Prices for information purposes

A customer who has taken out a subscription to a PRA's service has made a significant commitment. Prices tend to be higher than for any comparable media report and the licences are usually provided only on an annual basis. PRAs can charge relatively high prices because their information is usually difficult to replicate. They should have a reputation for fairness and reliability and their data is necessary for the subscriber to do his or her job well.

PRAs fill in the huge information gaps between prices that are set by governments and prices that are widely available in exchange data feeds. For example, an oil refinery may know the price at which their government requires them to sell kerosene locally. They can also see the price of WTI or Brent crude oil from picking up a newspaper or watching the business news. But this level of information would be nowhere near enough for them to make appropriate business decisions.

The refinery's procurement director needs to know the price of lots of different grades of crude oil in order to choose which will be the best value to purchase. At the same time the refinery's sales director needs to know the value of kerosene in the international markets in order to decide whether it is more profitable to sell the kerosene domestically or as an export cargo. This level of detail and this range of commodity prices can only be accessed with a subscription to a PRA price service.

Basis for transactions

Subscribers often need PRA data for more than just information that helps them understand their markets better. As our definition expresses it, they also use PRA prices "as the basis for physical or financial transactions". This form of usage will be addressed in greater depth in subsequent chapters, but, in short, benchmark usage is where two traders agree to use PRA pricing data as the basis of a deal between them.

The use of PRA information as an independent benchmark is common in the energy markets and in certain metals and agricultural markets. The main reason behind using a PRA's information as the basis for deals is that it reduces arguments during negotiations. Commodity markets can be so volatile that rather than arguing whether a North Sea crude oil delivery for next month should be sold for $40 per barrel or $140, most traders prefer to agree a deal based on the Platts assessment of North Sea crude oil and then spend their time focusing on whether the delivery should be at a premium of 40¢ or 30¢ per barrel to the Platts assessment.

At the time of the delivery, the two traders will look up the Platts assessments and see that Platts assessed the price over that period at, say, $50 per barrel. They will then apply the 35¢ premium that they agreed to this price and the buyer will pay the seller $50.35 per barrel.

In order to use a PRA in this way, both sides have to agree that Platts or one of its competitors is acceptable to them both and will provide a fair price that they can both access. Using the PRA benchmark allows the traders to focus on the details of a transaction that generate the small premium or discount, such as the repayment terms, physical quality and delivery schedule.

Neither side can control the overall commodity price nor would they likely ever agree in advance what it should be, and so they outsource responsibility for assessing that part of the deal to an independent PRA. This is equally the case for physical transactions and for derivatives deals such as futures, swaps and options, which can all be settled in relation to price assessments by a PRA.

Benchmark usage is extremely significant for PRAs. It means they are the preferred supplier of pricing data in a particular commodity market. This typically means they will be able to charge more for their subscriptions than their competitors and also that there is a much higher chance that their users will renew their annual subscriptions.

Benchmark usage is, however, the element of the PRA business that has come under greatest scrutiny in recent years and which has led to direct regulatory activity in the European Union. PRAs that supply prices that are used to underpin billions of dollars of trading activity are increasingly finding it difficult to be treated as simple media companies or publishers. PRAs are having to improve their price assessment procedures and their compliance structures in order to respond to the new pressures they are facing. Governments are particularly concerned that any manipulation of the commodity markets could lead to unhelpful volatility in wholesale prices that might ultimately affect the cost to the end consumer.

Raising the profile of PRAs

The higher profile that has followed increasing government scrutiny is a new phenomenon for PRAs. Even in the relatively obscure world of benchmarks, the PRAs have flown well below most people's radar. Other benchmarks have received significantly more attention, particularly since the global financial crisis. Much of the scrutiny has focused on the role played by the ratings agencies who provide credit assessments, while the formation of benchmarks such as LIBOR, the London Gold and Silver Fixes and foreign exchange spot rates have been subject to major investigation by the media, the government and in some cases by the criminal courts.

PRAs have generally stood up well to any investigations into their procedures and practices. To date there have not been any instances where any PRA has been shown to have deliberately published a false or misleading price. This is an impressive record given that the first commodity price assessments go back to the mid-eighteenth century and most of the largest firms have been operating for several decades.

Any bad behaviour has generally come from the side of the market participants that report information to PRAs. There have been instances where firms have reported fake trades or provided incorrect information to PRAs. There have also been cases where market participants have tried to 'corner' a market assessed by a PRA by buying up all of the available physical supply. Most recently, the European Commission has investigated whether some participants colluded to try to ensure that certain companies were prevented from participating in a price-reporting mechanism.[2] But in none of these cases has there been any evidence that the PRAs in question colluded with market abuse or behaved improperly.

The profile of the PRAs has also been raised by a run of major corporate transactions that have attracted media attention for their high valuations. Ownership stakes in pricing businesses are trading at a significant premium to traditional media or publishing businesses as investors value their record of growth and steady income streams from subscription revenue. The consolidation of the PRA industry is only likely to continue.

Conclusion

PRAs are an essential part of many commodities markets. They bring transparency to opaque markets, improving price discovery. Their users rely on PRA information to make better trading decisions and they generally appear willing to pay premium prices for their subscriptions.

PRA data also acts as a useful shorthand for traders looking to conclude physical or financial trades and who want to focus their negotiations on the specifics of the deal rather than on potential changes in the outright price of commodities. Without the information that PRAs provide, many markets would function much less efficiently, which would ultimately generate additional trading costs.

In the following chapters we will explore how PRAs operate, their history and the various ways in which they assess prices. We will also look at how they have responded to increased regulatory pressure and what the future could hold for PRAs.

Notes

1   Jeff Colgan (2013) Fueling the Fire: Pathways from Oil to War, International Security, vol. 38, issue 2, 147.
2   European Commission Memo: Antitrust – Commission confirms unannounced inspections in biofuel sector, Brussels, 9 October 2014.

Table 1.1 Selected commodity price providers*

	Founded	Sector	Region	Owner	Website
Agrarmarkt Informations-Gesellschaft (AMI)	2009	Agriculture	Europe	Group of German publishers	www.ami-informiert.de
Agriwatch	2000	Agriculture	India	Indian Agribusiness Systems	www.agriwatch.com
American Metals Markets	1882	Metals	North America	Euromoney Institutional Investor	www.amm.com
Argus Media	1970	All	Global	General Atlantic & Private	www.argusmedia.com
Asian Metal	2001	Metals	Global	Beijing Jinyi Information Technology	www.asianmetal.com
Baltic Exchange	1744	Shipping	Global	Singapore Exchange	www.balticexchange.com
Benchmark Mineral Intelligence	2014	Industrial Minerals	Global	Private	benchmarkminerals.com
Bloomberg New Energy Finance	2004	Renewables	Global	Bloomberg	about.bnef.com
Bunker Index	2008	Refined products	Global	Private	bunkerindex.com
Bunkerspot	2004	Refined products	Global	Petrospot Ltd	www.bunkerspot.com
C1 Energy	2000	Energy & Petchems	China	ICIS & CBI	www.c1energy.com
Cannabis Benchmarks	2015	Agriculture	North America	New Leaf Data Services	www.cannabisbenchmarks.com
CattleFax	1968	Agriculture	North America	Private	www.cattlefax.com
CCF Group	1997	Chemicals & textiles	China	Zhejiang Huarui Information Technology	www.ccfgroup.com
Chemical Data (CDI)	1979	Petchems & Plastics	North America	Private	www.chemicaldata.com
ChemOrbis	2001	Plastics	Europe & Asia	AccessTurkey Capital Group	www.chemorbis.com
ChinaTSI	2005	Metals	China	Heibei Tangsong Big Data Industry	www.chinatsi.net
CoalinQ	2001	Coal	Asia	Private	www.coaling.com
coalSPOT	2009	Coal	Asia	Private	www.coalspot.com
Cotton Outlook	1966	Agriculture	Global	The Outlook Group Limited	www.cotlook.com
CRU	1969	Metals & Fertilizers	Global	Private	www.crugroup.com

(continued)

Table 1.1 continued

	Founded	Sector	Region	Owner	Website
Custeel	2002	Metals	China	Chinese steelmakers	www.custeel.com
CW Group	2008	Petcoke & cement	Global	Global	www.cwgrp.com
DTN	1984	Agriculture	North America	TBG AG	www.dtnpf.com
e-coal.com	1998	Coal	Global	Private	e-coal.com
e-petrol.pl	2001	Oil	Poland	Information Market	www.e-petrol.pl
Enerdata	1984	Natural gas	North America	Private	www.enerdata.net
Energy Data Hub	2009	Oil & gas	North America	Private	www.energydatahub.com
EnergyTrend	2010	Solar	Asia	TrendForce	www.energytrend.com
Esoko	2005	Agriculture	Africa	Acumen, INI & Lundin Foundation	esoko.com
EUWID	1926	Forest products	Europe	Europäischer Wirtschaftsdienst	www.euwid-paper.com
F. O. Licht	1861	Biofuels & Agriculture	Global	Informa	agribusinessintelligence. informa.com/product/ fo-licht
FastMarkets	1999	Metals	Global	Euromoney Institutional Investor	www.fastmarkets.com
Fenwei Energy	1999	Coal	China	Private	www.sxcoal.com
Fertecon	1978	Fertilizers	Global	Informa	fertecon.agra-net.com
FOEX	1986	Forest products	Global	AXIO Data Group	www.foex.fi
Genscape	1999	Crude oil	North America	DMG Information	www.genscape.com
globalCOAL	2000	Coal	Asia	Industry players	www.globalcoal.com
Global Dairy Trade	2008	Agriculture	Global	Fonterra	www.globaldairytrade.info
IHS Chemical (CMAI)	1979	Petrochemicals	Global	IHS Markit	www.ihs.com/industry/ chemical.html

	Founded	Sector	Region	Owner	Website
IHS McCloskey	1987	Coal	Global	IHS Markit	www.ihs.com/products/global-coal-news-analysis.html
IHS OPIS	1977	Oil	Global	IHS Markit	www.opisnet.com
ICIS	1979	All	Global	RELX	www.icis.com
Indian Petro Group	n.a.	Energy & Agricultural	India	360 Analytics & Advisory	reports.indianpetro.com
Industrial Minerals	1967	Non-metallic minerals	Global	Euromoney Institutional Investor	www.indmin.com
Kallanish	2013	Energy & Metals	Global	Private	www.kallanish.com
Kortes	1991	Oil	Russia	Reuters	www.kortes.com
London Energy Brokers Association	2003	Generation fuels	Europe	Brokers' Association	www.leba.org.uk
Live Rice Index	2011	Agriculture	Global	Private	livericeindex.com
Lubes 'n' Greases	1995	Lubricants	Global	LNG Publishing	www.lubesngreases.com
Madan24	2012	Metals	Iran	Private	en.madan24.com
Marine Bunker Exchange (MABUX)	2012	Refined products	Global	Private	www.mabux.com
Market Research Company (MRC)	2003	Plastics	Europe	Market Report Company LLP	www.mrcplast.com
Metal Bulletin	1913	Metals	Global	Euromoney Institutional Investor	www.metalbulletin.com
MetalMiner	2004	Metals	North America	Azul Partners	agmetalminer.com
myCEPPI	2013	Plastics	Europe	Private	www.myceppi.com
MySteel	2000	Metals	China	Shanghai Ganglian E-Commerce	www.mysteel.net
Natural Gas Intelligence	1981	Natural gas	North America	Private	www.naturalgasintel.com
Net Energy	2005	Oil	North America	Private	www.ne2.ca

(continued)

Table 1.1 continued

	Founded	Sector	Region	Owner	Website
Novus Agro	2009	Agriculture	Nigeria	Private	novusagro.com
OMR	1985	Energy & Renewables	Europe	Independent	www.omr.de
The Packer	1893	Agriculture	Global	Farm Journal Media	www.thepacker.com
The Petrochemical Standard	2014	Petrochemicals	Global	Genscape	www.petchemstandard.com
PetroChem Wire	2007	Petrochemicals	North America	Private	www.petrochemwire.com
Petrosil	2002	Energy & Petchems	India	Private	www.petrosil.com
Plasticker	2006	Plastics	Europe	New Media Publisher GmbH	plasticker.de
Plastics Information Europe	1990	Petrochemicals	Europe	Kunststoff Information Verlagsgesellschaft	pieweb.plasteurope.com
Point Carbon	2000	Emissions	Global	Reuters	financial.thomsonreuters.com/PointCarbon
PolymerMIS	2011	Plastics	India	Vista Websoft	www.polymermis.com
PolymerTrack	n.a.	Plastics	Global	Private	www.polymertrack.com
Polymerupdate	2000	Petchems & Plastics	Global	Shalimar Infotech	www.polymerupdate.com
PRC Steel	2006	Metals	China	Zhejiang Pricesteel Technology	www.prcsteel.com
Prima Markets	2014	Biofuels & Agriculture	Global	IHS Markit	prima-markets.com
Profercy	2004	Fertilizers	Global	Private	www.profercy.com
PT CoalIndo Energy	2006	Coal	Indonesia	Industry & Argus Media	coalindoenergy.com
Public Ledger	1760	Agriculture	Global	Informa	www.public-ledger.com
PV Insights	2005	Solar	Global	n.a.	pvinsights.com
The Rice Trader	1991	Agriculture	Global	The Rice Trader LLC	www.thericetrader.com
RIM Intelligence	1984	Oil & gas	Asia	Private & QUICK Corp	www.rim-intelligence.co.jp
RML AgTech	2007	Agriculture	India	IvyCap & Thomson Reuters	www.rmlglobal.com

	Founded	Sector	Region	Owner	Website
S&P Global Platts	1909	All	Global	McGraw-Hill	www.platts.com
SCI Group	2004	All	China	Sublime China Information Group	intl.sci99.com
Scrap Price Bulletin (Iron Age)	1859	Metals	North America	Euromoney Institutional Investor	www.scrappricebulletin.com
Shanghai Metals Market	1999	Metals	China	Private	www.metal.com
Ship & Bunker	2012	Refined products	Global	Big Ranch Media Inc	shipandbunker.com
Shorcan	1977	Oil	North America	TMX Group	www.shorcan.com/en
SteelCN	2009	Metals	China	Beijing Chinese Steel Information Technology	www.steelcn.cn
SteelHome	2004	Metals	China	Shanghai SteelHome E-Commerce	en.steelhome.cn
SteelKey	2003	Metals	China	Xiamen Tianxin Software	www.steelkey.com
SteelMint	2009	Metals	India	SteelMint Info Services	www.steelmint.com
SteelOrbis	2002	Metals	Global	Private	www.steelorbis.com
Sugaronline	1999	Biofuels & Agriculture	Global	Private	www.sugaronline.com
SunSirs Commodity Data Group	2011	All	China	Zhejiang Netsun	www.sunsirs.com
Tankard	2013	Natural gas	Europe	ICAP, Marex Spectron & Tullett Prebon	www.tankardindex.com
Tecnon OrbiChem	1976	Chemicals	Global	Private	www.orbichem.com
The Tex Report	1967	Ferrous metals and coal	Japan	The Tex Report Ltd	www.texreport.co.jp
TradeTech	1968	Uranium	Global	Private	www.uranium.info
TZMI	1994	Non-metallic minerals	Global	Private	www.tzmi.com
Umetal	2006	Metals	China	RGL Group	www.umetal.com
Urner Barry	1858	Agriculture	North America	Urner Barry Publications	www.urnerbarry.com
USP/ESALQ	1901	Biofuels & Agriculture	Brazil	University of São Paulo	www.en.esalq.usp.br

(continued)

Table 1.1 continued

	Founded	Sector	Region	Owner	Website
UX Consulting	1994	Uranium	Global	Private	www.uxc.com
Wood Resources International	1987	Forest products	North America	Private	woodprices.com
Xinhua InfoLink	1998	Coal	China	Private	xinhuainfolink.com
ZH818	2011	Metals	China	Changsha Tongrui Information Technology	www.zh818.com

* For guidance only; best endeavours for accuracy

2   The PRA business model

Introduction

The business aspect of price reporting agencies (PRAs) remains a mystery to many, even to some of those who deal with them daily. Of course, every PRA will have a different business model. China's SCI Group with 1,500 employees will operate differently from a small consultancy that also produces some price information. Nonetheless, the very basic business model of most price benchmark providers has not changed much since Warren Platt's day: discover high-value information and sell it on a subscription basis.

The main refinement to that basic model is the growth since the 1970s of the use of PRA assessments in benchmarking, where two commodity traders reference a PRA price in their physical or derivative contracts. Providing information is therefore no longer the main driver of PRA success, although it remains an important driver of PRA subscriptions. PRAs now have at least two aspects to their business: an 'informational role' and a 'benchmarking role'. It is this second role as a provider of physical and financial benchmarks that is the key to PRA profitability and which makes PRAs such a crucial component of the industries that they serve.

Beyond their informational and benchmarking roles, many PRAs have also developed a third strand to their business model. PRAs are increasingly leveraging their core competencies in order to push into related businesses such as conferences, consultancy, training and data analytics. Some of the Chinese metals PRAs have even launched their own electronic trading platforms and are looking to provide financing and settlement solutions for their customers.

These additional 'added value' businesses aim to make a customer's core subscription more 'sticky' by embedding it within a range of additional offerings. The aim for PRAs is also to diversify away from pure reliance on subscriptions and to broaden their revenue base. This recognizes that at some point the PRAs may hit a limit of what they can charge for data subscriptions without antagonizing their customer base and so will need to find different ways to increase their bottom line. Additional services can also be an insurance policy for times when a weak commodity cycle is affecting renewal rates for subscriptions.

Value hierarchy

PRAs typically think in terms of a 'value hierarchy' of services and usage. This helps to guide their business decisions and the areas in which they invest. The various types of informational usage are at the bottom of the hierarchy while benchmark usage sits at the heights. The best way to understand the value hierarchy is that the lower down the item the less revenue it is likely to generate. Higher-ranked items will generate outsized profits but will typically be much more competitive and difficult spaces to occupy. Expanding informational usage may require the recruitment of a few more reporters, for example, while expanding benchmark usage could require a PRA to hire a number of expensive business development managers.

The first three examples of informational usage, which are the lowest three lines of a typical PRA's value hierarchy, all have two elements in common. First, they are all word-based rather than number-based: this is written news, analysis and reports rather than data. Second, success in differentiating and adding value to subscribers depends entirely on the PRA analyst's connection to the market. An analyst that is in constant touch with market participants will inevitably hear high-value information, whereas an analyst who has difficulty getting the market to take his or her calls will struggle to generate higher-value content.

We will look at a typical day for a PRA price reporter in more detail in a later chapter but it is worth thinking about how a PRA analyst can get closer to the commodity market that they are reporting. Some reporters, although not many, appear to achieve this closeness with charm or by building relationships through socializing with their contacts. But for most, the willingness of the market to share information with an individual price reporter from a particular PRA is a factor of how much the PRA's assessments are used by the industry. In this sense, the benchmark usage of the PRA directly impacts on their informational value. A benchmark PRA will have better contacts, greater access and therefore an improved informational flow that should lead to greater informational usage. Obviously, the opposite is true of a PRA with little or no benchmark status.

The direct link between informational access and benchmark status can be confirmed by those price reporters who have switched from one PRA to another

Table 2.1 The PRA value hierarchy

Benchmark usage	Derivative settlement price
	Major physical benchmark
	Reference price for term deals
	Reference price for spot trade
Informational usage (data)	Data for mark-to-market
	General price reference data
	Fundamental data
Informational usage (text)	Market analysis
	Specialist news reporting
	General news reporting

only to find that previously good contacts are now ignoring them or vice versa. It is a salutary reminder to price reporters that the value of your written work to the market can be largely dependent on the usage of your data.

The data side of the business at most PRAs swamps the value of the written publications. Data can be split into two categories: informational usage and benchmark usage. The value of data for informational usage again depends on how generally accessible the data is and to what extent it can help the individual subscriber make money.

Moving further up the value hierarchy and becoming a benchmark is the ultimate aim of any PRA. This is where the serious money is made. PRAs tend to follow the classic 80-20 rule of business whereby 80 per cent of the revenue comes from just 20 per cent of the products. The PRA value hierarchy can almost be seen as an inverted pyramid in which the majority of the revenue comes from a very small number of benchmarks at the top.

General news reporting

Like any journalistic enterprise, PRAs understand very well that information can be more or less difficult to obtain, while different types of information are also valued in very different ways by subscribers. Unlike newspapers and magazines, however, where information can also have an entertainment aspect, the value of information for a PRA subscriber is primarily a function of how much money the information can help the subscriber make.

In PRA terms, the lowest value information is non-exclusive news. This would be something like a report of BP's quarterly results or the news that Rio Tinto is selling off a small iron ore mine. News like this is very easy to obtain – the companies involved will send out a press release or else they might hold a media conference – and it is likely that the news will be widely reported. In cost terms, a reader can obtain this kind of information from a newspaper that charges a tiny fraction of a PRA subscription, while in terms of speed the news will usually be available significantly earlier on a newswire service like Thomson Reuters or Bloomberg.

PRAs therefore have no significant advantage in the general business news space and so they tend to be involved in this kind of non-exclusive reporting purely in the interests of offering their subscribers a full service rather than because this is their strength or a significant driver of profits.

Specialist news reporting

Where the PRAs should have an advantage is in the provision of more exclusive specialist news. PRA analysts speak to commodity traders and brokers that would not be on the calling list of general business news reporters or who would not speak to a newspaper reporter. Their role in pricing means that PRAs have privileged access to a very hard to reach group of subject matter experts who will be on top of every development in their market.

This access means that PRA staff should come across information relating to issues like a refinery maintenance shutdown or a potential strike at a mine before more general reporters. Specialist news reporting would ideally be 'market moving' – its dissemination will have consequences for the price of the commodity that is affected. One veteran reporter once summed up a good specialist news story up as one "where they can trade off the headline".

Specialist information helps subscribers make money by helping them reach better trading decisions. A flow of regular specialist news should ensure that the customer values their PRA subscription at a premium to a more general news service.

Market analysis

Good market analysis can also have a similar impact on how subscribers value their PRA reports. PRA analysts are supposed to be speaking to many more different players in the market – producers, consumers, traders, brokers, analysts and government officials – than any one subscriber could hope to speak to in a typical working day. A PRA overview of market activity should therefore, at least ideally, give the subscriber a more complete overview of their market that they might otherwise have had.

Again, the value of this information directly relates to its ability to make the subscriber money. If a Belgian electricity trader reads some fundamental analysis in a PRA report that makes him nervous about his long position and decide to close it off just ahead of a major market sell-off, then the amount of trading losses the trader has avoided will make him happily pay even the most elevated PRA subscription fee at the next annual renewal.

Fundamental data

One of the key categories of informational data is fundamental data, which is any data that relates to physical supply and demand of a particular commodity. Examples of fundamental data include German wind power output, agricultural harvest sizes, aggregated blast furnace output statistics and customs data.

Depending on how reliable, how exclusive and how up-to-date the information is, fundamental data can help commodity traders make a lot of money in the market. The difficulty for PRAs is that there is a lot of competition to supply fundamental data and the data itself quickly becomes commoditized: one firm will make a breakthrough and produce a new set of fundamental data that the market loves – ship-tracking software, for example – but within a year or two other providers will have replicated the set.

It is extremely difficult to retain exclusivity over fundamental data in the longer term, which is why PRAs are increasingly focused on the delivery mechanism for fundamental data. PRAs are pushing deeper into advanced data analytics and software platforms that enable modelling, customization of data and the aggregation of fundamental with pricing data. As a result, many of the acquisitions made by the largest PRAs in recent years have focused on data management.

General price reference data

Further up the value chain than fundamental data comes pricing data. It is much harder to replicate pricing data than fundamental data and so its value tends to be higher. The generation of pricing data requires investment in methodology design and in the price reporters or pricing platform that generates the actual prices. Still, not all pricing data is valued equally. Price information that is used as a general check or just for information purposes is the least valuable data.

Returning to the example in the previous chapter of the refiner looking to manufacture kerosene from crude oil, the refiner needed detailed information about prices in the crude oil and the kerosene markets and so the firm would have been prepared to pay for a PRA subscription as the information is unobtainable elsewhere. But the refiner needed general information on pricing for informational purposes only and so there is a limit to what they will pay for their subscription, especially when there are several PRAs competing for the business and the refiner has no particular reason to choose data from one PRA rather than from another.

Mark-to-market pricing

Similar limits apply to customers' purchase of price data for internal mark-to-market calculations. Mark-to-market is where the middle office of commodity firms needs to compare the positions that their company has taken in the market with daily information in order to check on the performance of their trading activity and their overall portfolio. A risk manager will subscribe to a daily feed of pricing data from an independent source like a PRA in order to compare the values that his or her firm is assigning to certain commodities that they buy or sell with the values that the independent source is assigning them. The risk manager will then investigate any major discrepancies and may decide to reduce a trader's position if his view of the market is diverging majorly from the independent pricing data.

No serious firm can operate in the commodity markets without applying mark-to-market in its risk management and so an independent data source becomes business critical: the business cannot operate safely without this data. This makes data for mark-to-market the most valuable of all of the informational uses of PRA data. But, as we saw with general price data, there is a natural cap to the amount that a subscriber will pay for mark-to-market data because the risk manager can choose data from any PRA, can take a feed from Reuters or Bloomberg or can use other data sources like broker information to construct an independent mark-to-market assessment.

Given this competitive environment, PRAs cannot charge too much for a subscription to their pricing data when they know the feed is only destined to be used in mark-to-market functions.

Reference price for spot trade

The top third of the PRA value hierarchy comprises benchmark usage. If a PRA produces prices that are used as benchmarks, then it is now operating in an environment where its data is not used solely for information purposes but also, in the words of our earlier definition of a PRA, "as the basis for physical or financial transactions". We will explore how PRA benchmark usage works in greater depth in the next chapter but, essentially, traders use PRA benchmarks as a shorthand when they negotiate trades.

The outright prices of commodities can be so volatile – Brent crude oil has traded as high as $145.61 per barrel and as low as $2.23 per barrel – that it can be very difficult for traders to agree on a fixed price for their deals. PRAs can provide a neutral assessment of outright prices that both sides can agree upon. This takes the guesswork out of trading and means that neither side risks massively losing out, particularly if they hedge this outright exposure. Many traders therefore prefer to trade commodities at "Platts plus 50 cents" or "PetroChem Wire minus $2" and to focus on negotiating the discount or premium rather than the outright price, which the PRA will assess.

In theory, there is nothing stopping two counterparties to a "spot" or short-term deal from choosing a different index each time they undertake a transaction. This is why usage in a spot transaction, although a major breakthrough, is less valuable to a PRA than use in a longer-term deal like an annual supply deal. A spot transaction, such as for a single cargo, may not be repeated or may not be enough to establish an individual PRA's dominance of a certain market.

Reference in a term deal

The longer the duration of the deal, the better the chance that the PRA will come to dominate the market. PRAs will therefore fight aggressively to establish benchmark status in any new commodity markets that open up and to displace their rivals in existing markets and we will look at how this plays out and the PRAs' various offensive and defensive strategies later.

A reference to their pricing in a lengthy supply deal – known as a "term deal" – between two counterparties therefore gives the incumbent benchmark provider some security that their pricing will not be displaced by a rival benchmark provider.

It also gives the PRA greater security of revenue. The two counterparties will not be able to cancel their PRA subscription until the term deal is complete and so the longer the deal, the longer the PRA can be assured of its subscription revenue.

Major physical benchmark

Not all commodities are of equal value or size. Becoming the benchmark for spot and term deals in a regional polymers market is a great achievement and will generate significant revenue, but the reputational and financial impact of becoming the benchmark for a major commodity like natural gas or crude oil will be an order of greater magnitude.

The definition of a major physical benchmark is that it is referenced outside the market to which it specifically refers. A benchmark for a regional polymer market is unlikely to be watched carefully by participants in many other markets that are not immediately related. In contrast, a major physical benchmark will be referenced by traders working in different markets and different regions.

The most important PRA-assessed commodity benchmark is Platts' Dated Brent assessment of North Sea crude oil. A major physical benchmark like Dated Brent is of interest to traders in crude oil around the world, to traders of refined petroleum products, to natural gas traders watching the oil-gas link, to investors in renewable energy, and to government policymakers.

The commercial potential of a major physical benchmark is huge as it will attract subscribers from different backgrounds. A major physical benchmark is also a 'must-have' product – access to the data is essential to most customers who cannot carry out their normal business activities without knowing precisely where the benchmark is being assessed. This allows a PRA to charge a premium for access to this data.

Providing the benchmark for a major physical benchmark also plays an important role in enhancing a PRA's reputation. It is easier for Platts to enter new markets and introduce its services to traders because traders in far-removed markets are still likely to have heard of Platts' Dated Brent and to assume that they can trust Platts' assessments, given that they are trusted in such a major commodity market. Similarly, Argus' usage in a major physical benchmark like European gasoline gave traders in the United States confidence to use Argus in their crude oil pricing.

Derivative settlement price

Major physical benchmarks typically see a derivative market grow up around them. These benchmarks are so important that traders want to manage the risk of the assessment going up or down too much by hedging their forward exposure with futures or options products.

Usage in a major physical benchmark that is linked to a derivatives market represents the jackpot for PRAs. First, usage as a settlement price for derivative contracts gives the PRA a high level of confidence over their benchmark usage and revenues. If it is difficult to unwind a physical term deal in order to change benchmark provider, then it is infinitely more complicated to change the settlement price of a derivative. By their very nature, derivatives relate to future periods, thereby giving the PRA more guarantees about how long their benchmarks will be used for. Derivatives are also now virtually all listed for trading or clearing on exchanges and exchanges are naturally slow to invest resources in listing unused, challenger benchmarks. This leads to a chicken-and-egg situation where customers cannot change PRA provider because there are no linked derivatives, while exchanges will not list the benchmark because there is no customer demand.

There is also substantial additional revenue to be gained by a PRA if its assessments are used as a settlement price for derivatives. Exchanges pay PRAs to use their benchmarks as a settlement price (see the chapter on exchange relations for further details), giving the PRAs an extra revenue source. Derivative usage means the PRA also derives revenue from customers that it would never otherwise reach. Many banks, hedge funds and proprietary traders are active in the Brent crude oil derivatives markets, for example, and so will subscribe to Platts' data, even though they have no interest in the underlying physical market. Without a derivatives market, PRAs struggle to sell their data to customers that are not immediate physical traders.

Non-core businesses

Beyond informational usage and benchmark usage, the PRAs also provide many other services to their customers. There has been a rush of acquisitions by the larger PRAs in recent years and it is notable just how few of these deals are in the traditional benchmark pricing space. Of the eight deals done by Platts between 2011 and 2016, only two (Steel Business Briefing and Kingsman) added additional benchmark exposure. The remainder of Platts' acquisition activity, apart from purchases of consultancies, was focused on data analytic tools and on new sources of data such as drilling rig counts or upstream information. The aim is clearly to expand Platts beyond a pricing agency for the commodities market into a general supplier of commodities data, analytics and data management tools.

The same driver can be seen, albeit to a slightly lesser extent, at Platts' rivals ICIS, which picked up data and analytics firms in Italy and Germany in 2011 and 2013 respectively. As a privately held entity until late 2016, Argus has had less appetite for larger deals and its corporate activity has been more focused on filling in the gaps in its traditional pricing offering – principally in petrochemicals and fertilizers – than on acquiring non-traditional businesses, although it has picked up some niche consultants and a conference business.

For all of the PRAs, these separate non-pricing businesses are intended to bolster the bottom line of PRAs by taking them into new spaces and generating additional revenue. But at the same time they are also intended in part as a marketing tool, albeit a supposedly profitable one, that will bolster the core benchmark business. Successful conferences, seminars and training courses should generate revenue for the organizing PRA but they can also have a powerful branding impact. A graduate trainee from industry who has attended a number of ICIS petrochemical training courses may, for example, come away feeling positive towards ICIS and may prefer to deal with them over Platts once he is installed on a trading desk. The risk is that the opposite might also be true. A very weak conference may tarnish the brand of the PRA that organized it.

Other common related activities for PRAs include concepts like publishing directories such as 'who's who' in certain markets or lists of firms active in certain commodities. Several of the Chinese metals PRAs have also made a big push into providing physical trading screen facilities for their customers with payment based on a brokerage model, although most have to date only experienced limited success.

PRAs as consultants

Consultancy is perhaps the area most fraught with concern for PRAs. This is true in both the financial sense and in terms of reputational risk.

On the financial side, consultants with extensive commodity experience tend to be expensive and some of their price tags can come as a shock to PRAs that are used to competing on salaries with media firms, rather than with well-established consultants such as McKinsey, FACTS Global Energy and BCG.

The different PRAs have tended to go down different routes. IHS was first involved in energy consulting before acquiring PRAs such as McCloskey Coal,

CMAI and OPIS and so in 2017 it was still viewed more as a consultant that is acquiring its own data sources rather than as a traditional PRA. This is also the case in many smaller firms, particularly in the fertilizer and agricultural spaces, where traditional consultants started keeping their own databases in order to assist their consulting work and ended up becoming de facto PRAs more by accident than by any particular design. Many of these smaller firms were so focused on their consulting work that they never really exploited the pricing side, making them obvious acquisition targets for larger PRAs whose model has been to retool and upgrade their reports and then sharply increase subscription rates.

ICIS and Argus have moved more organically into consulting, slowly acquiring staff as they pitch for and secure projects. Observers would class consulting in both of these firms as still an add-on rather than a core business: they exist to exploit profitable niches in which both firms have key competencies. Argus has, for example, done well with consulting projects on Russia and LPG/NGLs where they dominate the pricing model, while ICIS tends to consult primarily within its petrochemical stronghold.

At these firms, the concept behind consulting is not just to pick up additional revenue from existing customers but also to strengthen usage of their benchmark data. A power plant developer whose economic models were developed by consultants from IHS may find it easiest to use IHS McCloskey coal price data going forward as this will be easily compatible with the model.

PRA consultants often have a price advantage over rivals that are not linked to a PRA. A large part of project costs for consultants is acquiring market data from a relevant PRA. This inevitably gives PRAs who do not cross-charge their consulting arms for data a major cost advantage. Although one could argue that the PRA's pricing arms are essentially subsidizing their consultancy arms by not applying transfer pricing, PRA management would argue that the benefit to the overall business of getting their data locked into customers' systems and strategic planning has a significant benefit to the whole business.

As part of the McGraw-Hill publishing giant, Platts has had the financial firepower to be more aggressive on the consulting side than its two smaller rivals in terms of non-organic growth. Platts acquired BENTEK Energy in 2011 and the PIRA Energy Group in 2016. Platts also picked up consultants via its acquisitions of ferrous metals specialists Steel Business Briefing in 2011 and the Kingsman sugar analytics business in 2012.

Customers tend to follow individual consultants rather than brands, though, and Platts has suffered from consultants jumping ship after their lock-in period expires and simply starting up new advisory businesses. Kallanish, the PRA and advisory service founded in 2013, is largely staffed by former Steel Business Briefing experts, while some of the consultants from BENTEK have also moved on.

PRAs and advertising

Unlike the traditional news media, the larger PRAs rely on subscription revenue and do not derive significant income from advertising. This is partly because their subscription revenue is more than sufficient without the need to chase advertising dollars but also because there are some concerns around perceptions of impartiality. A PRA whose website was plastered with banners advertising a certain commodity trading firm might be perceived by that firm's rivals as being biased in some way towards the advertiser.

Smaller PRAs are likely to pay more heed to the potential of selling advertising, particularly if they publish more glossy monthly reports. Allowing individual firms to advertise their goods or services is still rare due to the potential conflict of interest implications, but selling advertising to more neutral parties such as technical service providers or conference organizers is more common. The use of PRA websites to promote job vacancies is also common among some of the Asian PRAs.

PRA revenue models

PRAs' core informational and benchmark usage is typically monetized through annual subscriptions. This allows them to bill in advance as well as making their revenue relatively predictable: subscribers are extremely likely to renew a subscription when the PRA provides an important benchmark price and so renewal rates above 90 per cent can be expected. Additional sales to new subscribers generate growth for the PRA as well as compensating for subscribers that have disappeared as the result of job losses or corporate events such as mergers and acquisitions. The repeatability and predictability of their revenues combined with relatively high margins is one of the factors that makes some PRAs such an attractive investment to private equity funds.

Other revenue from areas like conferences, training and consultancy will tend to be harder for the PRA to predict as this tends to be sporadic and its repeatability is less certain. Traders need pricing data from PRAs whatever the state of the market but spending on conferences and consultants is more discretionary and is likely to be cut in a market downturn.

Pricing policies around subscriptions differ widely from PRA to PRA. At some there is a very clear formula (for example, $1,000 per user per year) and subscriptions can be purchased online with a credit card. At other PRAs, pricing is more of an art than a formula and the cost of the subscription will vary according to how much an individual salesperson believes the customer is willing to pay. Most of the larger PRAs will want to understand their customer before they sell them a subscription. The PRA salesperson will want to understand if the subscription is for informational or benchmark usage, how many people are likely to access the subscription and from which parts of the business (front office, middle office or back office). The subscription rate will be set accordingly.

A subscriber that takes multiple reports will likely get a discount, while some very large firms may have global arrangements in place with PRAs that give them access to the PRA's full output for a fixed cost. Some subscribers may also push for special treatment if they are perceived to have a strategic importance in a particular market or if they are a major information contributor, although a PRA will have to be careful in such cases. The standard complaint by traders to PRAs is always that "you just sell me back the information I provide" and so acknowledging that this argument has merit by providing discounts represents a slippery slope for a PRA.

There is no particular reason why a subscription to a specific PRA report should cost $500, $5,000 or $10,000 and prices tend to vary widely between some reports and between PRAs. Many other industries have a 'cost–plus' model that sees them sell goods at the cost of production plus a specific mark up. This is not the case for PRAs, which will mostly tend to charge whatever they believe the market will bear, taking into account their competitors' pricing strategies.

There are a few rules of thumb to bear in mind. Typically, the cost of subscribing to a report about one of the petroleum markets will be higher than the cost of an electricity or generation fuel report, which will in turn be higher than the cost of a metals or agricultural report. This relates to perceptions of the relative financial strength of firms operating in each commodity sector and their willingness to pay for data. A second rule of thumb might be that a subscription from a PRA that is the incumbent benchmark provider will be more expensive than a subscription to a challenger PRA. The incumbent can afford to charge more because its reports are a business essential.

Another related rule of thumb is that PRA subscription costs do not appear to matter as much to users as the vocal complaints at every annual renewal cycle might indicate. The rising cost of PRA subscriptions is a constant source of criticism by traders. But no one in PRA history has ever switched benchmark provider to save money. A challenger PRA that sought to displace an incumbent by offering free data would not succeed. At the end of the day, commodity firms have so much money at stake linked to PRA benchmarks that the quality and the broad acceptability of the benchmark is much more important than any subscription cost, which in any case represents a very tiny fragment of a firms' operating costs.

Conclusion

These rules of thumb around PRA revenues indicate just why it is so essential for a PRA to advance as far as it can up the value hierarchy. The financial rewards available from occupying the benchmark space at the top of the ladder vastly outweigh the revenues that can be derived from the pure informational usage at the bottom. This explains why the larger PRAs devote so much attention to the design of their methodologies and to improving perceptions of their brands as well as why they invest so heavily in expensive business development staff.

Part of the knowledge economy, the PRA business model is a classic example of a 'weightless goods' industry. Weightless goods are intangible services and products, in this case intellectual property, that have high initial development costs but cost very little to reproduce and distribute. Weightless products can be distributed infinitely. Smaller PRAs in niche areas can struggle financially because of the high development costs of hiring price reporters, business development staff and building a reputation in a specific market. But once the initial fixed investment is made, achieving benchmark status in a major physical market, particularly one with derivative usage, enables the PRA to recover its initial investment and to leverage its intellectual property almost infinitely, either through subscription sales or through revenue from derivatives trading.

3   How price benchmarks work

Introduction

The simplest definition of a benchmark is that is provides a standard or a reference point against which something else may be compared. In the commodities markets, a benchmark is usually defined as a price reference point that is acceptable to both buyer and seller as a basis to settle a contract. This is why in commodities, the terms 'benchmark' and 'price index' are used interchangeably.

There are thousands of commodity prices published by price reporting agencies (PRAs) every day but only those that are used as reference prices in contracts are classed as benchmarks. There are also a select few critical benchmarks or 'super-benchmarks' that have an influence on the broader economy outside of their specific market: these would include Brent and WTI crude oil, the London gold and silver spot fixes and in the financial markets, LIBOR and EURIBOR.

There are two main reasons why the commodities markets make such heavy use of benchmarks in their day-to-day business. First, physical commodity deals vary greatly in terms of specifications. Deals can be either for import or export, while the size, quality, delivery, timing and payment terms all vary tremendously. If the price of every deal had to be negotiated from scratch, it would be very time consuming for the traders involved. This explains why market participants often prefer to link their deals to relevant benchmarks and then just negotiate the cost of the difference between their particular commodity deal and the more general benchmark specifications. This evolution away from arduous fixed-price negotiations has occurred in the majority of energy markets since the 1970s and took place most recently in the iron ore markets from 2010 onwards.

The second reason for the reliance on benchmarks is the immense volatility of most commodity prices, which makes it extremely difficult for traders to predict how prices will evolve even in the near future. Given this difficulty, many traders do not want to negotiate about overall price levels because they would never agree. Instead the two sides will agree on a benchmark index that will broadly capture price changes. The traders will then focus on discussing the size of the premium or discount to this index.

If we imagine an Indonesian importer who wants to buy a cargo of gasoline from a Singaporean trading house in one month's time, the two sides have two options for how to price the deal. The first option is that they agree an overall price in US dollars for the cargo. This would be called a 'flat-price deal' and this structure is much less common. The two sides would spend too long debating whether prices are likely to fall or rise over the month before the cargo is delivered, and there is a risk that one side would end up seriously out of pocket if prices move in a particular direction.

The more common convention would be to link the deal to a benchmark. In the case of the Singapore gasoline cargo, the most typical structure for a deal would be to link the price to published assessments of gasoline by Platts. The two sides would agree to use an average of a certain number of Platts' Singapore gasoline daily assessments as their index. In the case of Asian gasoline this would likely be the assessments for five days, whereas an Asian crude oil cargo might price against the average of all the assessments in a specified month. The two sides would then discuss whether the market conditions or the specific quality of the cargo means that the buyer should pay a premium or a discount to the standard Platts' assessment.

Benchmarks are used throughout the commodity supply chain. In the example above, the Singaporean trading house that was selling the gasoline would have already acquired the cargo from a refiner at a price based on Platts' assessments before it sold the material on to the Indonesian importer. The Indonesian importer would then look to break up the cargo into smaller parcels and sell it to fuel distributors, again using Platts' assessments where possible, in order to avoid generating additional risk by using different benchmarks, a concept known as 'basis risk'.

This benchmark system ensures that both sides can focus on the element of the price that they can control (the premium or discount) and not on the element that they cannot (the flat price). The counterparties can then use derivatives to hedge themselves against adverse moves in the underlying flat price by trading swaps or futures that also settle against the same benchmark.

Indexes are therefore a shorthand that reduce friction in negotiations. Both sides are taking on equal amounts of risk as both are exposed to an index that they cannot control because it comes from an independent PRA. Neither side should be at a disadvantage.

It is this kind of benchmark usage that is the ultimate aspiration for all PRAs. From a professional point of view, benchmark status means that the industry trusts a PRA's assessments to such an extent that they accept the PRA as the independent arbiter of much of their contract price. From a financial point of view, it is also enormously significant. Use of PRA assessments in a trading contract makes it absolutely essential that the two sides both subscribe to the PRA's data. The essential nature of this subscription means that the two sides will both be willing to pay a premium for their subscription. Benchmark usage also means that not only will the frontline traders, who are the principals in the transaction, need a PRA subscription, the firm's middle and back office will also need to subscribe in order to monitor and settle the trade.

Acceptability of benchmark

The two sides in a trade have to choose a PRA index that is acceptable to them both. If either the buyer or the seller believe that the PRA tends to favour producers or buyers, then one side will not trust the PRA to provide the largest price component of their deal. The two sides need to believe that the PRA index will reflect actual prices being traded across the marketplace and that its staff and methodology will deliver a fair assessment.

There are a few reasons why a particular PRA assessment will be recognized as a benchmark by the industry. The main reason is a question of habit: the market is just more used to one PRA rather than another. This is often because that PRA was the first to assess a particular commodity. In benchmarks and for PRAs, first-mover advantage is extremely important because it is so rare for the industry to switch from one PRA benchmark to another. The industry also chooses a PRA benchmark based on its methodology, perhaps because it feels a certain methodology is more representative or else is preferable for compliance purposes. The choice of a particular PRA benchmark may also depend on the availability of a related derivatives market. Many participants will want to hedge their price exposure to a PRA by taking the opposite position in the derivatives market and so they will need to know that there are also liquid swaps or futures available for any specific benchmark.

Switching benchmarks

Throughout the history of the industry, very few PRA benchmarks have changed hands. The majority of the switches have come in the energy market, which is the most competitive commodity sector for PRAs, although some petrochemical benchmarks have also moved from one PRA to another, with PetroChem Wire acquiring some benchmarks at the expense of Platts.

Because of its long history as a pioneer among PRAs, Platts is the incumbent benchmark in most energy markets and so by definition has the most benchmarks to lose. In energy markets, Argus has tended to be the second-choice PRA and so has picked up some benchmarks from Platts, although Platts has itself acquired the Asian light crude oil benchmark from the Asia Petroleum Price Index (APPI) and is currently pursuing the Japanese domestic petroleum markets, whose benchmarks have historically been provided by RIM Intelligence.

The three factors that have driven the selection of one PRA rather than another are first-mover advantage, frequency and methodology.

We have already mentioned the importance of first-mover advantage. Incumbency combined with industry inertia is nine-tenths of the battle in PRA benchmarks because the industry becomes used to a benchmark provider. With over a century in business, Platts is the incumbent in most energy markets, but Argus became the benchmark in European biodiesel and biomass, for example, principally because it was the first of the major PRAs to report those markets in depth.

Frequency is another key factor. Given the conservative nature of the commodity industry and the complications of switching, it takes a lot for traders to want to move. Frequency of assessment is one of the very limited issues that can drive a move. The first benchmarks to move from Platts to Argus were the European and Asian LPG markets, which responded to Argus' decision to move to daily pricing from the weekly assessment period that Platts was using. As markets develop, the market typically wants a greater frequency of assessments in order to capture growing activity levels. If the incumbent PRA is slow to respond, then the market may well switch.

The third factor in the choice of benchmarks is methodology. If first-mover advantage is the most important factor in establishing a benchmark, then methodology is the main factor that has led to switches from one PRA to another. Platts acquired the Asian crude oil benchmark from APPI because the incumbent's panel methodology was perceived to be producing erroneous results and the market had more faith in the Platts methodology. But on the reverse side, Argus acquired the European gasoline and US crude oil benchmarks from Platts because of industry concerns about the introduction of the Platts' market-on-close (MOC) methodology (see the chapter on MOC for further details).

There are very few examples of benchmark switches that were generated by a rival PRA doing something better than the incumbent, with the exception of frequency of publication. The power of incumbency is so strong that even great alternatives tend to be overlooked by the industry in favour of the familiar.

One of the few examples of a switch that was not based on a misstep by an incumbent is the switch from Platts to PetroChem Wire (PCW) in some US petrochemical benchmarks in the late 2000s. In this case, the switch was the result of the strong reputation of PCW's founder, Kathy Hall. The industry chose to follow Hall when she decided to leave Platts and start her own PRA. This was a unique occurrence and other price reporters have failed to repeat Hall's success in driving a switch when they change employers.

Switch prospects

There have been very few PRA-to-PRA switches in history and the chance of a new wave of benchmark switches is very small. Virtually all of the previous changes were the result of the incumbent PRA doing something out of the ordinary, such as changing its methodology, or else failing to respond to a shift in the market by ignoring the need for a change in frequency. The recent switches from Platts to Argus were the direct consequence of Platts changing its methodology to MOC. Without a major new change in methodology by Platts, it would be a surprise if any more benchmarks were to switch in the next few years. Any switch would, however, be extremely significant.

PRAs devote considerable resources to promoting a change in benchmarks, despite the industry's very limited record of switches. For PRA management, this is a low-probability, high-upside bet, given the enormous economic uplift of winning a new benchmark from a rival.

Looking around the global commodities markets, the biggest opportunity of all at present is in North Sea crude oil. Platts' Dated Brent assessment is the most valuable PRA commodity benchmark and over the next few years Platts will have to carry out a major design shift to its Brent benchmark, given the reduced production base in the North Sea. Any misstep by Platts could let a competitor in. Other opportunities for PRAs are to establish first-mover advantage in some of the newer markets such as LNG, where Platts currently has the advantage. LNG is such a significant opportunity because it also has the potential to disrupt regional pipeline gas markets. Agricultural markets are also still generally open for PRAs to establish benchmarks, although again Platts seems to be in prime position. New countries and regions could also open up and develop pricing hubs that PRAs would want to cover as soon as was practical.

PRA managements must make a difficult decision: should they allocate business development and marketing resources evenly across all the markets in which they compete or should they weight investment aggressively towards the two or three most promising opportunities? The difficulty of securing a switch means that if a PRA achieves just one switch per decade then that would be a very impressive record. A single switch anywhere would be a major revenue driver for a PRA and would represent a fantastic return on investment.

Why so few switches?

It is worth considering why so few commodity benchmarks have changed hands over the years, given the activity of the various PRAs' business development teams. The first and overwhelming factor is that most traders do not care much about benchmarks or PRA methodologies; they care about the profitability of their most recent trades. A benchmark generally has to diverge from expectations over a lengthy period and to cost some firms a lot of money before it will provoke any substantive reaction from the industry.

Benchmarks are a classic example of what economists call "path dependency". This is the continued use of a product or practice based on historical preference or use. The concept of path dependency suggests that, due to the previous commitment made, usage will continue even if newer, more efficient products or practices are available.

A commodity trader that has decided to look at pricing issues because of perceived deficiencies in the current PRA-supplied benchmark will face a host of difficulties. His or her trading manager may be sympathetic but frequently the firm's risk managers will be suspicious that the desire to switch benchmark provider is actually the result of a desire to mitigate or cover up potential trading losses. The company's middle and back office will tend also to push back because a benchmark switch may require them to take a second expensive PRA subscription, which they will also have to configure to feed into internal systems that are set up to take data from the incumbent PRA.

Even if the trader's firm understands the benefits of a change in PRA provider and is fully supportive, there is still the issue with the wider market. The problems that the current benchmark is experiencing are likely to be benefiting some part of the market, which as a result will be highly reluctant to switch. There is also an innate suspicion of anyone proposing a switch. When the trader talks to his counter-parties at other firms about changing benchmark provider, most will assume that the trader's firm has found an angle to exploit and so they will oppose the switch on general principle. A switch proposed by a natural buyer will typically be opposed by a seller, for example. Anti-trust rules also make it very difficult for companies to get together to discuss the need or not for a switch.

Even assuming the whole industry is united in favour of a switch in PRA benchmark provider, the initiative can still be derailed. Some companies will be locked into long-term supply deals and they will not want to change the contract terms to reference a different PRA out of fear that the entire contract could then be open to renegotiation. Traders will also have long-term exposure to the incumbent benchmark through the derivatives market. Brokers and exchanges will all need to be aligned in order to promote derivative contracts based on the new PRA provider's assessments and to assist counterparties to roll their derivatives exposure from the old benchmark to the new.

These stumbling blocks are not insurmountable as the list of benchmark switches over the past couple of decades has shown. But the enormous difficulties explain the rarity of switches and help to explain why first-mover advantage and incumbency is so valuable.

Rival benchmarks

There are also many commodity benchmarks that are not established by PRAs. Exchange benchmarks, official selling prices or posted prices, government-set prices and broker indices are all examples of commodity benchmarks that are not sourced from PRAs. There is inevitably, however, a significant interplay between the various types of benchmarks. Very few commodity markets are islands and so a benchmark that is set by an exchange will necessarily influence or be influenced by a benchmark in an adjacent market that is set by a PRA. Similarly, official selling prices or government-mandated prices need to take the market prices reported by PRAs and exchanges into account. Otherwise, they risk distorting the markets in which they hold sway.

Exchange benchmarks

Futures exchanges account for several of the most prominent global commodity benchmarks, typically in the form of the settlement price of a physically settled futures contract. The chapter on PRA relationships with exchanges deals in greater depth with how exchanges develop benchmarks and how they cooperate with, and in some cases compete with, PRAs.

Traditionally, exchange benchmarks have had the advantage or disadvantage of being directly regulated by governments, which gives potential users a greater sense of security. In contrast, the PRAs have historically been treated as media companies or publishers and their benchmarks are self-regulated. In recent years, though, this distinction has been blurred and with the 2018 advent of the European Union benchmark legislation, still more of the difference in regulatory status between PRA and exchange benchmarks will be erased.

Official prices

Some commodity price benchmarks are also set directly by sellers on a monthly basis and are known as 'posted prices' or official selling prices (OSPs). This approach is particularly common among national oil companies (NOCs). The NOC will publish a price each month at which it will sell its output of, for example, crude oil,

LPG or sulphur. These OSPs cannot be challenged by the buyer, although the two parties often agree discounts depending on the size, timing and duration of their agreement.

Posted prices were once common across energy markets in Europe and the US as well but most sellers have abandoned the practice. This is in part because sellers that set a posted price and stick to it immediately open themselves up to undercutting by rivals. Some sellers also ceased to post official prices because of the potential legal and compliance implications of taking full responsibility for establishing market prices. Apart from the NOCs in the energy markets, posted prices do, however, survive in some other areas such as some base oil and lubricant markets and some steel product markets.

Posted prices are in any case not set in isolation by the seller. A responsible seller that does not want to alienate its buyers will look at where PRAs are assessing either their own market or similar markets in order to judge where to set their OSP. The pricing team of the NOC is also likely to make use of one or more of the methodological approaches that the PRAs use in order to reach its official price. For example, most sellers carry out official or semi-official surveys of their buyers in the run up to setting their OSPs.

Posted prices and OSPs represent good potential targets for PRA benchmarks. Historically, markets have tended to evolve away from prices fixed by sellers towards genuine independent benchmarks and so PRAs look upon markets where such prices dominate as good future opportunities. In 2006, for example, BP decided to cease setting its BP Agreed Prices (BPAP) for European propane and butane and turned instead to Argus to set an independent index: the Argus North Sea Index (ANSI).[1]

Broker benchmarks

Another source of benchmarks is broker indexes, which are commodity price indexes established by over-the-counter brokers. These indexes will typically be based on the market activity that the brokers themselves observe. The main criticism of broker indexes is that there is a perceived risk that the largest customers could intimidate the broker and perhaps withdraw business if the broker does not adjust the index in their favour. There is also a concern that brokered indexes might not capture bilateral activity or trades done through brokers that are not part of the index mechanism.

Some brokers have neatly circumvented concerns about their independence from undue influence by launching indexes that are based on volume weighted averages (VWAs) of deals. Broker indexes based on VWAs have, for example, come to dominate the Canadian crude oil markets. The larger PRAs offer Canadian price assessments but so far the industry in Canada has preferred the VWA indexes provided by two rival brokers, Net Energy and Shorcan.

The PRAs' experience in Canada encapsulates one of the major dilemmas currently facing the energy PRAs: how to create benchmark methodologies that are transparent and clear but which are not at the same time easily replicable. The danger with the use by PRAs of VWAs as a benchmark methodology, as Shorcan and Net

Energy have shown, is that one VWA is very much like another, assuming similar access to the underlying deal data. This makes it hard for PRAs to differentiate themselves, especially when their subscription rates tend to be relatively high, whereas a broker may give away its index cheaply or for free as an added-value service to its main business, which is broking deals for commission.

Bioenergy specialist PRA PRIMA Markets is experimenting with involving brokers more closely in the price-discovery process. Rather than seeing brokers as potential rival benchmark providers, PRIMA has built its Discovery pricing platform with the specific intention of including intermediaries alongside principals in its electronic assessments. The concept behind the approach is that brokers, like price reporters, are incentivized to extract bids and offers from market participants in order to generate deal liquidity. Working with brokers has the added benefit of potentially reducing PRA manpower and therefore the overhead needed to run electronic price-discovery sessions.

Benchmark manipulation

The importance of benchmarks to the commodity markets means that there is inevitably a concern that benchmarks could be manipulated, particularly given the scandals in recent years around some of the financial benchmarks, such as the London Interbank Offered Rate (LIBOR). There have always been strong penalties in place for firms that have sought to manipulate benchmarks but in recent years governments have turned their focus towards preventing potential manipulation by raising compliance standards rather than simply detecting and punishing bad behaviour.

Attempts to manipulate benchmarks can take many forms but include: false reporting of trades to PRAs, misleading PRAs about market conditions, selling small volumes during the price-discovery mechanism in order to buy much larger volumes at a cheaper price, 'cornering' a market by withholding physical supply; taking a loss on a physical trade in order to benefit a much larger derivatives position; bidding for supply on date ranges where there is no or limited availability; bidding or offering very prompt material; and "stampeding the close" with exaggerated activity at the end of an assessment time period.

Any commodity market veteran will have a tale of some attempt or other to 'move the market'. It is not always easy to determine when a legitimate if aggressive trading play crosses the line and becomes market manipulation. PRAs have traditionally been self-regulating entities, which have had to resist pressure and be aware of potential attempts to manipulate. Ensuring the integrity of their benchmarks is paramount for PRAs, given the paramount importance of protecting their reputation for producing fair assessments. Since LIBOR, greater awareness of the risks of manipulating benchmarks have encouraged firms that contribute to price discovery to be more aware of their responsibilities and have also led to some innovation from PRAs that are trying to improve their price-discovery processes. Regulatory scrutiny has, however, proved to be something of a double-edged sword: firms are now more nervous of interacting with price reporters, which risks limiting the information flow to PRAs. The impact of this issue is explored in more depth in the chapters on PRAs and regulation.

Conclusion

Benchmarks are an integral part of the way many segments of the commodities markets do business. Without good quality benchmarks, traders would waste their time arguing the framework of every single deal and could make disastrous calls about the future direction of outright prices. Benchmarks are therefore hugely valuable to the commodity market and have a major commercial significance for the PRAs that provide them.

Establishing benchmark usage is a key objective for every PRA, particularly as it is so difficult for a rival PRA to displace an incumbent. First-mover advantage is enormous in the benchmark world and, generally, a rival can only displace an existing benchmark provider if there is a serious misstep by the incumbent. Despite the enormous difficulties of displacing an incumbent and the extreme rarity of switches, rival PRAs have to nonetheless invest heavily in marketing and in business development staff in order to be considered as a credible alternative during those rare moments when the incumbent stumbles or when a market moves away from posted prices or OSPs.

Note

1   BPAP Changes Name to ANSI, Argus Media press release, 5 October 2006.

4 Who are the price reporters?

Introduction

It is fair to say that no one ever told their careers advisor that their dream was to become a price reporter. And yet over 10,000 people around the world generate price assessments that are then distributed by more than 100 commodity information services. This chapter will look at how people enter the price reporting sphere, how they are trained and their career development prospects.

Not every one of those 10,000 immortals spends their entire day assessing prices. Many would consider themselves primarily to be analysts, consultants or brokers for whom reporting or calculating benchmarks is a part-time ancillary activity. Even those whose business cards describe them as price reporters do not spend all day every day assessing prices, simply because there is not enough trading activity in most physical commodity markets to require constant supervision. Most will have other work to do and will only turn to market assessments towards the end of the working day.

Increased use of technology and a trend towards the use of more mechanical approaches to reporting prices, as described in the chapter on methodologies, is also changing the role of price reporters at some of the largest price reporting agencies (PRAs). The traditional price reporter that was an expert in his or her market and who spent a large amount of time entertaining traders in order to build trust is now a dying breed. Price reporters are increasingly tied to their desks by compliance concerns both from their own employer and by those of market participants. With the change in emphasis of the price reporter's role, analytical skills are becoming more important than the social and investigative skills that were previously required.

Birth of a price reporter

Somewhere in a major capital city a 20-something journalist is looking for a job. He or she will likely have a degree in some form of the humanities and a desire to work in the media. But journalism is a competitive field and the search for a new job is proving a challenge.

Then our hero's luck changes. There is an opening for a reporter at a publisher that seems to specialize in business news, with a particular focus on the commodity markets. The publisher's name doesn't sound familiar and the job doesn't sound quite as prestigious as a role on the *New York Times* or the *Economist*. But on the other hand, reporting on OPEC or renewable energy could be quite interesting and so he sends off an application.

During the interview process, there are tests for numeracy and literacy as well as interviews probing the candidate's personality and business awareness. The interviewer does not require any specialist knowledge but wants to test the candidate's awareness of non-academic economics and ability to think logically. She asks our candidate questions like what factors might impact on German electricity demand and why oil-producing nations might have decided to form OPEC.

Our hero makes it through the tests and the interview process and is delighted to get an offer, especially when the job seems to pay surprisingly well. The proposed salary is a major improvement on anything the local newspaper, trade magazine or NGO newsletter might have offered and so our hero is delighted to accept.

Then one Monday morning soon afterwards, the process of converting an excited and slightly nervous young journalist into a price reporter begins. Our hero is introduced to the intricacies of arcane commodities like open-spec naphtha or metallurgical coal. Over the coming months our hero will absorb vast amounts of information about trading strategies, market structure, technical specifications, reporting methodologies as well as learning to understand the requirements of the compliance department. At a western PRA this training tends to be more or less formal depending on the firm and will rely a lot on individual mentoring by an editor or a senior price reporter. At the Chinese PRAs with their very large graduate intakes, the process tends to be significantly more formal and can even stretch out for six months in a format that approaches a mini university course.

At some point our hero will be let loose on the markets and will need to interact with stressed-out commodity traders whose bonus may in part depend on our hero's first attempts at reporting benchmark prices. Unsurprisingly, the attrition rate for new employees will be relatively high. Some will dislike the emphasis on numbers rather than words, and others will find dealing with market participants daunting, while others will leave to pursue more typical media careers. But many members of the new intake will stay and thrive.

Those that make it through the first two years tend to stay in the commodities sector for the rest of their career in some form or another. By then they will have become subject matter experts and their value is growing. Some price reporters will stay on the reporting side and will rotate within their firm to cover different commodities or be promoted to run a report or a market segment.

Other price reporters will cross the invisible line that separates the publisher from the commodity market and will become brokers, traders or analysts. The interchange between the markets and the PRAs generally depends on whether it is a bull or a bear market. In a bullish market for commodities where lots of new players are entering the markets and there is a lot of money around, PRA staff will tend to be more in demand and may choose to move for higher salaries. In a downturn, however, where commodity firms are making staff redundant, PRAs will look more attractive. In general, PRAs offer greater security of employment, albeit at lower wages, and so in depressed markets they will start to receive enquiries about reporting jobs from traders, brokers and analysts that have been laid off.

Whether or not the price reporter stays with a PRA or moves into the industry, his or her pay will tend to outperform that of their peers in traditional media or publishing firms. The price reporter will also gradually cease to think of themselves as part of the media world that seemed so attractive just a few years ago. Once a would-be journalist, our hero is now a 'pricing guy' – a small and generally under-appreciated cog in the wheel that drives the modern commodity markets.

A day in the life

Let us now take a look at a typical day in our hero's life and see just how a price reporter operates. We can picture our hero as a relatively new recruit to a global PRA who is working on the LPG/NGL desk in London and is covering the North Sea cargo markets for propane and butane. The rough outlines of his day will apply to most commodity markets and to most locations within a specialist PRA – of course, the day will look very different for price assessors whose primary role is as a consultant, analyst or broker.

The first thing to note is that our hero will not start work early. Very few people will be in the office by 10am and most will appear around 11am. This is in part the traditional journalists' aversion to early mornings but it also reflects the slightly offset nature of the price reporters' work. The price reporter will be at his or her busiest once the markets have closed, usually from the late afternoon onwards, so PRAs will tend to work a staggered shift, coming in mid-morning and leaving late in the evening at around 7 to 8pm.

Once our hero is behind the desk at 11am, his or her email and instant messages will start lighting up. Many commodity participants prefer to use instant messaging applications rather than phone calls and so the first login of the day is always a nervous moment. Will there be a dozen messages flashing up complaining about the prices that our hero published yesterday? Today is a relatively calm day and there's just one relatively polite query from a German trader asking for an explanation of yesterday's assessment. Our hero shoots him back a relatively detailed explanation of his decision and the trader accepts it with a terse "thx".

Inevitably, in a rising market, the buyers will complain that the price reporter is moving the price up too aggressively and the opposite will be true for sellers into a falling market. There will also be complaints from anyone who is caught on the wrong side of the market and whose trading strategies are not playing out. These kind of complaints are easily dealt with and our hero has learnt quickly who the natural bulls and the natural bears are and therefore who is likely to complain when the price moves up or down. Listening to the grievances of disgruntled commodity traders is all part of the job.

The tougher days for our hero are when one or two market participants are aggressively driving the market in a certain direction. It is at times like these that the rest of the market will take their frustrations out on the price reporter and blame the methodology that allows some of their rivals to exert pressure on prices. These are the times our reporter will need to get his editor or manager involved and will need to get out to visit customers to reassure them that their concerns are being heard.

Today is not one of those tougher days and after dealing with the single query, our hero will work through the overnight emails and will start liaising with his counterpart at the PRA's Asian operation. The PRA's Asian offices, primarily located in Singapore but also in Japan or China, are coming to the end of their working day just as London opens up and they now need to share their market assessments and reports with their colleagues in London. The handover from Asia is a crucial part of the day – in many commodities the supply-demand balance in Asia will set the tone for European trading.

Fresh information from Asia will also give the European price reporters something new to tell their contacts in the market when they start making calls in the afternoon. Commodity traders always prefer to trade information rather than to simply download what they know. The most rewarding calls are when the reporter has something new to tell the trader rather than just asking for information about market activity.

The Asian reports have been received, the market commentaries are edited and any pricing spreadsheets are updated. Depending on the PRA, some market reporters will now work on a news story or a longer feature for one of the PRA's reports or newsletters. Others might help out on a consulting project or prepare a presentation for a customer meeting or industry conference. There are also the inevitable internal meetings and the need for lunch.

By mid-afternoon, the decks must be cleared. Reporting the market now takes over. On Platts' desks that have adopted the eWindow methodology much of the information-gathering process is automated but for other markets and other PRAs, information needs to be gathered through a combination of phone calls, instant messages and emailed activity sheets from brokers and traders. Our hero is talking all the time to colleagues as well, not just his neighbours on the LPG/NGL desk but also checking what the reporters on the naphtha desk are hearing since the two products compete for some petrochemical uses. The office, which was previously fairly silent, now starts to get noisier as the reporters are either on the phone or shouting out to one another. Reporters will be calling out to each other to ask "who've you spoken to already?"; "what's crude doing now?" and "are your numbers in the spreadsheet yet?"

Major market participants that allow their traders to speak to PRAs can expect a call from a price reporter every single day, while other less active participants will be classed as an alternate-day or once-a-week call. In every case, the call will follow roughly the same pattern: an exchange of views on where the market is trading; a query whether or not the contact has done any deals today or seen any firm bids and offers; and a more general discussion about factors that might move the market, such as potential demand in Asia, local refinery shutdowns, and so on. The better the relationship the price reporter has built up with the trader, the more information he or she is likely to share.

Younger price reporters will all have heard the tales of the glory days of price reporting, which were long before anyone had heard of the concept of compliance. In those far-off days, there were no restraints at commodity firms about talking to price reporters and socializing was common. Reporters and their contacts would drink together and relationships tended to be deeper. In these more stringent times, the contact will tend to be more functional and the price reporter is just relieved if the firm is not one of those that has already banned its traders from speaking to PRAs.

After an hour or two of frenetic conversation, the noise level will die down once again. Most of the European markets close for normal trading at around 4.30pm and traders are usually willing to talk for another hour or 90 minutes. By 6pm the reporters should have gathered together all their information and be in a position to make their assessments of where prices should be set and to start on their market commentary.

The next period will see our hero discussing the final assessments and any likely issues with his or her line manager and submitting a commentary for editing. This can be a brief recital of who traded what at what level or a longer essay that also takes in all of the market fundamentals, depending on the reporter and editor's inclinations.

By now, it is well into the evening and the production staff are wanting to get their hands on the final assessments and reports so that they can be sent out to subscribers. The European staff also now need to check in with their colleagues in the US, usually in either New York, Washington D.C. or Houston, who are now coming into work and who need to know what happened in Europe and Asia. Once the handover is complete and the report is finalized, our hero's working day is done. He or she heads off into the London night, relieved to have got the report out on time but always with that slightly nagging feeling that tomorrow morning could bring a clutch of complaints.

Trends in employment

As in any job, older colleagues will tell the younger ones that everything was better in their day. In the case of price reporters, this is probably largely untrue. Most PRAs are more profitable now than at any point in their history and some of this increased revenue and investment filters down to the employees in terms of higher salaries and nicer offices. The greater emphasis across PRAs and their users on compliance and clarity in methodology has also greatly reduced the atmosphere of conflict that sometimes existed between price reporters and traders. With more predictable methodologies and transparent screen-based assessments, there is relatively little upside for a trader in lobbying or bullying an individual reporter to try to get him or her to accept a certain view of the market. The downside to which, of course, is that many firms and traders have simply stopped talking to PRAs altogether, reducing the relationship aspect of the job that many price reporters enjoyed.

Women in PRAs

The western PRAs generally have a decent balance between men and women in their staff, while the Chinese PRAs are if anything weighted towards female employees. In contrast, the commodity markets remain very male dominated and so most of a price reporter's contacts list will be men. The reduction in the tension between price reporters and their contacts brought about by clearer methodologies and greater emphasis on compliance has, however, helped to reduce the 'macho' quotient of price reporting. Price reporters are no longer expected to drink with their contacts or to endure abuse on a bad trading day, and this has undoubtedly benefited those female price reporters that were less comfortable dealing with testosterone-driven traders.

Despite relative equality at the level of price reporters, the PRAs still tend to be run by men. Just nine of the 37 members (24 per cent) of the senior leadership teams of the 'Big Three' – Platts, Argus and ICIS – were women in early 2017. Senior female executives also tended to be concentrated in support roles such as human resources, legal and marketing, rather than overseeing price reporting operations.

There are a few notable exceptions to this rule. There are plenty of female senior editors at PRAs. And at the highest levels, Hisako Mori has run RIM Intelligence since its creation, while Kathy Hall founded PetroChem Wire and Ellen Beswick founded Natural Gas Intelligence (NGI). Platts has also had two female presidents: Victoria Chu Pao from 2005 to 2009 and Imogen Dillon Hatcher, later Imogen Joss, from 2014 to 2015.

Overall, on a gender equality scorecard basis, most PRAs are significantly more equal that the commodity firms with whom they deal but women are still not fully represented at the very highest levels of management.

Conclusion

Price reporters are an unusual breed. Most of them are closer in background and temperament to their counterparts in the media or publishing and yet to succeed as a price reporter they need to hone their analytical skills and to brush up on subjects like economics and chemistry that they likely neglected in college. Price reporters find themselves spending large amounts of time talking to traders who typically come from engineering or mathematical backgrounds and inevitably they need to adapt to a different approach and worldview if they are going to succeed in building relationships with their contacts.

PRA salaries are also pitched somewhere in the middle of the two worlds: price reporters make higher salaries than counterparts in media and publishing, but their earnings are significantly lower than the traders and brokers with whom they deal on a daily basis.

A price reporter's prospects of a salary rise depend primarily on his or her responsibilities and on how well the PRA is performing financially, which in turn may depend on where we are in the commodity price cycle. The reporter's value will also depend on the importance of his or her experience in a particular market. A more opaque seaborne market like coal that is still highly reliant on phone calls and personal contact for price discovery may, for example, require greater experience and therefore better paid staff than a market where price discovery takes place entirely on a screen, making the experience of the reporter less relevant.

The trend towards greater reliance on screen-based market assessments or more mechanical methodologies such as volume-weighted assessments leads to some angst that the traditional price reporter is at risk of extinction. Will the PRA of 2050 still need price reporters that can handle angry customers and can wheedle information out of close-mouthed traders, or will all price discovery be handled by screens or by algorithms? While there will inevitably be some move to automation and indeed this is already happening, it is still hard to imagine a PRA entirely without price reporters. A PRA will always need staff capable of explaining and promoting its methodology and of dealing with queries and complaints, while machines are also still not yet able to compose a readable market commentary, although some traditional price reporters struggle with this as well.

Fears of the longer-term extinction of price reporters can be exaggerated. The more niche commodities that trade infrequently and on different terms and conditions will never be suited to more automated approaches. These at least will remain the sphere of the traditional price reporter operating in a strange niche between journalist and commodity market participant.

5 A brief history of energy PRAs

Introduction

Commodities are usually divided into three classes: energy, metals and agricultural, although some products do not fit neatly into these categories or they straddle the line between two classes. Price reporting agencies (PRAs) play a different role in each of the three classes: their role is limited in the agricultural markets but growing in the metals markets, where they are very significant to the ferrous metals industry. PRAs are, however, absolutely essential to the operations of the energy markets and the largest PRAs derive the majority of their revenue from energy.

The development of PRAs largely mirrors the development of the energy markets. Although commodity prices had been published for centuries, the 1973 Arab Oil Embargo ushered in a new era for commodity pricing by generating unprecedented energy price volatility, leading to a new focus on spot pricing and risk management. The events of 1973 led directly to the creation of several PRAs.

The next generation of firms was born in the early 1990s in response to the liberalization of the European and US electricity, gas and coal markets and to the opening up of new energy markets following the end of the Cold War. The last 15 years have seen a marked consolidation in the sector and the dominance of the 'Big Three': Platts, Argus and ICIS. In recent years, increased regulatory scrutiny of PRAs in the wake of various benchmark scandals, such as LIBOR, has forced the industry to tighten up its business practices and has acted as a further driver of consolidation.

The early years

The longest running commodity pricing publication is *The Public Ledger*, which is currently owned by Informa, and which has been assessing agricultural commodities traded in London since 1760. The *Public Ledger's* subtitle on its masthead: a *Daily Register of Commerce and Intelligence*, still could appear on the masthead of virtually any publication produced today by a price reporting agency.

The Public Ledger was building on a legacy of innovation in the agricultural markets. Agricultural products underpinned the very first exchanges, such as the Amsterdam Stock Exchange, created in 1560, and the Dojima Rice Exchange, created in Osaka in 1697. Agricultural derivatives were taken to the next level by the success and reach of the Chicago futures exchanges from the nineteenth century onwards. But perhaps because of the success of the exchanges in meeting the information and trading needs of market participants, agricultural markets stayed outside the mainstream of the development of the PRA industry, at least until very recently.

The major players in the PRA world have instead come from within the energy industry. The modern PRA industry was created in the US and is largely the invention of one man – Warren Platt of Ohio – who in 1909 established the first publications dedicated to the oil markets and to reporting oil prices.[1]

The father of the PRA industry

Warren Cumming Platt was born in 1883 in the US state of Ohio, the third of five children. His ancestor Richard Platt had moved from Hertfordshire in England to Connecticut in the mid-seventeenth century and by the time of Platt's birth, his branch of the family was well established in Ohio, where they worked as clockmakers, silversmiths and jewellers.

Platt turned his back on the family trade and dropped out of school to train as a journalist, later specializing in covering energy issues. He was in the right place: Ohio was the epicentre of the growing US oil industry. Just 13 years before Platt's birth, John D. Rockefeller had established Standard Oil in Ohio and had built it into the world's largest oil company.

Platt spotted a thirst for independent information about the oil sector and at the age of 25 he borrowed $2,500 in order to set up his own monthly magazine, which he called *National Petroleum News*. The magazine's stated aim was to level "the information playing field between independent oilmen and Big Oil by promoting transparency within the oil industry".

In 1911, Platt's newly founded business received a huge stimulus when the US Supreme Court ruled that Standard Oil was a monopoly and forced its break-up into 34 different companies, many of whose descendants are still key oil companies today.

The break-up of Standard Oil led to an explosion in demand for oil industry information and Platt responded by launching further publications, with a growing emphasis on disseminating price information, from his new headquarters in the heart of the US oil fields in Tulsa, Oklahoma. In 1953, and at the age of 70, Warren Platt sold his various energy publishing businesses to US publishing firm McGraw-Hill. He passed away in March 1963 in California.

Warren Platt focused on accuracy but also on the speed of delivery of information and he made full use of the latest technology in copying and in dispatching his reports. Platt's *Oilgram* publication, which was launched in 1923 and is still published today, was intended to provide up-to-date, reliable and independent data on pricing to oil companies on a premium subscription basis. Platt thereby created the basic business model for all of the PRAs that still operate today.

A major breakthrough for Platt and for the energy industry came in 1928 when his assessment of the price of US Gulf crude oil was used by leading oil companies as an independent reference point in their contracts. This was the first time that a published index had been accepted by the energy industry as a viable way of agreeing a mutually acceptable price point.

But the use of indexation remained the exception over the next few decades as oil prices remained largely range bound. With markets dominated by a relatively small number of companies and prices relatively stable, most energy deals were done on a fixed-price and long-term basis, which offered little scope for independent assessment or analysis.

Right up until the 1970s, there were few major developments in the PRA sector beyond the acquisition of Platts (the apostrophe was dropped in 2000) by McGraw-Hill in 1953 and the expansion of Platts into Europe in the 1960s, where the firm began to assess energy prices in the English Channel and in Rotterdam using the same methodologies as they had done in the US.

1970s–1980s: new PRAs emerge

In 1970 the first genuine rival to Platts emerged, when a British former military officer, Jan Nasmyth (1918–2008), who had grown frustrated at the opacity of the global energy markets during his work as an energy analyst with the United Nations, founded the weekly *Europ-Oil Prices* report from the basement of his house in London to cover European crude and products.[2]

Three years later in 1973 the Arab Oil Embargo essentially remade the global energy markets, ending decades of relative price stability, making price controls in much of the developed world untenable and opening up the modern era of commodity price volatility.

The clear instability of supplies from the Middle East also generated feverish exploration activity in the North Sea, Asia and Americas that generated new centres of energy resources and price discovery, as well as supporting a large number of new independent drillers, financing banks and traders that were to become key customers of the PRAs.

Nasmyth's timing had been impeccable. In 1976 *Europ-Oil Prices* was renamed as Petroleum Argus and in 1979 Argus began publishing its first daily spot prices for crude oil and petroleum, going head-to-head with Platts. Argus' move to daily pricing had been inspired by the aftermath of the Iranian Revolution, which had dramatically reduced global supply and sent oil prices shooting higher, generating further demand from the oil industry for information about markets and prices.

In 1983, former BP employee Adrian Binks joined Argus and in 1984 he took management control, after buying a partnership in the business. Binks began to develop Argus as an international player, opening offices in the United States and Asia and increasing the firm's focus on pricing.

The massive volatility unleashed in the 1970s was felt particularly hard down-stream in the petrochemical industries, generating a new interest in price indexation, benchmarking and hedging. Jack DeWitt created the first petrochemical reporting service in 1973 – DeWitt & Co – and in 1975 Platts expanded into the sector. In

1979, a former Platts' petrochemical reporter based in Paris, Humphrey Hinshelwood, set up his own reporting service – Independent Chemical Information Services (ICIS) – after spotting a gap in the market.

At around the same time, a raft of other PRAs were springing up to cover different aspects of the newly liberalized and vibrant energy markets. OPIS emerged in 1977, initially as the *Oil Express Newsletter*, to cover the US downstream and retail markets, where it achieved benchmark status in many of the West Coast refined products markets and, most famously, the Mont Belvieu hub for natural gas liquids. Across the Atlantic, the *London Oil Reports* were founded in 1980 as a rival to Platts and Argus, only to merge with ICIS in 1984.

The first gas-focused PRA emerged in the United States in 1981 when Ellen Beswick founded Natural Gas Intelligence (NGI). NGI started publishing the industry's first natural gas price survey report in 1983 as the US natural gas market began to develop and the firm went on to achieve benchmark status in a number of US hubs.

For the first time, PRAs also emerged outside the traditional energy trading hubs of the US and UK. RIM Intelligence was founded in 1984 to cover the Japanese energy markets and OMR was created to cover the German energy markets in the German language in 1985. RIM came to dominate the Japanese domestic markets as well as being used in a number of Asian crude oil benchmarks. RIM was more successful than OMR in expanding outside its home country in part because its decision to use English in many of its reports gave it a broader reach.

The 1990s: new markets open up

The end of the Cold War and the opening up of the Eastern Bloc and China during the 1990s created several new energy markets and brought a number of new energy companies into the global markets, offering significant opportunities for PRAs.

The existing PRAs were quick to open up offices in new locations with varying degrees of success. The most aggressive in their expansions were Platts, Argus and ICIS, establishing the pattern of dominance that remains to this day. In the Asian markets, Platts came to dominate the key Singapore crude and refined products markets, while sharing leadership in the Asian petrochemical markets with ICIS. ICIS itself later made a major investment in China when it acquired C1 Energy in 2014 (see Chapter 9 for further details).

Argus was arguably less successful in Asia but it made a major breakthrough in another newly opened jurisdiction: Russia and the countries of the former Soviet Union. Argus quickly established a major lead over its western competitors and built a very impressive operation in eastern Europe and central Asia from Moscow, although it faced indigenous competition in the region from Kortes, a Russian PRA founded during market liberalization in 1991, which was later acquired by Thomson Reuters. Poland also saw the development of a national PRA champion, ePetrol, which was founded in 2001.

At the same time as new jurisdictions around the world were liberalizing, a revolution was also taking place in the European generation fuel and electricity markets, which were being opened up to competition for the first time. The UK natural gas market began trading actively in 1994/95 and a genuinely competitive UK electricity market emerged in 2001 with the creation of the New Electricity Trading Arrangements (NETA) in 2001, which was renamed as the British Electricity Trading Transmission Arrangements (BETTA) in 2005.

Liberalization in the power sector forced European electricity producers to compete for customers by offering more competitive prices, making them focus on benchmarks, spot trading and hedging for the first time. It also reinforced similar developments in the generation fuel sector, creating further momentum in gas and coal trading.

The liberalization of the generation markets effectively created a whole new energy trading sector for PRAs to explore, allowing them for the first time to diversify from their traditional petroleum-based business lines. The emissions and biomass markets emerged later on as add-ons to the power and generation fuels markets.

Argus published its first non-oil report, the *European Natural Gas Report*, in 1995 and picked up a suite of US coal, gas and power reports through the 2000 acquisition of Fieldstone publications. Platts also entered the generation and fuels business through its 2001 acquisition of the FT Energy publications.

New PRAs also emerged to cover these new market developments. A former FT Energy staffer, Gerard McCloskey, created McCloskey Coal in 1987 to focus on the coal markets. McCloskey Coal and Argus later formed a partnership to publish joint coal indexes – the APIs – that have become the standard reference price in most thermal coal markets.

The first European gas-focused PRA also emerged when in 1993 a former Argus and Energy Intelligence employee, Patrick Heren, launched Heren Energy. Heren had noted the value of pricing data during his time at Argus and his firm's price assessments of European natural gas trading hubs, particularly the UK's National Balancing Point (NBP), went on to become important industry benchmarks.

Then in 2000, Point Carbon was founded in Oslo, Norway to focus on the newly developing European emissions markets. The firm was created by a group of Norwegian analysts who had realized that international governments who were negotiating the first climate agreements were hampered by a lack of information about global emissions.

2000s: consolidation begins

At the start of the new millennium, low barriers to entry and the development of significant new markets meant that there were a large number of independent PRAs operating around the world specializing in different markets or different jurisdictions.

Within the industry, Platts remained well established as the clear market leader. Platts benefited from its long history which made it the incumbent in virtually all of the well-established markets as well as from the financial strength of its parent McGraw-Hill. Platts' dominance of the traditional petroleum markets was virtually complete, with the sole exception of the LPG/NGL markets, which were in the hands of Argus in Europe and Asia and of OPIS in the US. Platts was also very active in the power and generation fuels space, although it lagged behind Argus, McCloskey and ICIS, and it had also become the first of the traditional energy-focused PRAs to report the metals markets.

ICIS-LOR had been acquired in 1994 by the Reed-Elsevier publishing conglomerate, later RELX, and was neck-and-neck with Platts in the petrochemical markets, with neither firm seemingly able to steal market share from the other, despite regular campaigns and attempts to lure away the other's staff. ICIS' position improved dramatically with its acquisition of Heren Energy in 2008. Heren's strength in European gas tied together ICIS' excellent position in petrochemicals and its somewhat weaker petroleum business as well as taking ICIS into the newly developing LNG market.

In 2007, McCloskey Coal was sold to publishing conglomerate IHS, while in 2010 Reuters acquired Point Carbon. The new wave of PRAs – McCloskey Coal, Heren Energy and Point Carbon – that had emerged to report the liberalized European energy markets of the 1990s had lasted less than 20 years as independent entities.

Meanwhile, Argus had been growing strongly and had established strong positions in LPG and coal, without breaking into a major market. This changed in 2003 when Platts introduced its new market-on-close (MOC) price assessment methodology in Europe. The MOC is dealt with in detail in a separate chapter but essentially standardized all of Platts' petroleum methodologies around a single time of day ('the window') during which traders would transact in an online platform.

MOC had been fully accepted in Asia in the 1990s and was almost entirely accepted in Europe. But it provoked uproar in the European gasoline market, which switched wholesale to Argus as the most realistic alternative. The importance of the European gasoline switch from Platts to Argus is difficult to overstate. The vastly increased revenues created by the switch enabled Argus to expand aggressively over the next few years, while the impact on the firm's credibility was huge. The energy industry became aware for the first time that it was genuinely possible to switch benchmark providers and that Argus was a realistic alternative to Platts.

This success ensured that subsequently when some US energy markets rejected Platts' attempt to roll out MOC, Argus was the natural beneficiary. Argus had become the official sour crude index for Middle East exports to the US from 2009 and subsequently became the benchmark in the US domestic crude oil markets as well as making some limited inroads in refined products. Some US firms found Argus' methodology to be more regulator-friendly than the changes proposed by Platts (see the chapter on MOC for further details).

PRA acquisition spree

The impact of the US changes continue to play out, with Argus hoping to leverage its newly gained strength in the United States to expand its position in Europe and Asia, while Platts seeks to claw back market share in its home territory. But with a new status quo in crude oil and refined products seemingly established for the short term at least, new markets such as bioenergy, LNG, the ferrous metals complex and the agricultural markets have become the latest battlegrounds for the 'Big Three'

PRAs. All of the 'Big Three' as well as publishing giant IHS have also shown a strong appetite for the acquisition of firms that gave them access to new data management tools and fundamental data to complement their pricing data.

Argus did ten deals from 2010 to 2015, while Platts did five and ICIS three, although the Platts and ICIS deals were larger overall. The standout deals for Platts in terms of benchmark acquisition was the purchase of the dominant iron ore PRA – Steel Business Briefing – in 2011 and its push into agricultural pricing with the Kingsman acquisition of 2012.

Argus used its increased revenues to push into fertilizers, petrochemicals and ferrous and specialty metals, while ICIS' M&A was dominated by the previously mentioned deal for C1 Energy in China. With its focus on the downstream petrochemical markets, ICIS had traditionally been the weakest of the 'Big Three' in the oil markets, despite its early acquisition of the London Oil Reports, but in 2015 it made a major breakthrough when global exchange ICE chose ICIS to provide the final settlement data for its giant Brent futures contract.

The elevated level of deal activity reflected the cash-rich position of the 'Big Three' but also an appetite for an exit by the founders of many smaller PRAs. Some of these were closing in on retirement and looking for a profitable sale of their businesses, while others were struggling with the new compliance burdens that reflected the increased scrutiny on the industry in the wake of the financial crisis and the investigation into rigging of numerous financial benchmarks, in particular LIBOR.

With relatively few independent PRAs left as targets, all three of the largest PRAs looked to broaden their revenue streams by adding consulting services, data management and conference businesses. The performance of these non-core activities was, however, weakened by the commodity price collapse seen from 2014 onwards, which threatened to cap some of the soaring growth rates seen by the PRAs in recent years by reducing customer budgets and reducing customer numbers through industry consolidation and the exit of many financial institutions from proprietary energy trading.

Increased consolidation

The next few years are likely to see further consolidation in the industry and the disappearance of some of the last remaining independent PRAs as potential lower industry spend and higher compliance costs effectively reinforce the dominant position of the largest players. It also looked possible that the 'Big Three' could become a 'Big Four' after information giant IHS Markit added OPIS to its various price benchmark businesses, which included McCloskey Coal, PRIMA Markets and CMAI in early 2016. It will be interesting to see whether IHS Markit looks to integrate its various pricing services and compete directly with the other PRAs as a single global entity or whether it will leave each to run as separate businesses.

The $650mn price tag that IHS paid for OPIS in 2016 was agreed at a very significant premium to the price that Platts had agreed in late 2010 to pay for OPIS. This earlier deal had fallen apart within months amid customer complaints that the combined Platts-OPIS business would be negative for competition in the US energy

PRA space. The new IHS deal for OPIS showed the elevated valuations that were being placed on PRAs after a run of revenue growth during the first decade of the century and as a result of the new interest from private-equity firms in data-driven businesses. Outside the PRA space, a rash of deals had shown just how valuable data businesses were becoming: the IHS Markit merger was worth $13 billion, while in March 2016 Verisk Analytics had paid £1.9 billion for energy data firm Wood Mackenzie and McGraw-Hill had paid $2.2 billion for financial news, data and analysis firm SNL Financial.

This upturn in interest in PRAs reached its peak with the partial sale of Argus in mid-2016 which stimulated enormous interest among the investment community and attracted dozens of expressions of interest. In May 2016, the family of the late founder Jan Nasmyth sold their stake in the business to US investor General Atlantic in a deal that valued Argus at around £950 million, which was way beyond most observers' initial estimates. As well as making the Nasmyth family and publisher Adrian Binks very wealthy indeed, the partial sale created millionaires among many of the senior Argus managers and editorial staff.[3]

The £950 million valuation of Argus easily surpassed the £854 million that publisher Pearson had generated by selling the *Financial Times* to Japan's Nikkei Group in mid-2015. The valuations of the two businesses showed the relative change in fortunes of the PRAs compared with even the giants of the traditional print media. The previously less fashionable end of the media spectrum now attracted the highest premiums.

With OPIS and Argus both on the block, 2016 was a major year for PRA corporate activity and just before the end of the year, there was one more deal. The management of RIM Intelligence, which was facing an assault from Platts on its position in its home Japanese domestic market, sold a 33.5 per cent stake in the business in November 2016 to Japan's QUICK Corporation, a subsidiary of the Nikkei Group. RIM had previously resisted takeover approaches from other international PRAs.

Next steps

After the wave of acquisitions and mergers, the energy-focused PRAs have achieved economies of scale. Platts and ICIS were already both part of major business conglomerates, OPIS has joined their number, while Argus and RIM have acquired partners with deep pockets. At the same time, though, the healthy profits of the PRAs and their increasing size is encouraging the development of a new wave of smaller, nimbler specialist PRAs, such as Kallanish in the ferrous metals space and PRIMA Markets in biofuels and agriculture, which are looking to carve out profitable niches for themselves.

As the energy-focused PRAs look towards 2020 and beyond, some uncertainties remain around further regulatory action and the impact of a sustained period of low commodity prices. But equally there are still major opportunities as new commodity markets develop and require benchmarks and risk management, which the PRAs are best-placed to deliver.

It is noticeable that the PRAs themselves are all gearing up for a new era. Senior

Table 5.1 Selected PRA corporate activity

Date	Entity	Purchaser	Overview of business
20-Dec-07	McCloskey Coal	IHS	The leading coal benchmark and info provider
04-Mar-08	Heren Energy	ICIS	Leading European gas publisher with power and emissions coverage
10-Dec-09	New Energy Finance	Bloomberg	Leading data provider for renewable energy
28-May-10	Point Carbon	Reuters	News and analytics for emissions markets
03-Jan-11	BENTEK Energy	Platts	Analytics for natural gas and related power markets
11-Jan-11	CBI China (C1 Energy)	ICIS	Leading Chinese energy and petchems publisher
09-Jun-11	FMB	Argus	World fertilizer market prices and analysis
29-Jun-11	Steel Business Briefing	Platts	News, pricing and analysis in steel and iron ore markets
28-Nov-11	Parpinelli TECNON	ICIS	Italian chemicals data and analysis firm
08-Feb-12	Fundalytics	Argus	European natural gas fundamentals data
15-Jul-12	DeWitt	Argus	Petchems pricing and advisory
31-Dec-12	LCI Energy Insight	OPIS	North American natural gas supply and market analysis
07-Jan-13	TABrewer Consulting	Argus	Consultants on hydrocarbon resins and C5 olefinic chemicals
08-Jan-13	Energy Publishing	IHS	Coal publications
14-Jan-13	Fertilizer and Chemical Consultancy	Argus	Two strategic consultants to petchem markets
01-Mar-13	GasBuddy	OPIS	Consumer app and website focused on North American retail fuel prices
31-May-13	Jim Jordan & Associates LP	Argus	Methanol pricing and advisory
06-Jun-13	Tsach Solutions	ICIS	German emission analytics firm
14-Nov-13	Kortes	Reuters	Reuters acquires independent Russian PRA
12-Mar-14	WaxData	Argus	Monthly publication covering petroleum, synthetic and natural wax
06-May-14	MetalPages.com	Argus	Metals PRA with focus on China and specialist metals
17-Jul-14	Eclipse Energy Group	Platts	Analytics for LNG and European gas and power
28-Oct-14	The Energy Conference	Argus	US fuel oil conference
12-Jan-15	MetalPrices.com	Argus	North American ferrous and non-ferrous secondary metal markets
27-Mar-15	NAVX	OPIS	European and South American retail fuel pricing, parking and vehicle charging
16-Jul-15	Petromedia	Platts	Bunker pricing and analysis for the shipping and fuel oil markets

Date	Entity	Purchaser	Overview of business
11-Feb-16	OPIS	IHS	IHS does major deal for largest non-Big Three PRA
15-Mar-16	Commodity Flow	Platts	Data visualization for waterborne commodity markets
06-May-16	PRIMA Markets	Markit	Data giant takes a stake in bioenergy specialist PRA
02-Jun-16	RigData	Platts	Data on north American rig activity
15-Sep-16	PIRA Energy Group	Platts	Major energy consultancy
26-Sep-16	Baltic Exchange	SGX	SGX acquires freight benchmark provider to strengthen exchange
11-Oct-12	Kingsmann	Platts	Sugar and ethanol price providers and consultancy
23-May-16	Argus Media	General Atlantic	Private equity investment in a leading PRA
15-Aug-16	FastMarkets	Euromoney	Metals pricing, analysis and data service
29-Nov-16	RIM Intelligence	QUICK Corp	QUICK acquires a 33.5% stake in RIM
03-Apr-17	DTN	TBG AG	US agricultural data provider

management changes took place in 2015 and 2016 at both Platts and ICIS, while Argus went through a period of management change after the arrival of its new strategic investor. The challenge for all of the PRAs will be to continue to generate significant growth in already healthy profits during the down–cycles of the wider commodity markets.

Notes

1   Platts: 100 Years, A Historical Perspective, www.platts.com.
2   Patrick Heren (2008) Lakeview, home of Jan Nasmyth's little platoon, ArgusOffline newsletter.
3   Striking It Rich, *The Economist*, 28 May 2016.

6 PRAs in the metals and minerals markets

Overview

The metals markets have used benchmarks provided by price reporting agencies (PRAs) in the ferrous complex – steel, iron ore, and coking coal – for several decades, with this process accelerating dramatically since 2010. In contrast, other parts of the metals industry have traditionally been dominated by exchange pricing and have seen less uptake of PRA benchmarks.

Pricing in the precious metals complex has been dominated by the spot London Gold and Silver Fixes and by CME Group's COMEX futures prices, while most of the key base metals have been priced in relation to settlement prices on the London Metal Exchange (LME, now owned by the Hong Kong Exchange). PRA pricing has, however, started to become more important for the aluminium and alumina markets in recent years, showing that there is a growing appetite for PRA pricing in base metals.

Unlike the energy pricing sector, where there tend to be one or two dominant PRAs, multiple firms are used in metals benchmark pricing, perhaps reflecting the less globally integrated nature of the industry, particularly in ferrous metals. The first metals publications – Metal Bulletin, AMM and Iron Age/Scrap Price Bulletin – each date back over a century and currently operate under the ownership of Euromoney Global Limited as does base and precious metals service FastMarkets. Platts is very active in the metals sector, while there are a number of specialist metals services such as CRU, MetalMiner and Kallanish, as well as a large number of very active Chinese pricing services. Argus entered the metals sector in 2014 and 2015 with its acquisitions of MetalPrices.com, which is particularly strong in North America, and Metal-Pages, which has more of an Asian focus.

First pricing pioneers

The first metals PRAs emerged in the nineteenth century in the United States. Iron-working and steel manufacture as an industrial sector significantly pre-date crude oil production and refining and so these publications significantly pre-date the first energy-focused PRA, Platts.

Irish immigrant John Williams and his son David founded weekly publication *The Iron Age* in April 1859 in Middletown, New York, after becoming frustrated at the lack of transparency in the US iron goods industry. Originally a hardware salesman in Ireland, Williams had fled his native land after an aborted rising against the British in 1848. Before founding *The Iron Age*, Williams Sr had worked as a salesman for a saw manufacturer in Middletown, while his son David had experience working as a printer.[1]

The Williams' launch came just three years after Sir Henry Bessemer had developed a new process for producing steel relatively inexpensively, which revolutionized the ferrous metals sector by opening the door for the first time to the mass production of steel.

The Bessemer process had an impact on the ferrous metals industry of the same order of magnitude as the break-up of Standard Oil's monopoly did on the US energy sector, driving increased competition and a massive upturn in interest in pricing issues and transparency.

The Iron Age expanded rapidly during the remainder of the century and David Williams opened branches across the United States. He had acquired a sole interest in the publication from his father in 1868, who died the following year while visiting Iowa to see whether the area would be suitable for settlement by Scandinavian immigrants. By 1901, *The Iron Age* was being shipped weekly to 50 countries, making it perhaps the first PRA to achieve a global subscriber base.

The publication changed hands multiple times during the twentieth century and in 2001 it was acquired by Metal Bulletin, which was itself later acquired by Euromoney. Although *The Iron Age* is no longer published in its original format, its scrap price offshoot *Scrap Price Bulletin* continues to be published to this day, providing regional scrap metal pricing for 18 major markets across North America.

Euromoney is also the current owner of another of the historic US metals PRAs, American Metal Market (AMM), which was founded as a weekly news and price report in 1882 and is the longest continuously published publication in the sector. AMM currently publishes around 1,300 metals prices, with a particular strength in the US ferrous markets.

Metal Bulletin

Although the very first metals PRAs to launch were American, the British publication *Metal Bulletin* was not far behind. *Metal Bulletin* was first founded as a weekly publication in 1913 in London by Lawrence Howard Quin, who initially named the publication *Quin's Metal Market Letters*. Quin had developed an interest in metals pricing while working for London's *Ironmonger* trade magazine and had decided to start his own information service. Quin's initial focus was on the base metals traded on the London Metals Exchange (LME) – copper, lead, tin and zinc – but Quin's coverage had a wider remit than *The Iron Age* and AMM as he initially covered 103 different markets across the precious, base, ferrous and rare metals space.

Metal Bulletin indices were used as benchmarks for contracts in the zinc and aluminium markets as early as the 1960s. *Metal Bulletin* currently assesses over 2,000 non-ferrous, ferrous, raw material and non-metallic mineral prices from around the world. *Metal Bulletin* prices are currently used as the settlement price for CME Group's European aluminium futures products.

The Metal Bulletin group was acquired by Euromoney Institutional Investor in 2007 for $408 million, joining its historical rivals The Iron Age/Scrap Price Bulletin and AMM in the same stable. Euromoney later further expanded its stable of metals pricing services by acquiring FastMarkets in August 2016. Euromoney paid £13 million for the London-based online platform, which provides over 120 proprietary price assessments as well as market analysis and real-time exchange data. The FastMarkets deal brought advanced technical capacity into Metal Bulletin, which the firm plans to leverage further with increased investment in technology.

Spot pricing emerges

Metal Bulletin's early strength in base metals pricing was unusual. The London Metal Exchange's (LME) domination of most base metal pricing globally ensured that many of the other metals PRAs of the time were primarily focused on the ferrous metals sector, particularly in North America and Europe, where the industries were more liberalized and price sensitive. Indexation to AMM or CRU prices was relatively common in the US.

In contrast, the Asian ferrous metals industry continued throughout this period to be dominated by state-owned steel producers, which tended to shun indexation in favour of fixed-price deals.

This generalized lack of interest in spot pricing and hedging explains why no PRAs emerged in the Asian metals industry until around the turn of the millennium when greater liberalization in China and the resultant economic boom led to the creation of a wave of new metals-focused Chinese PRAs and a greater focus on the Chinese metals markets by western PRAs.

Perhaps the key driver of interest in the Asian metals market was the explosion in iron ore trading that followed the breakdown of the traditional annual price negotiations. Until around 2010 the Asia-Pacific iron ore market was dominated by annual negotiations between Australian and other miners and Asian steel mills. The two sides typically agreed a fixed price in US dollars per ton for 12 months. The system worked well in eras of low price volatility but by 2010 high levels of price volatility had become a fact of life for miners and steelmakers alike. The run up in commodity prices had been followed by a crash during the global financial crisis and then a second rally on the back of soaring Chinese demand.

The wild swings in prices made fixing an annual price that was fair to both producer and consumer an almost impossible task. Each year, one side would be inevitably severely disadvantaged and this sometimes led to a failure to perform on contracts and a resultant breakdown in market trust.

Global mining conglomerate BHP Billiton eventually decided that enough was enough and by 2010 the firm took advantage of the shortage of iron ore in the market to push a new way of pricing onto its buyers. From now on, BHP would sell as much material as possible on a quarterly or spot basis with prices preferably linked to an index rather than outright prices. This move was soon followed by the majority of BHP's fellow suppliers such as Vale and Rio Tinto and was eventually accepted by Asian steelmakers.

The index that BHP chose was Platts' assessment of 62 per cent FE (cost and freight (cfr) China). Platts had begun publishing daily spot Chinese iron ore assessments in 2008 and The Steel Index and *Metal Bulletin* had quickly followed suit.

The Steel Index

Although Platts became the de facto physical benchmark for iron ore sales into China, the Asian ferrous market was unique among global commodity markets in adopting a different benchmark for its hedging requirements. Trade in cfr China iron ore swaps and later futures all settled against the index published by specialist ferrous PRA, The Steel Index (TSI). The Steel Index was the indexation arm of publisher Steel Business Briefing (SBB), which had been founded in London in 2001 by a small group of professionals from the ferrous industry.

The Steel Index settlement price underpins very active derivatives trade, which has made iron ore one of the fastest growing commodities globally in terms of traded activity. Iron ore has become the break out commodity of the last decade. Throughout the commodities space, analysts and price reporters are constantly discussing markets that have the potential to be 'the next iron ore'; to transform from a conservative pricing structure to one that captured the attention of investors and traders globally.

In one aspect at least, iron ore is highly unusual. It is hard to think of any comparable market where participants settle their physical prices on one generally accepted index and yet hedge their exposure on another equally well accepted index. In every other market, a single index has tended to dominate both physical and derivatives markets in order to avoid any basis risk between the two prices, which will inevitably differ slightly due to differences in their respective methodologies. Perhaps the only reason that this anomaly has survived is that both the TSI and Platts' indices are now produced under the same roof since Platts' 2011 purchase of Steel Business Briefing (SBB).

Some of the personnel involved in the creation of SBB later went on to set up Kallanish Commodities in London in 2013. The new firm publishes daily steel and energy news and market intelligence as well as providing training services.

Chinese pushback

Inevitably, there was some resistance to the use of PRA indexation in the Asian ferrous markets, particularly from Asian steelmakers who felt that their suppliers had bounced them into accepting the end of annual term negotiations. Chinese steelmakers, in particular, were quick to question the reliability of Platts' indexes. The Chinese felt that Platts' survey of the market was too limited and was too weighted towards the activity of the largest suppliers, which tended to take place at a higher price.

A number of attempts were made to provide alternative pricing models to the use of a PRA to settle physical contracts. The China Beijing Equity Exchange (CBEX) launched a spot trading service for metals, as did the China Beijing International Mining Exchange (CBMX), which began trading in October 2010. The hybrid broking platform globalCOAL, which provides the benchmark price for Australian thermal coal exports, also launched the globalORE physical iron ore trading service in 2012. To date, none of these platforms has achieved the level of success needed to displace Platts/TSI from their status as the major benchmarks for the Asian iron ore market. The only genuine rival to PRA pricing in Asia is the very active iron ore futures contract listed on China's Dalian Commodity Exchange. This contract is physically delivered and is not easily accessible by companies based outside China.

Further ferrous expansion

After iron ore spot trade and hedging proved such a marked success, there was an immediate campaign to promote a similar development in Asia-Pacific coking coal, also known as metallurgical coal, and in the Asian steel markets. In coking coal, it was the Platts' fob Australia index that emerged as the leading benchmark, although the TSI index is also increasingly popular. The first derivatives based on the Platts' coking coal traded in August 2011, although development in coking coal derivatives has so far failed to match the speed of developments in the iron ore sector, in part because of the relatively limited size of the market.

Several attempts have been made in Asia to push steel benchmarking based on PRA assessments along the same lines as iron ore and coking coal. Indexes provided by Platts and by Chinese metals PRAs Umetal, MySteel, SteelHome and Custeel (see Chapter 9 for further details) have all been proposed, although none to date has gained the same traction in benchmark pricing as Platts/TSI has gained in Asian iron ore. There are multiple PRAs in the Chinese metals sectors and some of them are huge operations, employing thousands of people, but many have struggled in recent years amid low steel prices that have led to a decline in their subscriber bases.

Steel benchmarking

A wide range of PRAs are used as benchmark suppliers in the US and European steel markets: CRU, AMM, Platts and TSI are all in use. AMM provides the benchmark for US Midwest busheling ferrous scrap, CRU for US Midwest domestic hot-rolled coil (HRC), while in Europe it is Platts and TSI that are the benchmarks for European hot-rolled coil and for ferrous scrap. SteelOrbis, which is headquartered in Turkey, and SteelMint, which is based in India, also provide ferrous benchmarks.

CRU is different from its competitors Platts and AMM in that the firm did not start life as a news and pricing business. Founded as the Commodity Research Unit in 1969 by Robert Perlman and John Horam, CRU views itself primarily as an analysis business that produces price indices in order to make its market analysis and forecasting more robust. CRU's price assessment division, CRU Indices, produces weekly assessments of carbon steel prices in the US, Germany and Italy. CRU's US Midwest hot-rolled coil assessment was the first index to have its data providers and methodology audited by a third party in mid-October 2013, following the publication of the IOSCO Principles (see the chapter on PRA regulation for further details).

Base metals

The base metals space has been traditionally dominated by the London Metals Exchange (LME), although there had been examples of the use of PRAs in producer–consumer contracts dating back to the 1960s when Metal Bulletin was used in European contracts for aluminium and zinc.

Issues with the LME's warehousing system emerged in the 2000s and this combined with the LME's sale to the Hong Kong Exchange in 2012 to encourage PRAs and rival exchanges in the sector to push hard into the LME's traditional territory.

CME Group focused on competing in the markets for hedging alumina and aluminium premiums. The US exchange listed US and Japanese aluminium based on Platts' assessments and European contracts based on Metal Bulletin prices. For alumina, CME used Metal Bulletin and Platts' assessments.

US information and consulting service MetalMiner also produces indexes for aluminium, zinc, titanium, carbon steel, stainless steel and nickel alloy. The firm focuses on providing information to metal procurement professionals. Its index methodology is based on volume weighted averages for North American material, adjusted for form, size and quantity.

Precious metals

Precious metals – gold, silver, platinum and palladium – are dominated by the twice-daily London spot market indexes (daily in the case of silver) and by activity on futures exchanges. As a result, PRAs have not to date been significantly represented in the precious metals sector.

The London spot indexes – originally known as the 'fix' or 'fixing' – are twice-daily or daily auctions that establish the spot price of precious metals. The first gold fix was held in the morning of 12 September 1919 by the five biggest bullion dealers of the day at the London offices of N.M. Rothschild & Sons. The system continued virtually unchanged until 2004, except that a second fix was added at 3pm in 1968 for the gold market. In 2004, the process moved to the telephone after N.M. Rothschild withdrew from the gold market. Barclays also replaced Rothschild as one of the fixing members.

The traditional system broke down in 2014. First, Deutsche Bank withdrew from the silver fix in January. This left just three firms committed to price discovery and the decision was taken that the process could not continue in its current form. Then in May the UK's Financial Conduct Authority (FCA) fined Barclays £26 million for systems and controls failures and for conflict of interest in relation to the gold fix over the nine years to 2013, including the outright manipulation of the gold price by a Barclays bullion trader on 28 June 2012.

The adverse publicity around the silver and gold fixes led to calls for drastic change in the price discovery mechanism, particularly in the wake of the LIBOR scandal. The fixes for the four precious metals had been operated by three fixing companies owned by the fix participants. These were wound down and ownership of the indexes was transferred to the London Market Bullion Association (LBMA), which is the trade association that represents participants in the London-based precious metals markets.

During 2014 and 2015 the LBMA awarded responsibility for the day-to-day management of the spot indexes to three exchanges.[2] ICE currently manages the gold benchmark, CME Group in partnership with Thomson Reuters manages the silver benchmark, while the LME manages the platinum and palladium benchmarks. The exchanges introduced electronic auctions as the new price discovery mechanism. From April 2015, the gold and silver benchmarks have been directly regulated by the FCA.

As well as the spot market, precious metals futures are widely traded around the world on dozens of spot and derivatives exchanges, with the most active contracts listed in the United States by CME Group's COMEX division and in China by the Shanghai Futures Exchange (SHFE). Between the exchange activity and the London spot benchmarks, the price transparency of the precious metals markets is relatively high, to the point that it has proved challenging for PRAs to find a useful role. One exception to this general rule is Metal Bulletin's FastMarkets service, which assesses physical premiums at various locations in Europe and Asia.

Mineral pricing

Industrial minerals are defined as minerals that are mined or processed for their special properties and which are used in a wide range of industrial and domestic applications. Industrial minerals typically include such commodities as graphite, alumina, bauxite, fluorspar, silica (frac) sand, lithium, magnesium, soda ash, TiO_2/zircon and rare earths. Many of these markets make use of third-party indexes in their spot and term contracts, although no derivative markets have yet emerged in the mineral sector.

The largest pricing player in the sector is Industrial Minerals, which was founded in 1967 by Peter Rowbotham as an offshoot of Metal Bulletin's mineral sands coverage. The firm is currently owned by Euromoney Global Limited, which also owns its sister publication Metal Bulletin. Industrial Minerals is the only pricing service that covers the full range of non-metallic minerals pricing but it has rivals in specific markets.

There is a very competitive market for providing pricing for industrial minerals with fertilizer applications, which is addressed in the chapter on PRAs in the agricultural markets, while alumina and bauxite are also increasingly covered by the larger global PRAs. In the more niche sectors of industrial minerals, there are also information and consulting services that supply prices, although pricing tends to be an aspect of their work rather than their absolute focus.

TZMI (TZ Minerals International), which was founded in 1994, specializes in the titanium minerals, zircon and TiO_2 pigment industries. Benchmark Mineral Intelligence was founded in London in 2014 by Simon Moores, a former manager at Industrial Minerals, to provide price data, analysis and forecasting services for lithium ion cathode and anode raw materials, particularly lithium, graphite and cobalt. There are also a large number of PRAs in China that offer some industrial mineral coverage (see Chapter 9 for further details).

The industrial mineral sector, with its long lead times for projects and complex logistics, has tended to be less volatile in price terms than the metallic mining industry or the energy sectors and so most price indices are weekly rather than daily and some prices in more specialist markets can remain unchanged for months at a time. Certain sectors also still rely on list prices provided by producers. This is the case for the US soda ash market, where the American Natural Soda Ash Corporation (ANSAC), which is the sales, marketing and logistics arm of three US soda ash producers, sets prices for some customers each quarter on a US dollar per tonne basis.

The industrial minerals sector is, however, changing quickly and there is a renewed focus on pricing issues. The initial disruption to the sector's traditional preference for long-term fixed-price supply deals came, as in so many other commodity markets, from the explosion of Chinese demand in the first decade of the millennium. As more independent producers enter the sector and seek finance for their projects, there has also been a drive to provide better quality pricing data to potential lenders at financial institutions. A third factor is more cultural and relates to the generational change experienced across all the commodity markets whereby younger managers prefer the use of independent floating benchmarks to the arduous annual fixed-price negotiation process.

Perhaps the final factor changing the sector's attitude to pricing is the boom in demand for industrial mineral components from the battery sector in recent years, which has seen a massive upturn in interest in markets for commodities such as lithium. This renewed focus on what had previously been fairly niche markets led to the establishment of new services such as Benchmark Mineral Intelligence and a renewed focus on pricing by Industrial Minerals. This renewed interest in pricing issues also comes at a time when the implications of the IOSCO Principles were starting to be felt across the commodity sector, even in its more obscure niches.

Conclusion

The history of metals PRAs is lengthier than that of the energy PRAs and indexation came early to the metals markets, particularly in US ferrous metals. Chinese iron ore trading based on Platts'/TSI assessments has also become perhaps the standout commodity of recent years in terms of its transformation from conservative bilateral pricing into one of the fastest growing spot physical and derivative markets.

Despite their storied history, metals PRAs have not achieved the prominence enjoyed by the energy-focused PRAs. Traditional energy market players like Platts and to a lesser extent Argus have in fact leveraged their strength in energy to expand into the metals markets, where Platts has achieved a leading position. The higher profit margins enjoyed by energy firms compared with their counterparts in the metals industry enabled PRAs in the energy market to charge significantly more for subscriptions than was the case for metals PRAs, giving them greater financial strength.

The metals PRAs also suffered in many cases from the regionalization of their core markets. In contrast to the global nature of the energy markets, many metals and minerals have tended to be consumed relatively close to home due to the higher costs of transport relative to the value of the commodity. Metals PRAs, with a couple of notable exceptions, tend to be focused on specific regions, such as the United States or China, and this has restricted their growth opportunities.

The recent surge in interest in risk management for the metals sector as evidenced by soaring iron ore volumes and greater interest in hedging products like steel and alumina looks likely to make the metals market a more tempting space for PRAs. Increased derivative volumes offer an additional revenue source to PRAs as well as subscriptions and massively increase the potential rewards of securing benchmark status. The prospect of greater rewards is likely to increase the competition among metals PRAs and could potentially provoke some further consolidation in the sector in the coming years.

Notes

1   www.scrappricebulletin.com/history-of-iron-age
2   Sakhila Mirza (2015) London Precious Metal Prices: Raising the Benchmark, The Alchemist, London: LME.

7 PRAs in the agricultural markets

Overview

The first commodities that humans traded were agricultural products. All the great empires of ancient history were firmly built on sophisticated agricultural supply chains. By 4,000 BC the inhabitants of what is now Iran were even making use of agricultural derivatives: clay tablets representing sheep or goats that could be exchanged without the difficulties of physically moving the animals. By the fifth century B-C, Socrates considered that "no one is qualified to become a statesman who is entirely ignorant of the problem of wheat".

As well as their lengthy history, the agricultural markets can point to a tradition of significant innovation. The first recognizable exchanges in Amsterdam and Dojima in Japan focused on agricultural products, while the first continuous assessments of prices in commodity markets come from *The Public Ledger*, which is still published today. Much of modern risk management theory was developed in the American Midwest in the nineteenth century by farmers, trading firms and their customers, all of whom sought to reduce volatility in the price of crops and livestock.

Agricultural markets are by far the oldest of the three broad classes of commodities, which are energy, metals and agriculture. Energy is the relative newcomer in the world of commodities but nevertheless has led the way in terms of the development of price reporting agencies (PRAs). The PRAs have in general failed to embrace agriculture, with a few notable exceptions, in the same way as they have the energy markets and to a lesser extent the metals markets.

This relative lack of penetration by PRAs is the result of a number of factors. There is a very long and storied history of exchange-based pricing in the agricultural markets, which has led to the dominance of benchmarks established by futures prices rather than by pricing agencies. The relative lack of development of agricultural pricing agencies may also reflect the difficulties of assessing prices in markets that are frequently subject to state subsidy or to political intervention. It is noticeable that the energy PRAs tended to develop alongside market liberalization initiatives. In contrast, the enormous political significance of agricultural markets and the overriding need to ensure food security, particularly in the developing world, mean that full price liberalization is not on the agenda in many key jurisdictions.

The largest firms in agriculture also control a greater share of the international traded markets than is the case in the energy and metals industry. The ABCD firms

– Archer Daniel Midland (ADM), Bunge, Cargill and Dreyfus – are giant producers, traders and processers, whose rise was chronicled brilliantly in Dan Morgan's 1979 classic account *Merchants of Grain*. Their vertical integration effectively acts as a barrier to greater price discovery and, as powerful incumbents, they are not necessarily incentivized to promote greater price transparency in the markets in which they operate.

Another factor that has tended to favour the energy PRAs rather than agricultural-focused PRAs is the pure economics of the sectors they serve. Agricultural producers and traders ship enormous quantities of material around the world, but agricultural products are significantly less valuable on a per-ton basis than energy products. Profits from agriculture tend on average to be lower than is the case in the energy sector and therefore the agricultural sector is generally less willing or able to pay the same subscription rates as would be the case for energy firms.

Primary agricultural production also tends to be fragmented across thousands upon thousands of small entities, even though the largest agricultural traders are huge entities that are comparable in scale to their peers in the energy markets. This fragmentation of the primary agricultural production base makes for a difficult target audience for PRA subscriptions, particularly for the larger global PRAs that are used to dealing with larger corporate entities like oil producers and miners. Argus' brief foray into reporting the agricultural markets in the late 1990s foundered on the difficulties in extracting sufficient revenue.

These factors ensure that the use of PRA indexation is still the exception rather than the rule in agricultural markets. Products tend to trade either on a fixed-price outright basis (US dollars per unit of agricultural material) or in relation to benchmarks derived from the dominant contracts listed on the agricultural futures exchanges.

Despite this relatively challenging operating environment, several PRAs have developed that specialize in supplying benchmarks to the agricultural sector, particularly on a regional basis. Many agricultural PRAs started life with an initial focus on consultancy, broking or advisory services, only to expand into pricing in order to develop their own proprietary data sets. In some cases, the data is now the primary business driver, while in other firms pricing remains very much an ancillary activity. As many suppliers of agricultural prices view themselves as information suppliers or advisers rather than pure PRAs, it is unsurprising that the debates around the role of the energy PRAs and the adoption of the IOSCO Principles have bypassed much of the agricultural pricing sector.

Things are, however, changing. In recent years the larger PRAs from the energy sector, in particular Platts, have invested in agricultural coverage, bringing a new perspective to the reporting of agricultural prices. As coverage of the energy markets is increasingly mature, energy-focused, PRAs are turning to the agricultural markets as a source of potential future growth, albeit likely at lower profit margins than their traditional energy businesses. The energy and the agricultural sectors are also increasingly interconnected because of the development of new markets for bioenergy – ethanol, biodiesel and biomass – that affect both energy and agricultural producers.

The Public Ledger

The first price reporting service that is still in business today is London-based publication, the *Public Ledger*, which is currently owned by Informa. The newspaper was founded in 1760 by publisher and merchant John Newbery (1713–1767). Rather than being known as the father of British price reporting, Newbery is instead better known in the UK as 'the father of children's literature' for his publication of the first ever books aimed specifically at children, including the Mother Goose series of rhymes. Originally covering politics and current affairs as well as commodity prices, the *Public Ledger's* slogan at launch – "Open to all parties, influenced by none" – could easily be adopted by any IOSCO-compliant PRA more than 250 years later.

During the course of its long life the *Public Ledger* has come to specialize in pricing and market commentary related to the agricultural markets. The publication currently provides news, analysis, and data for over 700 agricultural commodities as part of publishing giant Informa's Agribusiness Intelligence group, which has brought together a number of previously independent agricultural commodity analysis providers, such as F.O. Licht, Foodnews and Fertecon.

US agriculture

Although the first agricultural pricing service emerged in London, the heartland of the global trade in agricultural products for the past two centuries has been the United States. Many of the core pricing benchmarks used by the agricultural industry are derived from the futures prices listed on the Chicago Board of Trade (CBOT), which is part of CME Group, or on the New York Board of Trade (NYBOT), which is now part of ICE.

The Chicago Board of Trade (CBOT) opened in 1848 and introduced standardized futures contracts as early as 1865. The rival Chicago Produce Exchange (CPE) was founded in 1874, before morphing into the Chicago Butter and Egg Board and then in 1919 into the Chicago Mercantile Exchange (CME). Chicago was the natural choice for a major agricultural centre, given its close proximity to Lake Michigan and to the Mississippi River, its access to the fast-developing US rail network, and its situation at the heart of some of the world's most productive agricultural land. The development of agricultural futures contracts by CBOT incentivized investors to build up stocks of grain that could be consumed all year, which helped smooth out seasonal imbalances in supply and demand, reducing price volatility.

The CBOT later merged with the CME to form part of the modern CME Group. The CME Group dominates US futures trade in grains, oilseeds, livestock and rice and the settlement prices of these contracts are frequently used as reference prices in trades around the world.

Similarly, global trade in soft commodities tends to be dominated by the futures contracts listed on the New York Board of Trade (NYBOT), which was acquired in 2006 by ICE. NYBOT was originally founded in 1870 as the New York Cotton Exchange (NYCE) and later merged with the Coffee, Sugar and Cocoa Exchange

(CSCE). Now renamed as ICE Futures US, the NYBOT lists all of the key soft commodities and its settlement prices are referenced by the global trade.

Given the stranglehold of the US futures contracts over world agriculture and the key role played by US agricultural exports around the world, it is little surprise that so many specialist agricultural PRAs are based in the United States. Weekly newspaper *The Packer* has been reporting on the fresh fruit and vegetable markets since 1893, for example. The US markets also expect significantly more transparency than is true of other international agricultural markets, in part because of the significant volumes of fundamental and pricing data supplied by the US Department of Agriculture (USDA).

Soft commodities

The agricultural markets are divided into a number of subset categories: dairy, oilseeds and oils, forest products, grains and rice, and others. One of the most recognizable traded categories is soft commodities, of which the most active products are cotton, sugar, coffee, tea and cocoa. Pricing of these soft commodities is dominated globally by the futures contracts listed by ICE, although there are other exchanges around the world that list very active soft commodity contracts, the most notable being the Multi Commodity Exchange of India (MCX), India's National Commodity and Derivatives Exchange (NCDEX) and China's Zhengzhou Commodity Exchange (ZCE).

The dominant PRA operating in the cotton sector is the privately owned Cotton Outlook, which publishes the Cotlook A index and has offices in the UK and the United States. Cotton Outlook's added value relative to the New York cotton futures contract listed on ICE is that only US cotton is deliverable against the ICE futures contract, whereas the Cotlook A index is considered to provide a more robust guide to global prices. The very liquid cotton futures contracts listed in Zhengzhou, China and in India again tend to play a role as national venues for price discovery, hedging and speculation, rather than acting as international price benchmarks.

The Cotlook A index was first published in 1966 and caught on quickly. It has been the preferred reference price of the International Cotton Advisory Committee since the 1970s and since 1985 has been used by the US government in its agricultural support programmes.

The Cotlook A index provides a good example of how index providers need to revise their methodologies to reflect changing circumstances in the underlying physical market: Cotlook A has changed quality and geographical specifications several times since its creation. The original index created in 1966 referred to cif Liverpool, UK, reflecting the global importance of the Lancashire cotton mills. The index was later broadened out to refer to northern European in general, before incorporating the Far East from 2003 onwards.

The Cotlook A index is based on a relatively unusual version of a panel methodology. The assessment reflects the average of the cheapest five offers of cotton from a selection of 18 quotations for the principal upland cottons that are internationally traded. Cotlook explains its choice of methodology thus: "taking the average of the five cheapest quotations is a tried and tested means of identifying those growths which are the most competitive, and which therefore are likely to be traded in most volume". Such is the dominance of the Cotlook A index in the international cotton market that there have been very few attempts on the part of other PRAs to enter the cotton space, although China's CCF Group has carved out a niche for itself in the fibre intermediates markets, which are dominated by Chinese firms.

In contrast, the sugar markets have become a key area of focus and of competition for PRAs. This is largely because raw sugar has become in recent years a swing commodity that can be either processed for food consumption or else processed into biofuel before being subsequently blended into the gasoline pool. This ensures that reporting on prices and developments in the sugar market accurately is of interest to all of the energy-focused PRAs that have aspirations in the ethanol and bioenergy space. Platts, Argus and OPIS all report on ethanol prices and cover sugar to a greater or lesser extent. There are also other specialist services: Sugaronline, F.O. Licht and, most recently, PRIMA Markets.

The most significant specialist sugar market service is Kingsman, a consultancy firm founded in 1990 in Lausanne, Switzerland by ex-Cargill sugar trader Jonathan Kingsman. Kingsman was acquired in October 2012 by Platts for an undisclosed amount. In its news release announcing the acquisition, Platts was very explicit that the deal was intended to bolster the firm's position in ethanol while providing an entry point into the agricultural markets.

The Kingsman acquisition provided an example of the difficulties that the energy-focused PRAs face in their entry into the agricultural market. Platts' decision to raise Kingsman subscriptions towards the levels typical in the energy industry from the lower rates that subscribers had previously paid created some resentment in the sugar market. Rates of return for agricultural PRAs are typically below the levels their peers expect in energy, but without higher subscription rates, it is hard for energy-focused PRAs to justify internally their investment in developing agricultural pricing services.

The remaining soft commodities – tea, cocoa and coffee – have been relatively less explored by pricing services. Wholesale tea prices are set through auction processes in Mombasa, Kenya and the range of grades on offer has so far defied standardization either by an index provider or by an exchange. Trade in cocoa and coffee generally takes place on a flat-price US dollar basis or else in relation to exchange-listed contracts, although for both commodities there are wholesale price indexes published on a daily basis by trade organizations.

The International Cocoa Organization (ICCO) publishes a daily index – "the ICCO daily price" – which is a simple average of the quotations of the nearest three active futures trading months on ICE Futures Europe (London) and ICE Futures US (New York) at the time of London close converted into US dollars. The International Coffee Organization (ICO) publishes ICO Indicator coffee prices on a daily basis. Rather than relying on the futures markets, the ICO Indicators are derived from a market survey for the different growths of coffee. Polling takes place daily in the United States, Germany and France and the different results are then combined to generate a global index for each growth.

F.O. Licht, part of Informa's Agribusiness Intelligence group, also reports coffee prices through its *International Coffee Report*.

Grains and rice

The grains market is one of the agricultural sectors, along with fertilizers, where the uptake of independent price benchmarks is highest.

One of the key information providers in the grains markets is DTN (Data Transmission Network), which was originally founded in 1984 as Dataline. DTN was originally created in Omaha, Nebraska to service the information and technology needs of the agricultural sector by supplying and managing data on weather, plantings and commodity prices. DTN was acquired in 2011 by French conglomerate Schneider Electric, although in April 2017 Schneider sold the DTB business to Swiss private equity group TBG AG in a deal worth around $900 million.

The path of DTN's development reflects in many ways the opposite trajectory to that of the traditional energy-focused PRAs. While the energy PRAs started as data generators and have only recently invested heavily in data-management tools and systems, DTN started as a data supply and management business before moving upstream into its own data production.

DTN originally supplied information by FM radio broadcast before adding satellite and television capabilities, although the vast majority of its subscribers are now through online delivery portals, while its ProphetX trading and analytics screen has proved particularly popular. DTN also broadened its focus significantly with its 2007 purchase of *The Progressive Farmer* magazine, which has a circulation of hundreds of thousands across the United States.

DTN became the first US agricultural benchmark provider to be used in exchange-listed derivative trade in 2007 when it began to supply settlement prices to the Minneapolis Grain Exchange (MGEX).

Platts' aggressive entry into the agricultural space, following its acquisition of Kingsman in 2012, means that the firm is increasingly competing with specialist firms such as DTN. Platts has already registered some successes, particularly outside of the United States.

In November 2016 the first Australian wheat swap on a Platts' basis was traded between global agricultural powerhouses Louis Dreyfus and Cargill. The deal represented a significant milestone in that transactions for Australian wheat had previously always taken place on a fixed-price basis or priced against CBOT wheat futures. The swap was set to settle against the average of Platts' daily assessments of Australian Premium White physical prices in November 2016.

It remains to be seen whether this swap was a one off or the start of a trend towards PRA indexation in the key Australian grains market. Platts' position was bolstered by the trading of another swap based on its settlement price, this time for Black Sea wheat in March 2017. Further success by Platts in Australia or in the Black Sea could boost the confidence of traditionally conservative grains players in the use of indexation and could lead to further opportunities around the world.

Rice was the first commodity to ever be listed on an exchange: the Dojima Rice Exchange, which was established in Japan in 1697. Dojima ceased operations in the twentieth century, and despite its pioneering status, rice is perhaps the most significant global agricultural commodity that has not made the jump to major futures contract status. Rice contracts are listed in Chicago, Thailand, China and Japan, although rice futures trading has been banned on domestic exchanges in India since 2007. The extremely politically sensitive nature of rice pricing, given its status as the base foodstuff for so much of the world's population, ensures that price discovery has been relatively slow to catch on in the rice sector, despite the efforts of the weekly publication *The Rice Trader*, which has been in operation since the 1990s.

Price transparency has always been an issue in the rice market, particularly when so many deals have strong government involvement and when several key countries apply subsidies to either rice production or rice imports. Rice experienced the equivalent of the energy sector's 1973 Arab oil embargo when in 2007–2008 prices surged to new record levels, generating huge political concern.

The lack of price transparency in the market exacerbated fundamental supply-demand drivers and a new index provider, the UK-based Live Rice Index, was created in 2011 to provide robust price assessments for multiple grades of rice.

To date, however, rice continues to trade on a fixed-price basis and there has not been much use of reported assessments in physical supply contracts or in derivative trading.

Forest products

Pricing in the European forest-product sector has traditionally been dominated by two price providers. One is FOEX Indexes Ltd, which is headquartered in Finland and owned by AXIO FPI Holdings, while the other is EUWID, which is based in Gernsbach, Germany. FOEX provides benchmark indices for the pulp, paper, recovered paper and wood-based bioenergy/biomass sectors, while EUWID reports on wood products, pulp, paper, packaging, recycling and new energy. In north America, wood product pricing has also been provided by Wood Resources International.

In September 2016, FOEX became the first forest-product information service to adopt the IOSCO Principles. FOEX certified its PIX Pulp Europe Price Indices on the grounds that "IOSCO is the gold-standard for best practices in price reporting and adopting these principles will further enhance the reliability and reputation of the PIX indices."

Interest in indexation in the forest products sector has tended to come from the wood pulp side or, more recently, in the area of wood-based biomass. Biomass has attracted interest because of its use in power generation as a more environmentally acceptable replacement fuel for coal, which makes it of interest to both the traditional forest-product reporting agencies like FOEX and to energy-focused PRAs such as Argus.

The use of indexation by the biomass sector has yet to really take off in the same way as it did in the international coal markets. Many forestry players are still more comfortable with fixed-price deals, while some market participants are concerned that the very limited number of spot deals in the market each week could potentially expose the benchmark to undue influence.

Where indexation is used in the biomass sector, the most commonly referenced benchmark is provided by Argus, which is also heavily used in the international coal markets. Argus' European Wood Pellets cif NWE assessment is used as the settlement price for CME Group's European biomass derivatives. The use of derivatives in the biomass sector has been very limited indeed to date, although there is interest from some key players in seeing a market emerge for hedging products. The northern European APX-Endex exchange, later ICE Endex, also launched a biomass index in late 2008 and a biomass contract in late 2011, although this failed to gain traction and the project stalled with the acquisition of Endex by ICE. FOEX also provides biomass prices, which are used in certain parts of northern Europe, while Platts also supplies a weekly price, although the sector does not appear to have been a major focus for Platts to date.

Bioenergy

The bioenergy markets are perhaps the most competitive area for PRAs in terms of the agricultural sector, as bioenergy lies on the fault line between agricultural and energy markets. Energy firms are more used to arms-length trading and to PRAs than the traditional ABCD incumbents in the agricultural markets and the influence of energy sector practices has spilled over into bioenergy, making it feel more like an energy market than a traditional agricultural market.

Bioenergy comprises biomass, biodiesel and ethanol, all of which have become significantly more important since the turn of the millennium as politicians in the United States and European Union looked to diversify energy sources away from fossil fuels for reasons connected to the environment and to security of supply, while at the same time also offering new market opportunities to their domestic farmers.

Biomass has already been covered in the forest-product section and is currently dominated by Argus through its northwest European delivered assessment. Argus also sets the current European benchmark for biodiesel, while Platts currently supplies the leading benchmarks for ethanol in Europe and the United States. Other pricing agencies active in the bioenergy space include PRIMA Markets, OPIS in the United States and F.O. Licht.

Platts had always owned the ethanol market, both in the US and Europe. This is in part because Platts was the first to enter the ethanol space and in part because Platts has always traditionally provided the benchmark prices for gasoline into which ethanol is blended, at least until Platts lost the northwest European gasoline market to Argus in the early 2000s.

Platts' European ethanol assessments have received some negative publicity in recent years, ensuring that rival PRAs such as Argus and PRIMA have marketed themselves aggressively as alternative providers. Liquidity on the eWindow assessment platform has tended to be sporadic as a result of Platts' reluctance to broaden inputs into its T2 ethanol eWindow, while in 2013–2015 the European Commission raided a number of European ethanol and biodiesel firms as part of an investigation into potential collusion on pricing.

But just as Argus and PRIMA have ambitions to displace Platts in European ethanol pricing, Platts has its own ambitions to replace Argus in European biodiesel pricing. This new market emerged in the early 2000s and ICIS and Platts were the first to launch biodiesel assessments. Unusually for PRA benchmark pricing, this time first-mover advantage was not critical and it was Argus, which launched third, that established itself as the biodiesel reference price. ICIS lacked the reputation in adjacent markets, while Platts' market-on-close methodological approach was ill suited for a market that was just emerging and lacked standardization.

Argus' usage in biodiesel remains a sore point for Platts, given that Platts sets the benchmark for the two most closely related commodities: European ethanol and diesel. In 2016 Argus looked to further lock out any potential competition by adding European biodiesel to its Argus Open Markets (AOM) electronic bulletin board system. The system allows registered market participants to post bids, offers and initiate commodity deals in real time on the spot market but it is not technically a trading platform because any deals are ultimately done offline.

Use of a screen will undoubtedly make Argus' biodiesel benchmark more 'sticky' and harder to displace by other PRAs. At least, this has been the experience of Platts, which has rolled out its eWindow technology in the oil markets and in ethanol. One major downside is, however, that a screen offering tends to disintermediate over-the-counter brokers. This has been the experience throughout the Platts-based petroleum complex where bilateral transactions initiated on the eWindow screen have taken increasing market share from brokers.

The traditional PRAs are also facing competition in ethanol from a surprising source: the College of Agriculture of the University of São Paulo in Brazil (USP-ESALQ, Universidade de São Paul-Escola Superior de Agricultura "Luís de Queiroz"). ESALQ publishes a wide range of agricultural price references for the Brazilian market, but its ethanol prices have become a common reference point, particularly in the domestic market. ESALQ's methodology is based on a volume-weighted average of deals and its index is published weekly. ESALQ provides references prices for Brazilian exchange BM&F Bovespa. The importance of Brazilian ethanol in the global markets means that the ESALQ reference price could become an increasingly important reference price.

Fertilizers

Like bioenergy, fertilizers are another sector that are effectively an intersection point between different commodity markets. Fertilizers such as nitrogen occupy the line between the energy markets and the agricultural markets because some of the nitrogen that is sold to the agricultural sector is a by-product of natural gas. Meanwhile, mined fertilizers like nitrates or phosphates compete with other bulk commodities like coal and iron ore for dry-bulk freight.

These connections to other markets make the fertilizer sector a genuine hive of PRA activity. All of the big three energy PRAs – Platts, Argus and ICIS – maintain a position in the fertilizer markets. ICIS has done so for decades as an offshoot of their well-established petrochemical business, while Argus entered the space in June 2011 through its acquisition of specialist fertilizer pricing and advisory service FMB. FMB had been founded in 1982 in the UK to focus on nitrogen, phosphate, sulphur, potash and ammonia. Argus further bolstered its position in 2013 when it completed the purchase of the Fertilizer and Chemical Consultancy (FCC), which had been founded in 2004 as a provider of long-term outlooks and strategic consulting for the fertilizer markets.

As well as the large integrated PRAs, there are still other specialist fertilizer PRAs operating in the sector, which are also used in benchmarks. Fertecon, which was founded in 1978, is currently owned by Informa. Profercy, which was founded in 2004, is privately held. Consultancy and information provider CRU publishes *Fertilizer Week* as well as a large number of sector outlooks and cost reports. Privately owned, CRU was founded in 1969 as the Commodity Research Unit and covers mining, metals and fertilizers.

One of the quirks of the fertilizer market, which it shares with the international thermal coal and alumina markets, is the usage of multiple indices in the form of averages. Typically, the vast majority of commodity markets will select one PRA to supply its benchmark and that PRA will become dominant and be able to charge a premium for its services. Usually the industry will also encourage a second PRA as well in order to act as a check and balance on the incumbent and potentially as a replacement benchmark provider, should issues emerge with the primary supplier. In contrast, many fertilizer benchmarks are based on an average of the benchmark prices provided by two or three separate PRAs.

Several key markets – urea fob US Gulf and fob Egypt; DAP fob New Orleans, Louisiana (NOLA); UAP fob NOLA – make use in pricing of an arithmetic average of two assessments provided by ICIS and by Profercy. Elsewhere, other fertilizer swaps settle against the Fertilizer Index, which is published weekly by Argus. The Fertilizer Index is a three-way average of prices supplied by Argus FMB, CRU's *Fertilizer Week* and Fertecon.

The lack of consolidation among PRAs operating in the fertilizer sector makes it a competitive environment and ensures that margins are lower than they would be in the energy sector, for example. With so many players active, further consolidation would seem likely in the longer term.

Dairy and livestock

There has been relatively little penetration to date by PRAs into the dairy industry. The CME Group's US butter and cheese futures actually settle against monthly reference prices provided by the US Department of Agriculture (USDA), while the New Zealand Exchange also offers a range of dairy contracts with the support of dairy giant Fonterra, which are physically settled. Fonterra also owns the independently operated Global Dairy Trade trading and information service, which publishes price indexes for common dairy products.

Germany's EUREX lists European whey powder, butter and skimmed milk powder futures that cash settle to various indices. Eurex's whey powder index is provided by one of the few specialist European agricultural services, Agrarmarkt Informations-Gesellschaft (AMI). AMI is headquartered in Bonn and was founded in 2009 by a consortium of agricultural publishing houses, with German agricultural associations also holding a small minority share. AMI provides information, conferences and pricing for the European agricultural sector, primarily in German.

Pricing in the livestock sector is often based on indexes published by official bodies, such as the USDA in the United States, the Agriculture and Horticulture Development Board (AHDB) in the UK and by the various national bodies that report to the EU's Meat Market Observatory.

Those critics of PRAs who would prefer to see official indexes used instead as benchmarks might note the fate of the 'Georgia Dock' chicken pricing index published by the Georgia Department of Agriculture (GDA). The Georgia Dock index was used heavily in contracts but was suspended in December 2016 amid suspicions that misleading reporting had pushed the index significantly higher than other comparable indexes. A replacement index was launched in early 2017.

Despite the dominance of official pricing sources, there are some specialist reporting services operating in the sector such as the US-based CattleFax and Urner Barry. Urner Barry dates back to 1858 when Benjamin Urner, a successful printer from New York, created a single market report after noticing discrepancies in the various price circulars he was printing. Originally, Urner's market reporting was carried out by daily visits to the markets located between Fourteenth and Canal Streets in New York where he personally interviewed buyers and sellers before producing his weekly *Producers' Price-Current*. Urner's business later merged with the *New York Daily Market* Report, which was founded in 1873 by L. Frank Barry to become the Urner–Barry Company, which publishes information, analysis and pricing for the protein and seafood markets.

Rubber

Rubber generally trades either in fixed prices or in relation to the settlement price published by a futures exchange. Rubber is actively traded on the Singapore Exchange (SGX), the Tokyo Commodity Exchange (TOCOM) and the Shanghai Futures Exchange (SHFE). Rubber prices are also posted by entities such as the Malaysian Rubber Exchange and the Indian Rubber Board. PRA activity in the sector has to date been extremely limited. Sellers in Southeast Asia tend to benchmark themselves against the SGX settlement price, while Chinese buyers tend to look to the settlement provided by SHFE.

In an effort to promote improved price transparency, the International Tripartite Rubber Council (ITRC), which represents the three largest rubber producers – Indonesia, Thailand and Malaysia – announced the Regional Rubber Market (RRM) initiative in 2016. The RRM aims to improve price discovery and to stabilize rubber prices by creating an open forum through which producers can sell directly to end-users.

Oilseeds and oils

The soya complex, which comprises soy beans, soy bean meal and soy bean oil, is one of the most commonly traded agricultural commodities with over 50 derivatives contracts listed globally in the US, Argentina, India, Japan, South Africa and China, where there are huge volumes on the Dalian Commodity Exchange. The dominant contracts remain those listed on CME's CBOT in Chicago and these tend to provide the standard reference price for the soy industry.

Palm oil is another very commonly traded oilseed, with the standard reference price derived from the crude palm oil (CPO) futures contract listed in Kuala Lumpur on Bursa Malaysia. Although there are plenty of other palm oil contracts listed on exchanges in the US, Indonesia, India, Japan and China, all of them tend to price in relation to the Bursa Malaysia contract, which is where the true price discovery takes place.

Unusually, in terms of palm olein, which is a derivative product of crude palm oil, the most referenced physical index is provided by Thomson Reuters whose assessment underpins the CME Group's Malaysian Palm Olein calendar swaps contract. It is very unusual to see an assessment by a wire service such as Reuters or Bloomberg gain such wide acceptance in the physical commodity market. In this case, the use of Reuters can be attributed primarily to first-mover advantage. No other wire service or PRA was reporting palm olein prices in the way that Reuters, via its Kuala Lumpur bureau, was able to do. As the importance of palm oil in the biodiesel markets grows, it is likely that other PRAs will seek to compete more aggressively in this sector.

Grassroots developments

The vital importance of transparent pricing data to small farmers in the agricultural sector is demonstrated by the remarkable impact of schemes to provide farmers in the developing world with up-to-date pricing data via SMS services.

RML AgTech Pvt. Ltd. (RML), which was formerly known as Reuters Market Light, was launched in India in 2007 to provide a cheap phone-based information service to small farmers. The service sends data about market prices and weather as well as crop advice. A 2010 study by the World Bank indicated that farmers using the service earned an additional 8 per cent for their crops. The similar Esoko project in Africa has had equal success, generating an 11 per cent increase in farmers' income as a result of improved price information. The service was founded in Uganda as TradeNet in 2005 and renamed as Esoko in 2009. It operates in ten countries and has spawned a spin off agency in Nigeria, Novus Agro.

Although these services generate major social benefits, they are all for-profit firms and have a lot in common with the traditional western PRAs. They employ price reporters to verify prices in local markets using survey methodologies and they then distribute pricing information to their subscribers. The work of these PRAs enhances transparency and helps to address the information asymmetry that previously enabled middlemen to benefit at the expense of producers and consumers.

The main difference between these services and those offered by the western PRAs is in the customer base. The western PRAs' approach to selling subscriptions tends to be to focus on price rather than volume of sales, whereas the developing country services aim for a very high volume of users at a very low price point. The developing country PRAs are also focused purely on domestic markets – local markets – rather than covering the international wholesale trade that is the traditional strength of the western PRAs.

Conclusion

The agricultural markets are as disparate and as varied as one might expect of such an enormous sector and their use of price reference points varies accordingly. One aspect that almost all of these markets share is a great dependence on futures pricing, which stems from the very early introduction of exchanges in the agricultural sector.

PRA usage in agricultural markets is still very limited and likely to remain so without significant investment from the larger PRAs, first in developing new benchmarks and second in educating potential customers about their benefits. Platts appears to have the greatest appetite for this development work and has already achieved some success in Australia. It remains to be seen whether its competitors will follow suit and to what extent the revenues from agricultural pricing will justify the education work required.

It also remains to be seen whether agricultural players have the appetite to support greater PRA involvement in their industry. The integrated agricultural majors – the ABCD firms – are vertically integrated and are much less used than their counterparts in energy to price transparency in individual physical markets. The appetite to pay the level of PRA subscriptions that are typical in energy is also lower in the agricultural sector. The energy PRAs' attempts to raise subscription rates for agricultural customers affects their reputation and could risk potentially deterring market participants from supporting the development of PRA benchmarks.

The agricultural sector represents a difficult balancing act for the larger PRAs: if they raise subscription rates too high, the industry rejects them, but without the prospect of higher revenues, it is hard for PRAs to justify the investment in developing new benchmarks and coverage. Nonetheless, the success of services like RML, Esoko and Novus Agro in the developing markets shows an enormous thirst for better price transparency in the agricultural sector. The trend towards improved agricultural price discovery is likely to continue.

8   Petrochemical and plastics PRAs

Introduction

Petrochemicals and plastics are the end products in one of the hydrocarbon value chains that start with crude oil or natural gas. There are dozens of forms of petrochemicals and plastics, from major products like ethylene through to specialist lubricants for industrial applications. In such a broad and fragmented sector, it is little surprise that so many price reporting agencies (PRAs) are active.

Competition is fierce between the largest firms in the sector. The most important player among the PRAs is ICIS, followed by Platts. The IHS Markit group has a very strong chemicals offering under the brand of IHS Chemical, which builds on its acquisition of CMAI, while Argus also entered the sector with its 2012 acquisition of US-focused pricing and advisory firm DeWitt.

In the tier below the largest global PRAs, there are a number of smaller specialist PRAs operating that provide benchmarks in different regions. In the United States, there are PetroChem Wire and Chemical Data (CDI), while in Europe there are firms like Tecnon OrbiChem, MRC, Plastics Information Europe, ChemOrbis and myCEPPI. In Asia, which is the fastest growing centre for petrochemicals and plastics, there is Chemease, which was acquired by ICIS, Sublime China Information and SunSirs Commodity Data Group, all of which are based in China, while Polymerupdate is based in India.

Many of these second-tier firms have assessments that are used as a reference price, either in third-party contracts or by national customs authorities, although they are mostly in the $1–2mn per year range in terms of revenues. The division between full time PRA, traditional newsletter publisher, broker and consultant is often quite blurred among the smaller petrochemical information services.

In regulatory terms, much of the debate around the role and functioning of PRAs that culminated in the publication of the IOSCO Principles (see separate chapter on regulation) was focused on more politically sensitive areas, like crude oil, and the far downstream of petrochemicals and plastics was rarely referenced. This ensured that the regulatory debate passed by the majority of the smaller services in the sector.

One of the most notable aspects to PRA activity in petrochemicals and plastics is the relative fragmentation of pricing. In most other commodity markets, there is one dominant PRA that publishes the benchmark price and then one or two challengers who will publish price assessments but not be considered as benchmark providers. In contrast, in the petrochemical and plastics markets, PRAs have a better chance of occupying niche benchmark positions due to the disparate nature of petrochemical markets, which operate as distinct trading ecosystems. This fragmentation of benchmark usage ensures that the market is very competitive for PRAs due to potential challenges around gaining a competitive advantage. The size of the petrochemical and plastics derivatives markets is also smaller than for comparable energy products, again reducing the potential income for PRAs.

Petrochemical and plastics derivatives have still to take off fully to match oil markets' liquidity despite numerous attempts by exchanges to launch products either based on PRA assessments or on physical delivery. The main exception is China, which has seen significant liquidity in several petrochemical futures contracts, such as Linear Low Density Polyethylene on the Dalian Commodity Exchange. Actual manufacturers of plastic products tend not to hedge their exposure or may not want the cash commitment of posting margins. Petrochemicals with strong correlation to naphtha feedstocks such as aromatics have begun to see modest liquidity on the Singapore Exchange (SGX).

Another feature of these markets is that PRAs face competition from posted prices. Posted prices are sales prices that are set by a manufacturer often on a weekly or monthly basis and which are typically subject to undisclosed discounts. Posted prices are quite common in smaller markets with fewer sellers. Unlike in the more developed energy markets, there is still a lot of reliance on posted prices in the petrochemicals and plastics industries. In general, the more specialist the product, the higher chance that it will transact related to a manufacturer's posted price.

Market evolution

Prior to the 1980s most petrochemical or plastic products were bought and sold on a 'cost-price plus' basis, on a margin-sharing system, or on some combination of the two. This all changed in the 1980s when buyers took advantage of an oversupplied market and low oil prices to force through major changes in pricing. The buyers were looking for independent benchmarks that truly reflected the oversupplied spot market. They were able to turn to a new group of information and pricing services that had emerged during the previous decade.

Prior to the 1970s, the only real price reporting service for chemicals was the *Oil, Paint and Drug Reporter*, which William O. Allison had founded in 1871 in New York to report on news and prices for the chemical and pharmaceutical industries. The *Oil, Paint and Drug Reporter* listed hundreds of prices in its back pages and covered everything from aspirin to aromatics. The publication continues to live on, albeit after a series of reinventions. It became *Chemical Marketing Reporter* in 1972 and *Chemical Market Reporter* in 1996 before most recently becoming *ICIS Chemical Business* in 2006.

The *Oil, Paint and Drug Reporter* became a key reference point for the chemicals industry largely because it was the only source of pricing information available. This state of affairs was challenged by James D. "Jack" DeWitt, who deserves the title of the father of petrochemicals price reporting. DeWitt was working in the benzene business for Coastal Trading when he visited Shell in London. When he asked the Shell traders how they obtained information about the US benzene market, DeWitt was shocked to find that they waited for copies of *Oil, Paint and Drug Reporter* to be delivered to the UK by sea, by which time the assessments were already several weeks old.

DeWitt returned to the United States and in 1973 launched DeWitt & Co to provide pricing, analysis and consultancy. DeWitt produced weekly price assessments of the US markets and sent his reports by air around the world, dramatically changing the industry's information flow. After the early death of Jack DeWitt, his successors continued the business, eventually selling to Argus in 2012. The DeWitt brand name was finally dropped by Argus in early 2017.

Within a few years of DeWitt's 1973 launch, other chemicals information services quickly followed his lead. Platts began covering petrochemicals in 1975, while Tecnon OrbiChem was founded in London in 1976, initially in partnership with DeWitt but afterwards as an independent pricing and consultancy business. Tecnon became the first firm to expand pricing coverage into new areas like methanol, purified terephthalic acid (PTA), caustic soda, caprolactam and chlorine, using a survey methodology to provide monthly price assessments.

Chemical Data (CDI) was founded in 1979, while DeWitt and Platts both saw spin off competitors emerge. Three senior DeWitt staffers started out on their own account in 1979, founding CMAI, later acquired by IHS Markit, while also in 1979 former Platts' staffer Humphrey Hinshelwood founded Independent Chemical Information Services, later abbreviated to ICIS.

As a result of this explosion of pricing activity, the use of PRA benchmarks had become the norm in many of the larger petrochemical markets by the end of the 1980s.

The use of third-party benchmarks became increasingly accepted throughout the 1990s and the end of that decade saw the first attempts to develop risk management tools, such as derivatives, based on the most widely accepted PRA benchmarks. This process accelerated in the 2000s when spot physical trading really took off amid a boom in Asian demand.

Emergence of derivatives

The greater focus on spot trading and indexation encouraged exchanges around the world to show interest in petrochemicals and plastics for the first time. The London Metals Exchange (LME) was the first to offer plastics futures in May 2005. The LME made a very serious attempt to develop the market. It carried out significant market outreach, revised its original contracts in response to market feedback and launched regional contracts to attract commercial hedgers around the world. Despite all of their hard work, the LME contracts never really gained traction and were finally delisted in April 2011.

LME is far from the only exchange to have experienced difficulties with petrochemical and plastics derivatives. Trading volumes have generally disappointed and are a fraction of those seen in petrochemical feedstock markets like natural gas or naphtha.

The Multi Commodity Exchange (MCX) in India listed petrochemical and plastics contracts from 2005 onwards, while its local rival the National Commodity and Derivatives Exchange (NCDEX) launched futures contracts for polypropylene (PP), linear low-density polyethylene (LLDPE) and polyvinyl chloride (PVC) in 2007. None of the Indian contracts managed to establish themselves and even NCDEX's relaunch of PVC in 2011 failed to attract sufficient liquidity.

ICE took a different approach to the sector, focusing instead on the physical rather than derivatives side by acquiring the ChemConnect online trading platform in 2007. The platform had been founded in 1995 and hosted physical markets in the United States for natural gas liquids (NGLs) and for chemicals. ICE's big US rival CME Group launched ethylene and propylene futures contracts in 2009 and added polyethylene (PE) and PP futures in 2010, all of which settle to assessments from US-based PRA PetroChem Wire. These products continue to see steady trade but have not transformed into major derivative markets as yet.

The next attempt to generate interest in derivatives came in the Middle East, where the Dubai Gold and Commodities Exchange (DGCX) launched PP and mini plastics products in February 2014 and June 2015 respectively. Both quickly ceased trading.

Singapore Exchange (SGX) has had more luck than most of its rivals. SGX launched paraxylene (PX) futures in December 2014 followed by four polyolefins contracts, including PE and PP futures, in January 2015. SGX's PX contract settled to Platts, while its polyolefins contracts settled to ICIS assessments. By early 2017, SGX's petrochemical volumes were still growing, although from a relatively low level.

The only location that has successfully attracted high levels of liquidity to petrochemical and plastics derivatives is China. China's Dalian Commodity Exchange (DCE) lists a few petrochemical futures contracts that have attracted high levels of liquidity – LLDPE, PP and PVC – while the Zhengzhou Commodity Exchange (ZCE) has successfully listed PTA. It is notable that the Chinese contracts are all based on physical delivery rather than PRA assessments. China is without doubt the major player in the global petrochemicals industry at present, but the success of the petrochemicals futures contracts listed onshore appears to be more the result of strong speculative interest rather than a major uptake of risk management by Chinese commercial participants.

ICIS vs Platts

Of the three global PRAs, Platts has the longest history in petrochemical reporting but it is ICIS that is most focused on the petrochemical markets. Platts began reporting petrochemical prices from 1975 onwards, at a time when the previously stable downstream markets were still coping with the fallout from the 1973 Arab oil embargo that generated tremendous price swings. The Arab oil embargo sparked an interest in price indexation, benchmarking and hedging throughout the energy markets and the petrochemical sector was no exception.

In 1979 a former Platts' petrochemical reporter based in Paris, Humphrey Hinshelwood (1929–2001), set up his own reporting service – Independent

Chemical Information Services, later abbreviated to ICIS. Hinshelwood had stumbled into price reporting after a varied career as a music critic, theatre director and TV producer. His role as Platts' European correspondent covering the aromatics market convinced Hinshelwood that there was an opportunity for expanded petrochemical coverage that McGraw-Hill was not able or willing to cover.

Initially, Hinshelwood's new service only covered markets where Platts was not active but later ICIS went on to compete head-to-head with Platts across the spectrum of petrochemicals. ICIS then merged with the London Oil Reports (LOR) in 1984. This deal gave the firm access to coverage of the full range of petroleum markets but LOR never really consolidated a leading position in the oil markets and the merged firm never really gained traction outside the downstream markets. ICIS-LOR was eventually acquired by publishing giant Reed Elsevier, later RELX, in 1994, at which point Hinshelwood stepped down.

Under the ownership of Reed Elsevier (RELX), ICIS has made two major bets: first, the acquisition of Heren Energy in 2008 that gave ICIS a dominant position in European pipeline gas; and, second, its 2011 investment in C1 Energy and Chemease in China. This deal is discussed elsewhere on the chapter on PRA activity in Asia, but it represented a bet that major petrochemical benchmarks would emerge from China, the world's largest plastics player.

In terms of global market share, ICIS owns the majority of the major benchmarks, although Platts is strong in certain areas such as PX and benzene. In Europe and Asia, it tends to be a straight fight between ICIS and Platts, whereas the United States is more diverse. US benchmarks are split between IHS Chemical (owner of CMAI), CDI, ICIS, Platts, Argus (owner of DeWitt) and PetroChem Wire. Despite the very competitive nature of the market for petrochemical and plastics price reporting, it is notable that very few benchmarks have transferred from one price provider to another. ICIS, Platts and their rivals mount marketing campaigns, adapt their methodologies and poach each other's staff, yet still there have been relatively few changes in benchmark incumbency, with the exception of the US benchmarks that moved from Platts to PetroChem Wire in the late 2000s.

Perhaps there is not sufficient differentiation between the majority of the PRAs in the sector to warrant the industry changing benchmark provider. Most of them use some version of a survey methodology to arrive at their assessments, although Platts has migrated its assessments to its Market on Close (MOC) methodology (see the chapter on MOC for further details).

A group of former senior Platts' petrochemical reporters did try to challenge the status quo among methodologies by creating their own pricing service – the Petrochemical Standard (TPS) – in 2014. The unique selling point of TPS was that its price assessments were influenced by fundamental physical data derived from TPS' partnership with real-time commodity data provider Genscape. TPS claimed its assessment methodology would provide a "truly accurate alternative to outdated averaging and phone survey methods of petrochemical market pricing and analysis" but the service failed to make a significant breakthrough in benchmark usage and was fully integrated into Genscape in March 2016.

PetroChem Wire

The PetroChem Wire is a daily independent publication that focuses on coverage of the North American natural gas liquids (NGLs), olefins and polymers markets. PetroChem Wire was founded in 2007 by Kathy Hall, who had previously spent 12 years at Platts. Hall had noted that the petrochemical markets in the US were looking to OPIS for their NGL coverage, to Platts or CMAI (now part of IHS) for their base chemicals coverage, and to Platts or ICIS for their plastics coverage. PetroChem Wire was intended to be a one-stop shop covering all of these various markets. Hall had also spotted a gap in the market for greater coverage of US petrochemicals, which would always struggle to attract investment within the larger PRAs because of the relative dominance of the oil markets.

Hall had deep connections in the US industry and the market was quick to adopt PetroChem Wire as a benchmark. The firm's first reports were emailed out in July 2007 and its assessments were already being used as a pricing benchmark by market participants in January 2008. PetroChem Wire became the benchmark for US ethylene, propylene, polyethylene and polypropylene. Their assessments are used as the settlement price for the derivatives on those markets that are listed by CME Group.

Hall established a greater level of detail in PetroChem Wire's methodology for its first assessments than was typical at the time. Whereas rival methodologies would cite a delivery location as "US Gulf", PetroChem Wire would specify the exact locations and terminals, increasing market confidence in her assessments. PetroChem Wire also makes use in its methodology of a strict ranking of information. Its price reporters will consider firm bids and offers first, followed by deals done on an outright basis, followed by deals done on a floating price basis, followed by information from the derivative markets. The firm also publishes some volume-weighted averages (VWAs) based on confirmed deals.

US PRAs

IHS Chemical publishes four daily market services for the chemical markets: North America Olefins & Polyolefins Daily, North America Aromatics Daily, Europe Aromatics Daily, Asia Aromatics Daily. These are based on its 2011 acquisition of Chemical Market Associates, Inc. (CMAI), which had been founded in 1979 in the United States to provide business intelligence and consultancy to the petrochemicals market.

Argus similarly entered this sector through acquisitions. Its first and most major deal was for US market intelligence, pricing and consulting firm DeWitt in 2012. DeWitt was founded in 1973 in Houston, Texas. Argus later expanded its footprint in the industry through a number of other smaller acquisitions. In 2013 Argus acquired TABrewer Consulting and Jim Jordan & Associates (JJ&A). TABrewer Consulting was founded in 2003 by C5 olefinic specialist Tom Brewer, who had enjoyed a strong working relationship with DeWitt, while JJ&A was founded as a consultancy and analytics firm specializing in the methanol and ethers industries by industry experts Jim Jordan and Marybeth Maloy Gebauer.

Around this time Argus also made a number of acquisitions in the fertilizer pricing sector (the chapter on PRAs in the agricultural markets for further details). Then in 2014 Argus also picked up WaxData, a monthly publication specializing in petroleum wax, natural wax and synthetic wax. This flurry of deal activity turned Argus into a serious player in the petrochemicals and plastics markets, particularly in the United States, although it still has a way to go to challenge IHS, ICIS and Platts.

The other active PRA in the US petrochemical markets is Chemical Data, which was founded in Houston, Texas in 1979. Chemical Data publishes two monthly reports: one on petrochemical and plastics analysis and the other on feedstocks and fuels analysis. Chemical Data, also known as CDI, has benchmark usage in the PE and PP markets.

Other PRAs

There are a number of other smaller specialist PRAs operating around the world. Polymerupdate was founded in 2000 in India, while ChemOrbis was founded in 2001 in Tukey. Both started life with the intention of becoming major online trading marketplaces for petrochemicals and plastics but both have become increasingly valued for their price benchmarks. Polymerupdate's methodology is based on its assessment of standard repeatable orders and of concluded deals. The Petrosil Group launched in India in 2002 to cover chemical and energy markets, using a survey methodology to assess prices.

Founded in 2003, Russia's Market Report Company (MRC) prepares reports on the polymer markets in Russia and the rest of the former Soviet Union. Since 2010, MRC has been working together on pricing with ICIS. Also active in central and eastern Europe is myCEPPI, which was founded in Hungary in 2013 to cover a range of plastics prices and to provide consultancy services. The firm uses a market size weighting system to combine prices for multiple grades and multiple countries together into a single Central European Plastics Price Index (CEPPI). Another market intelligence provider is Plastics Information Europe (PIE), which publishes polymer price indices on a monthly basis that are calculated from the average monthly market prices of various plastic materials, weighted according to western European consumption volumes. Also covering the polymer markets are India's PolymerMIS and UK-based PolymerTrack.

In some of these smaller firms, price reporting or index calculation is not their main revenue driver but tends to be more of an offshoot of their other activity, which might be to generate news subscriptions, bespoke or sectoral reports and consultancy. The smaller firms do play an important role, however, by making price information available either for free or on a much cheaper basis than the larger, more specialist PRAs can afford. This ensures that some form of petrochemical pricing information is generally available to the smaller partic-ipants in the market, which may only require very general price indications for one specific product.

Chinese firms

As the most important global location for petrochemicals and the location of the world's most liquid petrochemical futures contracts, it is unsurprising that China hosts so many petrochemical information services.

The Chinese PRAs are dealt with in greater detail in the chapter on PRAs in Asia, but the most notable in terms of petrochemical coverage are the SunSirs Commodity Data Group, C1 Energy/Chemease – part of the ICIS family – and SCI Group. All of these PRAs are enormous by non-Chinese standards, employing almost 3,000 people between them, which is the same staffing level as the 'Big Three' of Platts, Argus and ICIS require for their entire global operations across all commodities. Nonetheless, none of these Chinese firms has been used in international contracts to date.

Base oils

Base oils, lubricants and petroleum wax are niche, high value products that occupy the border between petrochemicals and refined products. As a result, there is substantial competition among PRAs to report these markets.

The longest established PRA in the sector is ICIS, which is widely used as a benchmark for floating price deals. Surprisingly, Platts has never launched any base oils coverage, despite competing hard with ICIS across the rest of the petrochemical spectrum. Instead, ICIS faces competition from Argus, which launched its own global base oils report in 2010 and which acquired US monthly publication WaxData in 2014 to bolster its coverage of the sector.

Other regional pricing services are also active. China's SCI Group covers paraffin wax, while India's Petrosil Group publishes reports on base oils as well as other energy and petrochemical markets. In the United States, where these markets still rely heavily on producers' posted prices, local coverage is provided by the Lubes 'n' Greases stable of publications, which were launched in 1995.

Conclusion

The relatively complex nature of the petrochemical and plastics markets, which have so many specifications and different products to cover, represent both a challenge and an opportunity for PRAs. The challenge comes from the fact that reporting all of the many and varied markets is very labour intensive relative to the potential rewards, given that petrochemical and plastics players tend to operate on lower margins than their cousins in the oil markets. There are also relatively limited opportunities to make additional revenue from the derivatives markets, given the limited take up of risk management tools by companies in the sector.

The opportunity similarly comes from the very fact that the sector is so broad and diverse, both in terms of products and geographical location. This opens the door for smaller niche PRAs to establish a profitable business in a way that would be difficult in markets like energy and ferrous metals, which are increasingly dominated by a small number of large global players.

9   PRAs in Asia

Overview

Asia has always been one of the three key commodity trading regions of the modern era, along with northern Europe and the United States. Traditionally, though, Asia was seen as the little brother and received less attention than its two bigger siblings. This all changed from the turn of the millennium onwards. Since then Asia has been the fastest growing region in terms of overall commodity demand, principally driven by economic booms in China and to a lesser extent India, while demand in Europe and the United States has slowed. Commodity market participants all over the world now look at Asian demand as one of the most important factors to consider in their trading decisions.

As well as the demand story, many Asian countries have also liberalized their economies and have moved towards an increased use of market pricing. This greater openness has provided new opportunities for the western price reporting agencies (PRAs) either through organic expansion or through acquisitions.

At first the western PRAs treated China essentially as a mining operation – they invested in gathering information that they could sell internationally. There was relatively little emphasis on selling information into China because of concerns about copyright abuse and the perception that local players would be reluctant to pay the same subscription rates as international firms. But with time some PRAs came to the realization that it was in fact possible to develop services selling data into China, and even to develop Chinese-language information and pricing services designed purely for domestic consumption.

The growing liberalization of the Asian commodity markets has also encouraged the development of local pricing and analytics services, particularly in China and India. Indigenous Asian PRAs have a relatively lengthy history. RIM Intelligence was founded in Tokyo in 1984, while the Hong Kong–based Asia Petroleum Price Index (APPI) was a key oil marker for many years. But local activity has stepped up dramatically in recent years with the emergence of a raft of well-capitalized Chinese PRAs that employ large numbers of analysts and are prepared to sell reports at price points well below the levels that western PRAs were used to in their home territories.

To date, though, none of the regional PRAs has managed to break out of their domestic market and gain international acceptance. Some minor benchmarks have emerged from China in areas where Chinese firms dominate global trade, such as

Chinese PRA CCF Group's assessments of the fibre intermediates markets. But a PRA benchmark for a major commodity has yet to emerge from China, despite many attempts to develop indigenous price points.

Perhaps the relative lack of international penetration of Asian PRAs and of Asian-derived global benchmarks to date can be linked to concerns about government intervention. Firms operating in economies that still have a relatively high level of government control could be potentially subject to official intervention. Some Asian governments, particularly the Chinese authorities, have a record of intervening in commodity markets to dampen price growth or what they perceive to be excess volatility.

The first Asian PRA: RIM Intelligence

Until the emergence of China as the major player in the Asian commodity markets from 2000 onwards, Japan and Singapore were generally the two locations where PRAs focused their efforts in Asia. Singapore is the central trading hub for Asian commodities and where most of the key trading firms have their regional headquarters. Japan represented the demand side of Asia: the country's dramatic economic growth since the Second World War combined with its relative lack of natural resources to ensure a relentless focus on access to commodities and guaranteeing security of supply. Japan developed a vibrant oil refining system and its trading firms were the most advanced of the Asian market participants.

It is no coincidence that Japan was the first Asian nation to produce its own PRA. RIM Intelligence was founded in Tokyo in 1984 to cover energy markets in the Pacific Rim, hence its name. The firm's genesis, like that of so many of the western PRAs, was in the oil-price shocks of the 1970s, which generated unprecedented volatility. RIM was also responding to the growth in importance of the Japanese petroleum sector, where Japanese trading houses and refiners had established themselves as major global players in the crude oil and refined product markets.

RIM produces reports on crude oil, refined products, LNG, LPG and petrochemicals. Its strength has traditionally been in its assessments of the Japanese market, but in recent years the firm has expanded into assessing other international markets, such as the Chinese domestic and import markets. RIM has always been perceived to be very close to the Japanese trading community and its usage in formulas such as the Indonesian Crude Price (ICP) was felt to reassure Japanese market participants that they were receiving a fair price.

RIM was not considered by IOSCO to be one of the four main oil-price reporting services (Platts, Argus, ICIS, OPIS) during its investigations, but it was referenced as a key second-tier service in much of the material generated during the research and preparation of the IOSCO Principles. RIM subsequently adopted the IOSCO Principles, publishing a report into its compliance with the Principles in terms of its crude oil and condensate reporting in August 2015 and reports into the rest of its price assessments followed in March and April 2016.

As one of the last relatively small independent pricing services that also has benchmark usage, RIM has been the target for takeover approaches by larger PRAs over the years but has preferred to stay independent. RIM did, however, accept a substantial minority shareholder in November 2016 when Japan's QUICK Corporation acquired a 33.5 per cent stake. QUICK is a financial information service provider founded in Japan in 1971 that is a subsidiary of the Nikkei Group and which has traditionally focused on generating and distributing securities and financial information. The deal was intended to facilitate the development of new indexes and database management tools that could potentially appeal to the financial community.

The deal with QUICK also strengthened RIM at a time when it was coming under a sustained assault from Platts, which from 2015 onwards began to focus hard on the Japanese domestic market, where RIM had traditionally been dominant.

Almost 11 years after suspending its domestic Japanese assessments, Platts rolled out its eWindow system to the Japanese domestic market in late 2016. Platts also produced more material in the Japanese language and even pushed downstream by introducing Japanese lorry rack assessments in November 2016, competing in what had traditionally been a stronghold of RIM pricing. In April 2016, the Tokyo Commodity Exchange (TOCOM) had announced that it would use Platts rather than RIM assessments for its new balance-month contracts for gasoline, gasoil and kerosene, which were scheduled for a 2017 launch.

It remained to be seen how RIM would respond to the new threat from Platts to its core Japanese domestic business. The tie up with the QUICK division of the Nikkei Group may help to provide RIM with the firepower and global reputation to take on Platts and regain any lost ground in the domestic market. The technology available through the QUICK tie up also gives RIM the potential to move its price discovery process to a screen-based methodology. RIM has traditionally employed methodologies based on price reporters' survey assessments but Platts' introduction of a screen-based system to Japan has proved popular with market participants.

APPI: a democratic PRA

The other longstanding Asia-based PRA was the Asia Petroleum Price Index (APPI), which was published by Hong Kong-based Seapac Services. APPI was for many years the benchmark price for crude oil in the Far East and APPI assessments were used to price crude oil blends from countries such as Australia, China, Indonesia and Malaysia. APPI has steadily fallen out of favour since the late 2000s due to concerns about its reliability and most of its benchmarks have since been captured by Platts.

APPI was founded as a weekly service by the accountancy firm Peat Marwick in Hong Kong, which later became KPMG Peat Marwick, and later transferred APPI to Seapac Services. APPI was forced to move to biweekly pricing, set on Tuesdays and Thursdays, in 1990 when the price volatility generated by the first Gulf war made its prices out of date almost immediately.

APPI has been half-jokingly described as the world's only democratic PRA. Instead of being set either by PRA price reporters or by a volume-weighted average of trade, its benchmark prices were established by an adjusted panel methodology. A panel of participants representing crude oil producers, refiners and traders sent in submissions ("voting") on the price of the prices of the various crude oils that APPI covered, with the highest and lowest panel submissions discarded from the published average.

APPI Tapis developed as a major benchmark for Malaysian crudes, while official selling prices from Indonesia were originally based entirely off APPI assessments, particularly of Minas crude oil. Problems emerged with the APPI methodology in the late 2000s as its Asian benchmarks became increasingly disconnected from other crude oil markers. The declining physical volumes underpinning exports of Tapis and Minas made the benchmark prone to supply constraints, while at the same time the panel methodology employed by APPI led to some unusual outcomes. For example, by the late 2000s APPI Minas tended to be structurally much lower than comparable grades: the refiners submitting assessments to the panel preferred low prices, but producers were also comfortable with a lower outright benchmark because Indonesian tax assessments were based on APPI Minas.

In response to the concerns around the reliability of the assessments, Australia and Papua New Guinea shifted away from using APPI in favour of Platts' Dated Brent in 2009. This move prompted Seapac Services to revise the methodology of its benchmarks in mid-2010, but for most market participants the changes were too little, too late. Malaysia and Vietnam both dropped APPI and switched to Platts' assessment of Dated Brent in 2011.

Oddly, Indonesia was the first country in the region to reduce its dependence on APPI, but the last to make the final break. Indonesia had traditionally used APPI as its pricing benchmark, but it later moved to a 50/50 formula based on prices supplied by APPI and RIM Intelligence. Then in October 2006, it adopted a bizarre new formula comprising Platts, RIM and APPI assessments in a ratio of 47.5/47.5/5, before revising this once more in July 2007 to be based on a 50/50 formula of Platts and RIM.

At the same time, the Indonesian LNG formula continued to make use of APPI through to the late 2000s, with Indonesian LNG based on Platts', RIM and APPI assessments in the ratio 40/40/20, as late as February 2012.

With the loss of Indonesia, APPI effectively ceased to exist as a reference benchmark provider.

The next wave

RIM and APPI were the first Asian PRAs and the intense competition both faced from larger and well-capitalized western PRAs such as Platts shows just how difficult it is for smaller regional PRAs to compete in the modern globalized and highly regulated environment. Both found themselves losing ground to Platts' greater marketing reach and its arguably more predictable pricing methodology. Both also suffered from the relative decline in importance of their core markets: in RIM's case, the decline of Japanese domestic energy demand and in the case of APPI the decline in crude oil production of the Minas and Tapis crude oil streams in Indonesia and Malaysia respectively.

In contrast to these stories of decline, the global commodity markets from the first decade of the millennium onwards were dominated by the rise of Chinese demand, which propelled Chinese firms to the forefront of the international commodity markets and made Chinese market fundamentals of interest to a global audience for the first time. The surge in interest in China combined with greater liberalization in the Chinese domestic market to ensure that Chinese pricing was one of the largest and yet most challenging opportunities for the international PRAs.

The rise of China

The major issue facing every PRA in China, whether foreign or domestic, is the strong government preference for regulated and exchange-traded futures benchmarks rather than PRA indexes. To date, the powerful China Securities Regulatory Commission (CSRC) has only allowed domestic exchanges to launch physically-settled futures, with no financially-settled PRA reference prices permitted. The National Development and Reform Commission (NDRC) is also believed to have switched in March 2013 from PRA prices to exchange benchmarks for its domestic fuel price index. This government focus on exchange prices rather than PRA assessments makes it difficult for pricing firms to create major benchmarks that will be used officially, in areas such as tax or customs formulas, as happens in other countries.

In the early years of PRA activity in China, however, the lack of state sponsorship was the least of anyone's problems. China initially presented the international PRAs with severe difficulties, largely due to the tremendous issues that they experienced with unauthorized distribution. PRAs found that their reports were being translated into Chinese and shared widely, not just within firms but across companies. One PRA manager in Asia complained that even the copyright notices on their reports were being faithfully translated into Chinese. At the same time, Chinese companies were not used to paying the relatively high subscription rates that western PRAs had become used to commanding in their home markets. The combination of these two factors ensured that for most PRAs China was quite disappointing as a revenue source relative to its importance in the global commodity markets.

In response to this challenge to their traditional sales strategies, the different international PRAs followed different strategies. Some PRAs decided to treat China as a purely export location – they looked for raw information on pricing or on market fundamentals that they could sell internationally, rather than focusing on selling international reports into China or on developing their coverage of the Chinese domestic market.

ICIS, in contrast, decided to invest in China and its investment in domestic reporting service C1 Energy gave it the biggest footprint in China of any of the western PRAs. The deal was not large by the standards of ICIS's parent, the information giant RELX (then Reed Elsevier), but it still represented a substantial bet on China. The justification for the investment was two-fold. ICIS management argued that to be successful in China in the long term, ICIS needed to embed itself fully into the domestic market and to provide Chinese customers with a Chinese face. Second, ICIS took the view that as the centre of gravity of the commodity markets shifted towards the east, the next wave of major benchmarks would come from China. As always in benchmarks, first-mover advantage is crucial.

C1 Energy

C1 Energy was the first independent oil and gas PRA to be founded in China and provides domestic assessments based on both survey and volume-weighted average methodologies. It was founded in May 2000 and has offices in Shanghai, Guangzhou, Beijing and an overseas branch in Singapore. C1 was acquired by leading Chinese information provider CBI China in December 2007. By this point, ICIS had already taken a stake in CBI China as part of a strategic alliance between the two firms. The merger of C1, CBI's existing operations in energy and ICIS's existing operations in China created a substantial firm focused on Chinese energy and petrochemicals markets. ICIS increased its stake in CBI in August 2010.

The C1 acquisition was considered so strategically important to ICIS that its then managing director, Christopher Flook, moved to China for almost two years to oversee the integration. The deal has made ICIS into a major player in the Chinese domestic markets and has given the firm a reach in the Chinese downstream that none of their competitors can match. Probably the only disappointment is that C1 has yet to produce a major benchmark that has been adopted outside China.

Fenwei Energy

Platts is believed to have looked at the C1 acquisition as well but instead it has focused on building its own reporting team in China and has undertaken occasional tie ups with local firms, such as its cooperation agreement on coal with Shanxi-based Fenwei Energy.

Fenwei Energy, which is also known as SXCOAL, operates China's largest coal information platform, China Coal Resource, and has become China's largest supplier of coal information and consultancy services since its launch in 1999.

The partnership between Platts and Fenwei dates back to October 2013. The two firms announced that they would create daily Chinese coal price assessments under the brand of the China Coal Index (CCI). The concept behind the tie up was to combine Platts' international credibility with Fenwei's credibility in the domestic Chinese market. The two firms later expanded their partnership to include metallurgical coal pricing from April 2015 onwards.

Fenwei hit the news in November 2016 when China's state economic planner, the National Development and Reform Commission (NDRC), announced that it was investigating Fenwei for "problems" with its data. Fenwei had already suspended its spot physical thermal coal price index, which is used in China as the domestic industry benchmark, after saying that its prices did not reflect the majority of business transacted in the country. The NDRC had been pushing back against a surge in spot coal prices in late 2016 and the investigation of Fenwei was taken by most industry observers as an attempt by officials to promote lower prices in the Chinese market rather than as any reflection on Fenwei's reporting.

Fenwei's run in with the Chinese authorities provided a neat illustration of the difficulties of producing independent pricing benchmarks in an economy that is still very much subject to state control.

Xinhua Infolink

Coal price reporting agency McCloskey Coal, part of publishing giant IHS since 2007, followed a similar partnership strategy to Platts. McCloskey entered into an arrangement with a Chinese domestic PRA, Xinhua InfoLink, in 2003 and the two launched a joint report, *China Coal Monthly*.

Xinhua InfoLink was founded in 1997 in Beijing to provide news, data and research on the Chinese industrial economy. Since 2007, the firm's commercial arrangements have been handled by the China News Industry Information Centre (CINIC).

SCI Group and Sunsirs

Two of the most important Chinese PRAs are the Sublime China Information Group (SCI Group) and SunSirs – China Commodity Data Group. These are two of the Chinese PRAs that have the greatest potential to expand their reach significantly outside of their home market. As well as publishing pricing information, the two firms also organize conferences and provide consulting services.

SCI Group was founded in 2004 and was originally known as Chem99, reflecting its initial focus on the Chinese petrochemical markets. SCI was founded by seven partners working out of a small office but grew quickly and soon expanded into providing assessments of prices across the energy, metals and agricultural sectors.

A hugely ambitious firm, SCI published a 10-year strategic plan in 2015 under the title of "SCI benchmark: the one to trust for commodities". The scale of SCI is impressive. The firm employs 1,500 people, of whom 800 are analysts, most of whom work on its own campus. (To put that into context, Platts employs slightly over 1,000 people while Argus has around 800 staff.)

SCI claims to have 3.5 million registered users and 4.3 million daily visits to its website. The firm also operates a US subsidiary, Eminent Creation Inc. (ECI), which aims to adapt SCI's enormous database for use by a US audience as well as organizing Chinese business visits to the United States. SCI also has probably the best slogan of any PRA anywhere: "My Information, Your Wealth".

SCI takes pricing methodologies extremely seriously and has created the SCI Price Assessment Standard (SPAS) to define its procedures for assessment, evaluation and publication of prices. Price discovery is focused on a 4.30pm timestamp.

SunSirs – China Commodity Data Group is one of the major rivals to SCI. It also covers the range of energy, metals and agriculture. SunSirs is perhaps best known for publishing the China Bulk Commodity Index (BCI), which is a monthly index of the performance of the Chinese economy based on the performance of 100 different commodities within China.

Established in 2011, SunSirs focuses on eight sectors: energy, chemicals, rubber and plastics, non-ferrous metals, steel, textile, building materials and agricultural and related products. It collects transaction data from more than 100,000 market participants and from the three Chinese commodity futures exchanges.

Like SCI, SunSirs is huge by western standards: it employs 50 experts, 200 senior editors and more than 500 data analysts. SunSirs' data is frequently cited in the

Chinese media and is widely consulted by China government agencies. The service is part of the Zhejiang NetSun group, which was founded in Hangzhou by Sun Deliang in 1997 and is listed on the Shenzhen Stock Exchange. Zhejiang NetSun operates a number of business-to-business websites and e-commerce sites that match buyers and sellers.

CCF Group

One of the few Chinese PRAs to have established benchmark exposure is CCF Group, which has come to dominate the fibre intermediates markets, where China is the key global player. CCF Group is operated by Zhejiang Huarai Information Consulting, which was founded in 1997 to provide consulting services relating to the chemical fibre and textile industries. The firm also provides price assessments of some chemical and petrochemical markets.

CCF's success again shows the value of first-mover advantage in establishing benchmarks. It was the first PRA to cover the chemical fibre market and has never been displaced. CCF also benefits from a tie up with the China Cotton Textile Association and the Chine Yarn-Dyed Weaving Association, with which it operates a joint information website at tteb.com.

Chinese metals PRAs

Since the beginning of the millennium, China has become the main price driver for ferrous metals: the various types of steel, iron ore and coking coal. At the same time the metals markets have liberalized around the world, moving away from fixed-price long-term contracts to spot contracts and hedging with derivatives. The principal beneficiary of these changes amongst the international PRAs has been Platts, both through its own Asian benchmarks and through the Asian benchmarks it acquired in its acquisition of Steel Business Briefing (SBB) in 2011.

Despite the international adoption of Platts' prices for iron ore and coking coal, four major Chinese PRAs have nonetheless emerged as specialists on the domestic ferrous markets and have experienced tremendous growth in recent years: MySteel, SteelHome, Umetal and Custeel. Below the big four, there is also a group of smaller metals PRAs that are very active: Asian Metal, PRC Steel, Steel CN, ChinaTSI, SteelKey and ZH818.

At first glance, this may seem like a large number of PRAs to cover a single industry: Chinese ferrous metals. But the Chinese steel markets are simply enormous. At the end of 2015, it was estimated that there were 150,000 companies involved in the Chinese steel trade and that between them they employed over 1 million people.

The Chinese metals PRAs already have more than a decade of operations behind them. All date back to the first few years of the new millennium when liberalization of both the internet and of the metals sector created a very positive environment for the launch of new Chinese PRAs. The year 2000 was the time when the Chinese internet business really exploded and there was a surge in registrations of internet technology companies, even though most entrepreneurs had not yet worked out how to make money out of the new technology.

MySteel was founded in 2000 in Shanghai and added an English-language service in 2002. The original drive to create the information service came from the Shanghai Steel Association and MySteel founder Zhu Junhong who as chairman and general manager of the Shanghai Steel Association persuaded several influential firms and individuals to invest in the development of the MySteel platform. The firm has three core aims: to construct an information channel; to construct a trading platform; and to become a research hub.

SteelHome was set up in 2004 by Wu Wenzhang, Custeel in 2002 and Umetal in 2006. The size of the three firms' operations is huge by the standards of western PRAs and their information-gathering operations are extremely sophisticated.

Founded in 2002, Custeel is an integrated metallurgical website that operates under the auspices of the China Iron and Steel Association and is funded by 16 large-sized steel manufacturers and enterprises. Custeel's focus is developing e-commerce for the Chinese iron and steel industry but it also acts as a consultant and provides research and pricing services.

Oversupply hits

In 2014 and 2015, the Chinese steel markets experienced chronic oversupply and steel prices were very low. This affected the profit margins of all the firms operating in the ferrous industry in China and led them in many cases to cut back their subscriptions to PRA services, a trend which was exacerbated by the strong competition between the PRAs in the sector. The Chinese metals PRAs responded by trying to diversify away from their total reliance on their traditional core businesses: information, research and pricing. Their preferred solution was to try to leverage their excellent customer reach and their strong website offerings by launching spot trading platforms.

Whereas for the western PRAs, the top of the business value hierarchy is providing benchmark pricing data, the Chinese metals PRAs are constantly trying to move beyond data. Their business models are very different. MySteel once expressed the value hierarchy for the sector as: data at the bottom, then consulting services, followed by matching buyers and sellers, then operating a trading platform and, finally, at the top of the value chain, providing financial services such as lending and payment facilitation to customers.[1]

This attempt to diversify into e-commerce and become what MySteel termed "the closed biosphere" had only limited success. The majority of Chinese steel production is still sold bilaterally on a term contract basis or else via large distributors such as trading houses. This left the Chinese PRAs to fight over relatively low levels of spot volumes. The PRAs also ran into issues of standardization since different steel mills provide different quality specifications under different classifications. At the same time, some smaller steel users tended to prefer to transact through a trading house that has a stable supply relationship with a major steel mill than to pay to transact through a third-party platform.

The PRAs were also not the only ones interested in developing business-to-business platforms for steel transactions. The PRAs even faced competition from some of their biggest customers: major Chinese steel mills such as Baosteel, Hebei

Steel and Jiangsu Shagang had also already launched their own sales platforms in response to the market downturn. At the same time, specialist internet trading sites such as Banksteel, Zhaogang and ggang.cn emerged to serve the steel markets. By the end of 2015, there were an estimated 300 websites dedicated to steel trading, the most sophisticated of which also offered online financing and payment management.

This desire for greater integration along the value chain was not all one-way traffic. While the PRAs were trying to move into e-commerce, ggang.cn's owner, GangGang E-Commerce Shanghai Co. Ltd, decided to move into the pricing side, investing 120 million Chinese yuan (around $17.5 million) into SteelCn in 2016.

A moderate improvement in the steel price in 2016 and early 2017 sparked some renewed optimism in the sector, but the e-commerce drive looked to have run out of steam for most of the PRAs, meaning that many players with large staff numbers were still under pressure. High levels of competition and lingering doubts over the long-term health of the underlying physical market ensured that the picture for the Chinese metals PRAs remained nowhere near as rosy as for the energy-focused PRAs.

India

India is often touted as the next big location for PRAs. Its relatively fast pace of economic development ensures that demand for all classes of commodity is growing strongly while India has several highly sophisticated companies that are confident operating in international markets.

India has two successful commodities futures exchanges – the Multi Commodity Exchange of India (MCX) and the National Commodity & Derivatives Exchange Limited (NCDEX) – and the country pioneered online steel trading with the 2001 launch of the mJunction platform, a 50/50 venture between local steel producers Tata Steel and SAIL.[2]

India has seen the development of a few domestic pricing agencies: Agriwatch and RML AgTech in the agricultural markets; Indian Petro Watch in energy and agriculture, the Petrosil Group in energy and petrochemicals, SteelMint in ferrous metals, and Polymerupdate and PolymerMIS in the plastics markets. But, despite all of the positive macroeconomic signals, India is a long way from fulfilling its potential as a location for price discovery. Its domestic PRAs are very small compared with the Chinese PRAs, for example, while there has not been much direct investment in India by the western PRAs as has been the case in Singapore, Japan and China. Western PRAs have instead tended to cover India from Dubai or Singapore.

The relatively limited nature of price discovery in India partly stems from the nature of the Indian economy. Until relatively recently the Indian government operated a fairly comprehensive regime of subsidies that distorted the domestic market for many commodities. The Indian commodities business is also dominated by a small number of very large players, such as Reliance Industries and Essar in the energy markets and Steel Authority of India Limited (SAIL) in the ferrous markets. The relatively low level of domestic competition makes price discovery more of a challenge.

Ongoing efforts to make state owned players more responsive to international markets and to reduce subsidy levels may change the picture for Indian price discovery. This would likely encourage greater investment both from western and domestic agencies. PRAs need free markets to assess and without truly free markets they struggle.

Conclusion

Europe and the United States are mature markets in terms of PRAs, while Africa and South America currently offer relatively limited opportunities. Of all the regions, Asia has the greatest potential. It is the part of the world with the fastest economic growth rates and it is also home to world class commodity players like Reliance, the Japanese and Korean trading houses and the Chinese majors. Increased market liberalization in Asia since the turn of the century means that there are more and more opportunities emerging for PRAs in markets like electricity, LNG and coking coal.

Asia has developed its own PRAs and the Chinese PRAs, in particular, are huge in terms of scale and ambition. It is an amazing statistic that there are as many people employed by PRAs in China as in the rest of the world combined.

Yet for all the undoubted potential of Asia as a location for price discovery and reporting, relatively few major PRA benchmarks have emerged from Asia to date. The energy markets still look primarily to Brent and WTI, the agricultural markets to Chicago and New York, and the metals markets to the London Metals Exchange (LME). Indian and Chinese demand drives the gold markets, for example, and yet the daily gold fix is set in London and the primary futures benchmark is listed in New York. Perhaps the only significant commodity benchmark that has emerged from Asia in recent years is the iron ore price assessed by Platts/The Steel Index.

The central planning that is so central to so many Asian economies may be acting against the interests of the PRAs in Asia. In Europe and the United States governments have typically stayed out of the issues surrounding the pricing of commodities, only intervening to punish uncompetitive behaviour. When rival companies could not agree on a pricing basis, it therefore made sense for them to select benchmarks produced by independent PRAs. The development of PRAs in the west was a relatively haphazard and organic process that took place over more than a century. The industry in Asia is unlikely to follow the same path.

Unlike their western counterparts, governments in Asia expect to play a role in developing benchmarks. The Singaporean government is deeply involved in attempts to establish an LNG benchmark in Singapore, while the Japanese government is attempting the same in Japan. Meanwhile, the Chinese authorities have been pushing hard to make China a major commodities pricing hub and are backing efforts to develop a major crude oil benchmark in Shanghai.

Officials across Asia believe that establishing commodity benchmarks in their country will be a positive step for their national development. They are absolutely right, of course. But the irony is that government involvement can actually inhibit rather than enhance the development of benchmarks. The risk is that commercial companies do not provide honest feedback during the research process for fear of offending their host government. The explicitly national identity of projects that are backed by a specific government also tends to reduce the chances of success. The Malaysia government is unlikely to back an LNG benchmark sponsored by the Singaporean government, while it is hard to imagine Korean LNG importers deciding to make use of a benchmark promoted by Japanese officials. In contrast, many of the most important commodity benchmarks cross national borders, such as Platts' Dated Brent, which uses crude oil from the United Kingdom and from Norway in the assessment or the Cotlook A cotton index, which uses locations across the Far East.

There is also a concern that some Asian governments will be unable to resist the temptation to 'manage' the benchmarks that they have sponsored. Governments in China and India take great interest in commodity prices and intervene in the markets at will. Prices can be capped or subsidized if they are considered 'excessive'. The experience of Fenwei Energy and its assessments of prices in the Chinese coal market in late 2016 shows that the Chinese government is not afraid to intervene in the operations of PRAs when their price assessments contradict the official line.

Benchmarks tend to develop from industry need for risk management rather than being imposed from above and so for Asian benchmarks to develop, national governments will have to allow local firms to select the assessments that deliver the most transparency and accuracy, irrespective of whether these come from abroad or at home, or from futures exchanges or PRAs. Only at this point, will the full potential for PRAs in Asia be unlocked.

Notes

1   Bai, Rui (2015) presentation: Steel eBusiness in China and Automotive Steel Chain.
2   Steel e-commerce – set for a resurgence? (2016) S&P Global Platts Metals Insight, volume 11, issue 19, 1.

10 PRAs and environmental issues

Introduction

Environmental concerns have been growing around the world in recent decades. Since the Industrial Revolution of the nineteenth-century, the concentration of carbon dioxide (CO_2) in the atmosphere has increased, leading to a global rise in temperatures as well as to other severe environmental consequences. The phenomenon of climate change has been widely attributed to the current dependence on the use of hydrocarbons in the energy sector as well as to other factors such as deforestation. The energy industry's reliance on hydrocarbons has also been blamed for increased global emissions of sulphur dioxide (SOX) and nitrogen oxide (NOX), which cause acid rain and harm organisms from plants to people.

High-level efforts by international governments to push the world towards a low-carbon future represent a potential challenge for the largest price reporting agencies (PRAs). After all, the largest PRA players derive the majority of their revenue from their assessment and analysis of the traditional, hydrocarbon-based energy markets.

The increased focus on the environmental consequences of fossil fuels both by consumers and by national governments has already begun to reshape the energy markets that the PRAs assess. The PRAs have to date proved themselves remarkably swift to react to any such new developments, whether these lead to the development of new markets or to changes in the underlying specifications of traditional energy commodities. As political initiatives drive the adoption of new standards, new commodities or new environmental certificates, PRAs move quickly to occupy these new spaces by providing assessments of prices and reports of trading activity.

Governments have adopted five different but complementary strategies to mitigate climate change, each of which lead to opportunities for PRAs that can partially mitigate the potentially negative consequences on their businesses of a reduction in the use of fossil fuels.

First, there has been and continues to be significant investment in renewable technologies, such as wind, solar and hydroelectric power. This has led to the development of new markets for PRAs to assess such as those for solar panels and cells and their core component, polysilicon.

Second, there has been a drive to mitigate the environmental impact of existing energy sources, for example, by reducing the sulphur content of transport fuels or by encouraging the switch from coal to gas in the electricity sector.

Third, the development of bioenergy has received government support. Bioenergy comprises ethanol, biodiesel and biomass, all of which are currently assessed by PRAs.

Fourth, governments have designed schemes to encourage the energy markets to 'price in' the environmental impact of their products by creating tradeable certificates or permits for emissions of CO_2, SOX and NOX. Schemes such as the European Union Emissions Trading Scheme (ETS), US Renewable Identification Numbers (RINs), the California carbon markets, renewable energy certificate (REC) markets, the Regional Greenhouse Gas Initiative (RGGI) CO_2 market and US SO_2 and NOX markets are all assessed by PRAs.

Fifth and finally, there has been renewed interest by some countries in developing new nuclear power units. Nuclear technology does not emit harmful greenhouse gases, although it does have its own major environmental issues in terms of the treatment and disposal of radioactive waste.

The larger energy-focused PRAs keep a close watch on developments in the environmental markets, although it is notable that they have been swift to enter markets that are adjacent to their existing offerings, such as bioenergy, but slow to enter markets that are further away from their core businesses, such as polysilicon, which is dominated by smaller specialist information services. The experience of polysilicon confirms that the emergence of new markets can present an opportunity for new specialist PRAs to emerge and to become the de facto benchmark, as was already demonstrated in the early 2000s by the success of Point Carbon in the European emissions space.

Renewable technologies

Renewable energy is defined as energy derived from sources that are naturally replaced, such as wind, rain, tides, waves, sunlight and geothermal heat. Renewable energy is primarily used for electricity generation. Renewables are the fastest growing energy sector and 2015 was the first year since the Industrial Revolution in which renewable energy accounted for the majority of all new electricity generation brought online.

Renewable technologies are developing fast, partly as a result of government stimulus programmes around the world, and as a result the cost of generating electricity from renewable sources continues to decline.

In terms of PRAs, there is a relatively limited scope to develop traditional price assessments of the majority of renewable energy sources. Many renewable technologies operate on fixed government incentives, while the energy-focused PRAs already assess prices in the wholesale electricity markets that are supplied by renewables.

The only renewable technology where PRAs have been active is in solar energy. Solar energy is considered to be one of the most promising of the 'new energy' technologies. Solar energy harvests the power of the sun to generate electricity through photovoltaic cells. Solar energy has received substantial support from governments around the world, although this has made the industry and its component commodities rather exposed to political decisions on whether to increase or reduce subsidies for solar-generated electricity.

Given the relatively high profile of the solar market, it is unsurprising that it has attracted interest from PRAs and from exchanges, particularly in Asia, where China is currently the world's largest polysilicon consumption market as the largest manufacturer of solar cells and panels.

One of the first information services to launch a solar-focused service was PVinsights, which provides research, consultancy and pricing for the solar market and its components from its headquarters in Taiwan. PVinsights assesses polysilicon, solar modules, solar wafers and other related products on a weekly basis. The pricing methodology applied by PVinsights relies on a traditional telephone-based survey approach that requires significant editorial judgment in order to reach an acceptable consensus price.

Unlike in better established markets where the trend is towards more mechanical assessments, PVinsights promotes its services based on its editorial involvement in price assessments.

> In our opinion, applying judgment to the price discovery process remains today the best method to determine privately traded solar PV component prices. Our experience in making informed, accurate judgments is one of the most important values we offer to PVinsights.com subscribers.

PVinsights suggests that the failure of attempts in the solar markets to eliminate judgment by creating a neutral data collection process for contributors to submit actual purchase and sales contracts have had limited success because: "most solar PV companies prefer to keep their business contracts private and out of the hands of a third party; and 2) any company could submit false documents".

Another price reporting service for the solar sector, EnergyTrend, was founded in 2010 as an offshoot of Taiwan's TrendForce, a giant market intelligence provider to the technology industries. EnergyTrend covers a number of 'green energy' fields, including solar, lithium batteries and electric cars. In the solar markets, EnergyTrend provides pricing for polysilicon, wafers and cells. Like PVinsights, EnergyTrend relies on surveys both by phone and via written questionnaires to establish the inputs for its price assessments, which are then averaged to produce a final index.

Bloomberg New Energy Finance (BNEF), a subsidiary of the giant Bloomberg media empire, is another very active player in the solar and new technology space. BNEF was originally founded in 2004 as New Energy Finance by Michael Liebreich and was acquired by Bloomberg in 2009.

BNEF is not primarily a pricing service, although it does produce price assessments. Its main driver, though, is to be the key information source for developments in renewable energy. It provides financial, economic and policy analysis as well as databases of assets, investments and companies in the clean energy industries.

BNEF publishes the Wind Turbine Price Index, which is an index of the price of wind turbines on delivery and an outlook for the next 24 months, and the Solar Spot Price Indexes, which are weekly pricing updates, as well as the Solar Shipments Index, which is a monthly reference point for shipments from major Chinese and Taiwanese cell and module makers. Bloomberg again relies upon a survey methodology to derive its indices, whereby panel members submit assessments that are then reviewed by analysts and prices that are more than 50 per cent away from the average are rejected. The indices are updated daily, although the official spot index is provided on a weekly basis.

Of the traditional energy-focused PRAs, only ICIS has so far dipped its toe into the solar industry. ICIS launched a polysilicon service in June 2011, which provided price assessments based on Asia solar-grade polysilicon grades 6N–9N. The locations for the assessments were free on board (fob) Northeast Asia and delivered China. But ICIS later ceased publication of these assessments when liquidity fell in the underlying physical markets.

As well as PRA activity, solar price discovery also takes place on the Singapore Solar Exchange (SSX), which operates an online portal for over-the-counter trading in solar cells, wafers and polysilicon as well as traditional voice broking support. The SSX is a spin off from energy brokerage Ginga Petroleum (S) Pte Ltd, Asia's largest independent energy commodity broker and was founded in Singapore by Sakura Yamasaki. The SSX is planning to establish an index based on trades and bids and offers observed in their market, which would differentiate itself from the panel survey approach used by the other solar assessment services.

Changing specifications

Although the headlines have been dominated by the development of new markets such as those for emissions or bioenergy, the greatest impact of the growth in awareness of environmental issues has been the reshaping of the traditional energy markets. Every time a specification changes or there is a major shift in market dynamics, this represents a challenge for the incumbent PRA which has to manage the transition carefully in order to protect its benchmark status and avoid missteps that could let in a competitor that is swifter to respond.

In the global oil markets, it is generally Platts that is the incumbent and so has the greatest number of specification changes to manage. In particular, the sulphur specifications of gasoil/diesel have been reformed a number of times in recent years in different jurisdictions around the world in order to promote lower sulphur content. Platts is the dominant PRA establishing gasoil/diesel prices in the three core markets of the United States, northwest Europe and Singapore and has been obliged to revise its methodologies in accordance with changing official standards, which are trending globally towards a maximum sulphur content of ten parts per million (10ppm).

A further upcoming change is the shift away from fuel oil to marine diesel or even LNG as the primary fuel for large seaborne vessels. Fuel oil powers the overwhelming majority of all intercontinental shipping but with a sulphur content of up to 3.5 per cent, fuel oil is responsible for significant emissions of sulphur dioxide, which causes acid rain and human respiratory diseases, particularly in port cities such as Hong Kong. From 2020, the International Maritime Organization (IMO) has mandated a switch away from fuel oil to fuels with a maximum sulphur content of 0.5 per cent. This will have an enormous impact on the fuel oil markets, which are dominated globally by Platts.

None of the specification changes has led to date to a change in the PRA that the industry has established as the key underlying benchmark. Platts has been able to manage sensitively all of the transitions to tighter sulphur standard, while Argus also successfully handled the 2010 transition from its Eurograde gasoline benchmark to the Eurobob standard that enforced a stricter and larger ethanol component in the European gasoline pool. Although changing specifications for environmental purposes do force the relevant markets to consider the benchmarks they use, specification changes are usually so well signposted by governments that the incumbent PRA has plenty of time to make the relevant change. The energy industry is typically also so preoccupied with the changes needed in order to meet the new standards, such as increased refinery investment, that changing the benchmark PRA is usually the last thing on anybody's mind.

The generation fuels markets have also felt the impact of shifting environmental standards and here it is less a case of tighter specifications within the same fuel and more a case of a steady shift from one fuel to another. The push to reduce the use of thermal coal in electricity generation around the world has led to an increased focus on replacing coal with gas-fired generation, with the gas either coming from pipeline supplies or increasingly from LNG. To a much lesser extent, electricity generators are also seeking to replace coal with biomass (see the chapter on PRAs and agriculture for further details of PRA activity in the bioenergy sector).

This increased focus on natural gas, which is considered the 'cleanest' of the fossil fuels has driven a dramatic growth in LNG production and trading since 2000. Whereas previously LNG trade took place on very long-term contracts that left little room for PRA assessments, the recent production boom has seen the development of a spot LNG market that can be assessed by PRAs.

This has opened a new front in the battle between the larger publishers. Following its acquisition of Heren Energy, ICIS dominates pricing in the European pipeline markets and in particular in Europe's NBP and TTF gas hubs, which are often referenced in European LNG import pricing. In Asia, which is the heart of the global LNG market, it is Platts that has taken the lead through its Japan/Korea Marker (JKM). Japan's RIM Intelligence also has ambitions to establish a Japanese import benchmark. The US market tends to price in relation to the Henry Hub natural gas futures contract as listed on CME Group.

Argus has the most to lose of the major PRAs from a global switch from coal to gas because it dominates international coal pricing in partnership with IHS McCloskey. Argus is therefore also pushing hard on the gas side, and has had established some contract linkage in the Dutch TTF market, although it has yet to establish a key LNG benchmark.

Bioenergy

Bioenergy provided virtually all of the world's energy needs prior to the Industrial Revolution, with wood and other plant products used for heating and for cooking. Industrialization from the nineteenth century onwards led to the development of coal power and later of gas, while the transport revolution in the twentieth century led to the development of oil resources. While bioenergy remains an important source of energy in the developing world, it has largely been displaced in the advanced economies by hydrocarbon-based energy sources.

Bioenergy in the context of wholesale energy markets comprises ethanol and biodiesel, which are used in transport fuels, as well as biomass, which is used in power generation. These technologies, which are considered less environmentally harmful than fossil fuels because of their renewable nature, have become increasingly viewed as a useful halfway house between hydrocarbons and truly clean energy sources like wind, solar and wave. As such, bioenergy has attracted significant government support in many jurisdictions, particularly Europe and North America.

The activities of the various PRAs operating in the biomass sector are covered separately in the chapter on the agricultural markets.

Emissions markets

Any discussion of the various emissions markets around the world inevitably leads into a world of TLAs (three-letter acronyms) that are baffling to the non-initiated. The multiplicity of schemes around the world and even across different US states ensures that there is no shortage of markets in environmental certificates for PRAs to assess.

In Europe, there is the EUA (European Union Allowances), the CER (Certified Emission Reductions) and ERU (Emissions Reduction Units), while in the United States there are a multiplicity of markets, including the California carbon markets, renewable energy certificate (REC) markets, the Regional Greenhouse Gas Initiative (RGGI) CO_2 market and the SO_2 and NOX markets. There are also other initiatives around the world, particularly in northeast Asia, including seven pilot schemes in China.

These various emissions certificate markets are covered enthusiastically by Argus, Platts and ICIS among others. Nonetheless, the initial market leader in the European carbon markets was Point Carbon, a start-up analytics and pricing firm founded in Oslo, Norway by Per-Otto Wold and three partners. The four partners worked at the Fridtjof Nansen Institute in Norway, which does research on international negotiations. During their work, they realized that when international governments were negotiating the first climate agreements, they were hampered by a lack of information about global emissions or which countries were emitting the most carbon dioxide (CO_2).

Point Carbon was set up in a very different way from a traditional PRA. Its focus was analytics and data delivery rather than pricing. Nonetheless, its price reports became a key source of mark-to-market data for the European emissions market. Point Carbon was eventually acquired by Thomson Reuters in 2010 and its analytic services are now available through the Thomson Reuters Eikon screen. The deal took place not long after Reuters' major rivals Bloomberg had acquired New Energy Finance, showing the two media giants' strong interest in bolstering their coverage of the environmental markets.

Point Carbon's success in integrating news and pricing data with the delivery of fundamental data in easy-to-use and innovative formats into traders' desktops was a lesson for the traditional PRA industry and in many ways prefigured the investments in data delivery, analytics and management systems made by the largest PRAs over the last decade or so.

Developing new assessments

At the Paris climate conference (COP21) in December 2015, 195 countries adopted the first-ever universal and legally binding global deal on climate change. The agreement sets out a global action plan to put the world on track to avoid serious climate change by limiting global warming to well below 2°C. The Paris Agreement will inevitably accelerate the ongoing changes in the energy sector that have taken place in recent years, such as the adoption of bioenergy, the reduction of sulphur in transport fuels and the global shift from coal to gas in power generation.

These changes will inevitably be reflected in the work of PRAs around the world. PRAs have already established a strong track record of responding to any government changes in fuel standards. The emergence of new environmentally driven markets has also provoked a swift response from PRAs, which have been quick to provide price assessments for new markets, whether these emerge in bioenergy, renewables such as solar, or the various environmental certificate markets.

PRAs have a positive role to play in the transition to a lower-carbon global economy. Independent price assessments will be required to support the development of these new markets, either as benchmarks or for mark-to-market purposes, and PRAs are best placed to provide these assessments. Greater price transparency in newer markets such as polysilicon encourages other participants to enter those markets and to increase investment. Financial institutions are also happier to lend to projects where there are clear price indicators and some sensible forward price projections. Without independent benchmarks and analytics, it is also difficult for governments to quantify the impact of their decisions and to understand whether legislation or subsidies are being correctly deployed. As the founders of Point Carbon discovered, it is virtually impossible to have a sensible discussion about environmental initiatives without hard data to back up the arguments.

PRAs can be therefore very helpful in the development of environmentally driven markets. We should, however, be clear that PRAs' interest in providing benchmarks and assessments to these markets does not come from any particular interest in environmentalism within PRAs themselves but is more the consequence of sound business sense.

As information services, PRAs are typically neutral about the environmental impact of the markets they assess. A PRA would not differentiate between providing prices for highly polluting 3.5 per cent sulphur fuel oil or for the components of solar panels on the basis that it is the role of PRAs to reflect and assess markets rather than to moralize about them. It is clearly the role of governments to drive changes in the energy markets, but PRAs will be quick to respond as they are always looking for new markets to assess in order to expand their revenues and profits.

Nuclear energy

After a couple of decades in the wilderness following the Chernobyl disaster of 1986, interest in nuclear energy has experienced something of a renaissance in recent years. The previously vociferous lobbying by environmental groups concerned about the impact on the environment of radioactive waste has been tempered by a growing awareness that it will be very difficult for the world to achieve a reduction in harmful carbon emissions without the use of nuclear energy, which does not emit gases blamed for global warming. Nuclear power has come to be seen as an emissions-free and reliable source of base load electricity generation, which can help bridge the gap between the current dependence on fossil fuels and a potential clean energy future.

There are a large number of new nuclear reactors under construction in China, while South Korea, India, Russia, the United Kingdom and the United Arab Emirates are also planning or progressing new nuclear plants. The sector suffered a major public relations dent with the Fukushima nuclear disaster of March 2011 but concerns about global warming means that an expansion of the global nuclear fleet still looks highly likely.

The primary fuel for nuclear energy is uranium, which is mainly mined in Kazakhstan, Canada, Australia, Niger, Namibia and Russia. There are two main benchmark providers in the uranium space: the Ux Consulting Company LLC (UxC) and TradeTech. The two firms' benchmarks tend to be used either separately or as an average by uranium traders. Platts and Argus also publish uranium assessments, while UxC reports a Broker Average Price (BAP) based on information provided by Evolution Markets and Numerco Ltd.

TradeTech provides consulting services as well as producing publications and pricing data. Its predecessor company, the Nuclear Exchange Corporation (NUEXCO), was the first organization to publish a weekly assessment of spot uranium as early as August 1968. This assessment was used as a reference price in long-term contracts from the 1970s onwards. From 2011 onwards, TradeTech began assessing uranium prices on a daily basis, reflecting the greater price volatility that followed the entry of a number of new buyers and sellers into the market.

TradeTech's NUEXCO Exchange Value is TradeTech's assessment of where spot and near-term transactions for significant quantities of natural uranium concentrates could be concluded at the close of the trading day. This assessment, and other similar assessed benchmarks published by TradeTech, are based on a combination of transaction data and firm bids and offers as uncovered by the firm's price reporters. TradeTech also publishes a volume-weighted average price based on recent transactions.

UxC was founded in 1994 as an affiliate of the Uranium Exchange in order to provide information and consulting services to the nuclear and uranium industries. UxC is primarily a consulting firm that provides bespoke consulting services and publishes special reports, but its Ux Prices have nonetheless become a key benchmark. The Ux Prices are referenced in many uranium fuel sales contracts and were referenced in the US-Russia intergovernmental deal on highly enriched uranium (HEU). The Ux Prices are also used as the settlement price for the CME Group's uranium futures contract. The Ux Prices are published weekly and price assessments are based upon the most competitive offer of spot uranium that UxC's price reporters can uncover at the time of publication, taking into account certain quality, quantity and origin parameters. This 'best offer' methodology appears to be unique within the commodity markets, where PRAs typically base their assessments on panels, surveys or deals heard done in the market.

Due to its inherent political sensitivities, uranium remains a relatively niche market dominated by specialist agencies that combine price reporting with in-depth consulting services. It will be interesting to see if greater take up of nuclear energy around the world will lead to an increased competition in the uranium benchmark space or whether TradeTech and UxC will retain their current dominant positions.

Conclusion

The PRAs' drive to expand the portfolio of markets that they cover is made more urgent by the potential risk to their existing businesses. For Argus, for example, a global shift away from coal represents a serious commercial risk, given the revenues that benchmark coal pricing generates for the firm, while for Platts the shift away from fuel oil in the shipping sector could potentially see a consolidation in the sector that might lead to lower subscriber numbers. The traditional energy-focused PRAs therefore do have some risk related to their existing revenue streams in a carbon-constrained world.

Diversification into new environmental markets will offset the potential risk of declining revenues from traditional hydrocarbon assessments to some extent. But it is unlikely that capturing the benchmark for products like uranium, polysilicon or lithium, which is used in batteries, could ever represent more than a tiny fraction of the potential revenue opportunity of a traditional oil or coal benchmark.

The longevity of some of the environmental markets is also a concern for PRA managers looking to hedge themselves against the potential threat of environmental reform to their core hydrocarbon business. Some environmental markets such as those for carbon certificates are purely government constructs and can be reformed or abandoned at will, while other markets such as solar and bioenergy are still heavily dependent on government subsidies, which again are always subject to the risk of reduction or withdrawal.

Assessments of hydrocarbon markets will likely remain the core revenue driver for the larger PRAs for the next few decades as there is little immediate sign of a wholesale shift away from carbon-based fuels. PRAs will nonetheless play their part in driving the development of new sources of energy by providing transparency and indices to developing fuel markets. There is no 'new oil' on the horizon, however. Whatever fuel source comes to dominate the future is unlikely to be anywhere near as profitable for PRAs as traditional hydrocarbons have proved to be.

11 PRA pricing methodologies

Introduction

A methodology is the recipe that produces a price assessment. It is both a user's guide to how a price reporting agency (PRA) comes up with its price assessments as well as a 'how to' guide for the individual price reporter covering the market. The presence of a fixed, written and public methodology should in theory ensure that users of PRA pricing data can understand exactly how the assessment was derived. The methodology also acts as a guide to market participants about the format in which they should present any information that they wish to be included in the price-discovery process.

In each commodity market, a PRA lives and dies by the methodology that it selects. Industry debates rage about the best way of assessing prices. Reputations within the PRA sector can be made or lost on the design of a methodology and the market's response to it. In reality, though, there are only a relatively limited number of ways to design a methodology to establish commodity prices, although each broad type of methodology can be tweaked to reflect the particularities of specific markets.

There is a very special skill involved in designing a methodology. The way the price assessment is structured has to capture the way an individual commodity market operates, with all its quirks and uniqueness. At the same time, the methodology has to ensure that the resulting assessment will be fair to all sides – buyers, sellers and middlemen traders. Methodologies cannot be too complex or obscure. After all, they have to be quickly grasped by impatient traders, non-specialists and regulators. And finally, methodologies have to be practical. The perfect academic benchmark design may founder on the realities of a quiet day in August when two thirds of market participants are on their yachts. Methodologies have to work every single day of the year and have to be able to stand up to vastly different trading conditions.

Methodologies matter. Almost every time a commodity market has changed from using one PRA's assessment as a benchmark to another rival provider, the root cause has been users' preference for a different type of methodology from the one that the incumbent provider was either using or suggesting. The choice of methodology can cost or make PRAs millions of dollars a year.

Given the importance of methodologies, is no surprise that the IOSCO Principles for oil price reporting services devoted so much attention to issues around their design and to the processes by which methodologies are revised. IOSCO focused on ensuring that methodologies were clear and public. The Principles also obliged PRAs to discuss potential changes with their users before altering their methodologies.

In this chapter, we will trace some key developments in the design of PRA methodologies and look in detail at some of the most commonly employed methodologies in benchmark commodity pricing. There have not been any previous attempts to classify the various forms of price assessments and there will be inevitably plenty of room for debate about the family resemblance between the various approaches to commodity pricing issues. Nonetheless, this chapter will attempt a taxonomy of methodologies.

Trends in methodologies

It was not all that long ago that many PRAs used to refuse to make their pricing methodologies public. This was either on the same principle that stops restaurants from revealing their 'secret sauce' – a fear that competitors would copy their approach – or else because they felt that revealing how they assessed prices would enable traders to work out how to influence those prices. This approach has now almost entirely disappeared, although some price reporters may regret the passing of the days when they had to answer less detailed critiques of their decisions from traders.

The more opaque approach tended to raise questions from some market participants as to whether price reporters were even working to any methodology at all. The trend now is towards ever greater disclosure. Even those PRAs that were slow to formalize and publish their methodologies were anyway forced into full disclosure in order to comply with the IOSCO Principles, which were issued in October 2012. (See Chapter 14 on PRAs and global regulation for the background to and drafting of the Principles.)

The IOSCO Principles require "the formal documentation and disclosure of all criteria and procedures that are used to develop an assessment, including guidelines that control the exercise of judgment, the exclusion of data as well as the procedures for reviewing a methodology".

The IOSCO Principles also require "transparency of procedures by which PRAs will advise stakeholders of any proposed changes to a methodology, including the opportunity for stakeholder comment on the impact of any changes". Again, most PRAs were already requesting customer feedback before making any changes to their methodologies as a point of good faith and also in order to minimize the risk of a significant adverse reaction from the market to any changes. But since the publication of the IOSCO Principles, these previously voluntary consultations have become a major compliance point.

As well as the trend towards greater transparency in the provision and discussion of methodologies, another trend has emerged in recent decades: this time towards greater 'automation' or 'mechanization' of pricing. The role of the individual price reporter as the final arbiter of pricing decisions has declined in importance as methodologies have become increasingly based on screen-based pricing or on volume-weighted averages.

Proponents of automation argue that a more mechanical price assessment process produces more predictable benchmarks. Automation reduces the role of the human element – the price reporter – who may exhibit conscious or unconscious biases, or who can make mistakes on a difficult day, or who may simply not be very good at the job. Automation also leaves a clear trail for regulators to follow: inputs x and y generate price z, with none of the grey areas or judgment calls that are so difficult to document or to explain at a later date.

On the other hand, the opponents of automation would counter that the price assessment process can be compromised without skilled human oversight to oversee the quality of the inputs and to provide a sense-check to the final result. An algorithm cannot properly understand and assess an opaque commodity market, the critics would say. An automated system may provide predictable pricing but its very predictability may also leave it open to undue influence by market participants.

One of the undeniable arguments against full automation of the price assessment process is that it inevitably leads to the deskilling and devaluing of price reporters. A price reporter who is an expert in his or her market and who can sit face-to-face with a senior trader to justify an assessment has a certain standing in the marketplace and a corresponding economic value. A price reporter has significantly less value if their responsibilities are mainly to run a program to average various trade files or to copy down the last traded price from a screen-based system. Some cynics might suggest that this trend suits PRA management. Automation at its most extreme makes price reporters virtually interchangeable. This in turn leads to reduced pressure on wage bills as there will be little difference between the output of senior price reporters and their less experienced and cheaper colleagues.

As trading screens and bulletin boards proliferate across the PRAs, perhaps we are witnessing the birth of a new industrial revolution in price reporting. The skilled individual craftsman is increasingly giving way to the less skilled but more interchangeable machine operator.

Expert judgment methodology

This is all a very long way from the situation that prevailed at the birth of the commodity PRAs. The very first PRA assessments were generally the result of the skilled judgment of a single market expert, such as Warren Platt or the Williamses, who assessed the metals markets in *The Iron Age*. These pricing pioneers would look around the market, often literally visiting auctions or physical marketplaces. They would discuss recent developments with their contacts and would apply their deep market knowledge in order to come up with a reference price. These were gentlemen – and in those days they were all men – who could use their experience to essentially 'feel' what the correct price assessment ought to be for each day, week or month. At a time of lesser scrutiny, their assessments would typically be accepted by the markets as the best approximation that anyone was likely to reach.

The strength of this approach, which we could categorize as the 'expert judgment methodology', is that it is very difficult for an individual trader to manipulate an assessment generated by a subject-matter expert with considerable experience and self-confidence.

Table 11.1 Summary of methodology approaches

	Methodology	Key advantage	Key disadvantage
1	Expert judgment	A true market expert will make the right assessment	Depends on the individual reporter to get it right
2	Fixed panel	Locks in commitment from key market players	Potential suppliers of key information may be missing
3	Floating panel	Flexibility to capture key market information	Editorial selection problematic; less prestigious
4	Non-adjusted panel	Eliminates editorial involvement	Bad inputs can skew the final assessment
5	Adjusted panel	Removes outliers that could negatively affect pricing	Arbitrary judgement call; could eliminate key information
6	Hybrid panel	Both trades' and panellists' views are reflected	Small trades could skew the assessment
7	Survey	Allows greater context to emerge	Only as good as the price reporter and his contacts
8	Volume-weighted average	Based on actual trade; no judgment calls	Lacks context; timing can skew assessment
9	Market-on-Close	Transparent and allows easy price comparison	Limited underlying liquidity and participation
10	PRA physical delivery	Perfect convergence between assessment and commodity	Limited participation; unregulated process
11	Derivative based	Can reflect market practice; potentially highly regulated	Risk of circularity in assessments
12	Relative value	Enables assessments in illiquid markets	Dependant on stable relationships in relative value
13	Best offer	Clearly shows where sellers are operating	Does not clearly identify buying levels

The obvious weakness of this methodology is that it is entirely subjective and the quality of the assessment depends totally on the quality of the price reporter. A reporter given carte blanche to set the benchmark entirely on his or her own judgment risks being railroaded by aggressive market participants. There is the risk that assessments are unpredictable by the market and that the absence of the core assessor through sickness or leave could see his or her replacement reach a very different conclusion. Modern compliance departments also tend to frown upon expert judgments, which by their very nature tend to be lightly documented and hard to explain to regulators.

Not every price reporter is a Warren Platt and the expert judgment methodology is only as good as the expert behind it. As a result, the expert judgment methodology has largely died out in the professional PRA world, although it still survives in niche markets where price assessments are provided by specialist consultants that undertake price assessments as an adjunct to their normal advisory work.

Panel methodology

One of the most standard methodologies employed by PRAs across all sectors is the use of pricing panels. The use of panels was the obvious next development for PRAs after they began to move away from the expert judgment methodologies employed by most of their founders. Panels, of various types and in various formats, continue to be employed successfully to this day across a wide number of commodity markets.

Under the panel methodology, the PRA seeks to eliminate the subjectivity inherent in the expert judgment methodology by inviting a group of industry participants to submit their views on pricing. These are then combined through different calculations, usually involving an averaging process, in order to produce the PRA's final price assessment.

The strengths of the panel methodology are numerous, which is why it continues to be employed so frequently to this day. By using a panel, the PRA eliminates the risk of any poor performance by its own price reporter. The PRA can easily defend its assessment to the market: after all, the market's inputs were the direct source of the assessments. A third and very important advantage is that panel members feel a sense of ownership in the final assessment. The use of a panel draws the industry into the PRA's methodology and gives them comfort that their views are being taken into account. It is very difficult for a rival PRA to displace a panel methodology since it would have to persuade market participants that it could improve on a process that already directly incorporates their views.

One disadvantage of the panel approach is that there are markets in which some key firms are either unable or unwilling to participate. This would be the case with Middle East oil, for example, because the state-owned oil producers would never agree to participate directly in the price formation process because of political sensitivities. It is also increasingly the case in the new trading environment that some firms will be uncomfortable with their traders participating so openly in price discovery and so their compliance departments may prevent them from participating in panels.

The panel approach works well in markets where there is a good range of buyers, sellers and traders. It is less successful in markets where there is an imbalance favouring one side or another, or where both sides of the market are actually looking for the same price outcome. This often ended up being the case in the pricing panel for the Indonesian crude oil Minas that was operated by the Asia Petroleum Price Index (APPI, see the chapter on Asian PRAs for further details) where oil refiners and producers both tended to submit lower-than-expected prices, the former in order to reduce their procurement costs and the latter in order to reduce their tax bills.

Another important key weakness of the panel methodology is that it has the potential to generate an assessment that is at odds with the actual deals concluded in the market. If a certain commodity has been trading consistently at $50/ton all week, then a panel methodology would clearly have failed in its purpose if it ends up generating an assessment of $40/ton, either because the panellists were not aware of where the deals had been concluded or because they on average preferred a lower assessment.

A panel methodology is best employed in markets that are assessed on a weekly or monthly basis as many panellists may be reluctant to commit themselves to providing price assessments every day. This may be because of an individual trader's time constraints or because firms are concerned about the level of commitment involved in ensuring that there is an authorized person available to provide the assessment every single day. Panels therefore suit markets where prices are not too fast moving and weekly or monthly pricing is the norm; these tend to be downstream markets such as plastics or specialist chemicals.

Despite these limitations, panels seem likely to remain a mainstay of the assessment process and are one of the most commonly used families of PRA methodology. Within the family, there are various refinements of the panel methodology, which can be employed individually or in various combinations, such as the fixed panel, the floating panel, the adjusted panel, the non-adjusted panel and the hybrid panel.

Fixed and floating panels

Under a fixed panel system, the PRA selects its panellists in a relatively formal way, perhaps by having the participating firms sign legal agreements that oblige the firm to supply information to the PRA. The PRA will then employ the same panellists every time it makes its assessment. The advantage for the PRA is that it has a strong commitment from its panellists and there may be a degree of prestige involved for the firms that are invited to participate in a relatively formal panel.

Presumably, if the PRA is credible, it will have selected the most important and knowledgeable market participants for its panel. This will enhance its credibility and, as discussed above, will make it hard for rivals to displace a methodology based on the inputs of the most important market participants. The weakness of a fixed panel is that the PRA may be missing out on key information providers. Perhaps there is a small Malta-based trading house that would not typically warrant an invitation to participate in a fixed panel, but one month is responsible for significant market activity and is therefore for that period the best-informed player in the market.

It is in cases such as this that a floating panel methodology is more effective. Under a floating panel system, the PRA has the flexibility to invite different participants to offer their market views without being restricted to a fixed and limited list. This ensures that the PRA can contact a broader list of customers and can attempt to capture the views of the most active players, which may fluctuate with time.

This flexibility to contact the most active players is a key strength of the floating panel system. Another benefit is that the PRA is protected from a low response rate when a number of players are out of the market for vacations or an industry event. The PRA can simply keep calling around until it has sufficient responses to be credible.

The weakness of the floating panel is that it reintroduces editorial subjectivity into the process. The individual price reporter gets to determine who to call and how frequently, which is the kind of judgment call that the panel methodology was supposed to limit. A more informal panel set up also has the potential to be treated less seriously by its panellists and certainly there is no prestige involved in being part of a panel when anyone in the industry could also be considered as a panellist.

Non–adjusted and adjusted panels

A non–adjusted panel is perhaps the first truly mechanical form of methodology in that once the inputs are submitted by the panellists, the final price is produced automatically. Under this methodology, the price reporter first contacts the panellists for their views or they submit them in some electronic format. Once the PRA has built up the data set of panellists views on that day, the inputs are averaged to generate the assessment. There is no editorial interference in the averaging process. This eliminates any judgment calls by individual price reporters, particularly if the panel is a fixed one. Even in the case of a floating panel, use of a non–adjusted approach limits the influence that PRA staff have over the benchmark.

Perhaps the most successful and widely referenced unadjusted panel assessments are those provided by London's Baltic Exchange for the shipping markets. Since its first index launched in 1985, the Baltic Exchange – a subsidiary of the Singapore Exchange (SGX) – has used panels of shipbrokers to assess standard international shipping routes. For its physical indexes and assessments of the dry bulk forward curve, it uses an unweighted arithmetic average of all of the assessments submitted by panellists. These non–adjusted panel assessments are major global reference prices and are also used to settle freight derivatives.

Non–adjusted panels are, however, the exception rather than the rule. Most panel methodologies make use of some basic tweaking in order to reduce the risk of manipulation or of an off–market input skewing the whole assessment. The Baltic Exchange uses an adjusted panel methodology for its assessments of the forward wet freight market. It averages the brokers' assessments using a weighting related to the brokers' market share based on the previous month's cleared activity. The Baltic says that "this is intended to enhance the accuracy of the curve in a market where there are often few brokers involved and widely varying expertise".

Adjusting panellists' submissions according to market share is a fairly unique approach. The most common adjustment that benchmark providers apply is to eliminate the highest and lowest panel submissions when calculating the final assessment. This can be done in various ways: perhaps the highest 10 per cent and the lowest 10 per cent of panellists' submissions are excluded from the averaging process. Or perhaps the PRA eliminates any price that is outside a certain distance (either by percentage or in outright per unit value) from another reference point. This could be another marker, or the previous assessment price or the average of the initial pre–adjusted panel average. Under this methodology, a PRA may exclude panel prices if they are more than $5 above or below the previous settlement, for example, or if they are more than 15 per cent away from an adjacent benchmark such as Brent crude oil futures.

The value of adjusting panel inputs is clear. It avoids outlying prices from influencing the final settlement, whether or not these prices were provided by panellists with ill intent or through lack of market awareness. To keep the standard of their panels high, many PRAs will review panellists' submission records and will suspend or expel panel members found to be consistently submitting prices that are then discarded during the panel adjustment process.

The weakness of panel adjustment is again that it introduces editorial judgment calls into what is supposed to be a relatively mechanical process. The PRA has to set the adjustment parameters and these are by definition going to be arbitrary. Why throw out submissions that are 10 per cent off market rather than 5 per cent or 15 per cent? The risk also exists that the price that was thrown out was the correct one. Commodity markets are in constant flux and the sharpest traders hold the best information. It is possible to envisage situations where the best-informed trader can see the market surging higher before some of his or her slower competitors and therefore submits a high number into the panel, only for this price to be subsequently eliminated because it is 15 per cent above the average submission. The risk in such cases is that the adjusted panel will always be playing catch up to the market. The adjusted panel relies on information reaching the majority of firms and these firms then establishing a consensus. The risk for the PRA is that it inadvertently eliminates the views of those who are operating with the latest information. In the worst case scenario, the PRA could end up consistently ignoring inputs from the traders with the freshest information or even sanction them for consistently being too far from the consensus of the panel.

Hybrid panel methodology

One of the key weaknesses of any panel methodology – whether fixed, floating, adjusted or non-adjusted – was already identified above: a panel of the great and good of a particular commodity market may all submit assessments around $350 per metric ton but meanwhile actual physical deals have been reported at $325 per metric ton. The panellists may not have been aware of these deals or may have chosen to ignore them in their submissions. The fact remains that if they were done legitimately and the PRA has heard about them and confirmed them, then it would trouble a decent price reporter's conscience to publish a panel price of $350 while knowing all the time that this was way above the reported level of deals in the market.

After all, in the markets you will often hear the phrase "You can't argue with a deal." A reported, confirmed and repeatable trade usually represents the top of the information hierarchy when it comes to assessing prices. While individuals' views are important, and bids and offers are crucial guides to market levels, an actual deal is hard to argue with, given that hard cash and the actual commodity have changed hands at the price indicated.

In order to try to reduce any variance between the price produced by a panel methodology and the deals done in the market, some PRAs employ a hybrid panel methodology – a format that was pioneered by Peter Caddy of Argus for his firm's international coal assessments.

A hybrid panel methodology, sometimes referred to as a mixed panel methodology, is one where the panel's output is blended with data from deals. This format uses an adjusted floating panel to provide half of the final assessment, while the other half of the assessment comprises the volume-weighted average price of all reported deals during the assessment period. This methodology therefore ensures that reported trades are taken into account and are weighted equally with the output of the panel.

This hybrid panel approach has proved to be very robust and is well accepted by the coal market, for example. The use of a panel gives key industry stakeholders a voice in the assessment but the use of a hybrid panel methodology avoids some of the concerns around panel pricing by also introducing an element of actual traded levels.

The potential weakness of this hybrid panel approach is that there is the danger that one small trade has a disproportionate impact on the index, given that 50 per cent of the final assessment is derived from reported trades, however small they might be in volume terms. The scenario could emerge where the opinion of a panel of 20 or more industry experts controlling millions of tons of sales and purchases is only given an equivalent validity to one small 15,000 metric ton deal, simply because of their equal weightings and because this is the only trade that has been observed during the assessment period or that has been reported by traders.

There is also a risk in terms of a potential lack of consistency given that a hybrid panel methodology may be obliged to default to using the panel's assessment to establish 100 per cent rather than 50 per cent of the final index in the absence of any confirmed trading activity.

Survey methodology

A very large number of PRA methodologies state that their price reporters will carry out a "survey of market participants" in order to establish the correct level of prices. The documents sometimes give further details such as the kind of participants that will be contacted, such as producers, consumers, banks and brokers, or else the way in which the survey will be carried out, either by telephone or electronically through email or instant messaging services. Sometimes the methodologies even spell out a target number of participants to be surveyed: "up to 15", "at least 20", etc.

Surveys sit in the family tree of PRA methodologies somewhere between expert judgment and panels. They share their DNA with both. A survey approach usually allows a decent amount of flexibility to the individual price reporter. The reporter will typically call around the market to gather information on bids, offers and deals, as well as listening to the views of key market participants and discussing with them issues such as supply and demand and the behaviour of related markets.

A survey methodology takes what might be termed a more holistic approach than a pure panel methodology. With a panel, the price reporter's primary role is to note down the assessment provided by the individual panellist and to incorporate it into an adjusted or non-adjusted averaging process. In a survey methodology, the price reporter does not have necessarily have to treat the market participant's view with as much reverence. Their view is a very useful indicator but it can be challenged or ignored if it does not fit with other participants' views or with other evidence. In a panel methodology there is generally some form of obligation to average the price inputs received from panellists, whereas this is not necessarily the case with surveys.

The ideal survey is essentially a series of mini interviews with market practitioners where their views are solicited, challenged and noted. The price reporter should have sufficient command of the market to push back where appropriate and to seek the 'why' that lies behind the individual participant's view. If a trader is calling the market at a high level, it may be because he has transacted there, because he has seen bids and offers around that level, because he knows of a supply outage or a new buy tender. Maybe the trader's judgment is affected by the fact that he has a long position in the market and so wishes for a high assessment, or maybe even because he knows a rival company has a short position.

The view of a panellist does not necessarily come with any background, whereas a survey carried out by an experienced price reporter should build a framework of context that supports the final assessment.

The difference between a survey and an expert judgment methodology is that the price reporter in a survey approach is expected to be diligent in contacting all sides of the market and to reflect their views in his or her final assessment. In contrast, an expert judgment could see the expert in question produce an assessment purely from his knowledge of fundamentals and trends without contacting even a single participant. In the survey approach, the price reporter is the interviewer of the market, whereas when expert judgment is the preferred methodology, the price reporter is the star of the show.

The strength of the survey methodology is also its greatest weakness: it is somewhat on the fuzzy side. PRA compliance departments are increasingly careful to control that their staff have indeed called as many participants as they are supposed to and have weighted their calls fairly between different sides of the market. Nonetheless, it is not always easy for a price reporter to reach everybody they want to on every single occasion. And increasingly many of the most important firms are unwilling to provide information through surveys for compliance reasons (see Chapter 14 on compliance for the background to this unfortunate trend towards disengagement with PRAs by many key commodity market participants). A survey is after all only as good as the person carrying it out and the people to whom they manage to speak.

The survey approach remains extremely common throughout the commodity markets and some market participants value their interactions with price reporters who, in theory at least, can speak to everyone in the market and are therefore important conduits for news and gossip.

Surveys are unlikely ever to go out of fashion because of the flexibility they offer, particularly in the more opaque commodity markets, and because there will always be more information to be gleaned from a conversation than from a screen. That said, the survey methodology has come under increased pressure from the reduced number of firms that are comfortable allowing their traders free rein to speak to PRA reporters. There are also economic forces at work: price reporters that are comfortable handling survey methodologies will typically need to be more experienced and thus better paid than those administering more automated methodologies.

Volume-weighted averages

Expert judgment, panels and surveys tend to dominate in more illiquid or niche markets where trades are rare and levels are hard to determine. At the other end of the scale are methodologies that rely purely on volume-weighted averages (VWA), also known as trade-weighted averages (TWA). The use of VWAs is an entirely automated methodology where the PRA seeks to confirm the price and volume of as many actual trades as possible before averaging the price of the deals in proportion to their volume. This average then forms the final assessment.

For their inputs into the VWAs, PRAs either rely on the deals they can unearth and confirm in the market, or else increasingly they rely on deal files provided either by traders, brokers or physical exchanges. These deal files are either anonymized or else the PRA in question may have some form of non-disclosure agreement in place with market participants in order to receive the file with full details attached. Typically, in order to prevent individual traders from selectively reporting deals that benefit their position, a trading firm will have an 'all or nothing' policy in place for submissions: it will report all of the deals it concludes or none.

Again, as for all automated methodologies, the advantage of the volume-weighted methodology is that it requires no judgment call by the price reporter and can therefore be easily defended to the market. And if "you can't argue with a deal" then you certainly can't argue with a VWA that aggregates all of the trades into a single assessment.

There is no subjectivity involved in a VWA and no need for the price reporter to ever speak to a single market participant, except to check a trade identification. This makes VWAs ideal for markets where several key market participants are unwilling to interact with PRAs or for PRAs that do not want to spend heavily on experienced price reporters.

VWAs are far from suitable for every market. For a VWA to be meaningful, the average needs to be composed of numerous inputs, meaning that there have to be lots of transactions in the market. As a result, the VWA methodology tends to be most heavily used in markets where small deals take place in large numbers, such as wholesale natural gas and electricity or US crude oil and refined products (the so-called pipeline and wire markets). In seaborne commodity markets where there might be only a few very large trades each week, a VWA would be meaningless.

One concern about VWAs is that it can make it hard to line up the value of commodities in different markets. We could imagine a day that started quietly but where a surprise announcement by OPEC at lunchtime sent the markets shooting higher. If the majority of gasoline trades took place in the morning before the news, while the majority of jet fuel deals took place later in the day, then there will be a major discrepancy between the VWAs for gasoline and for jet fuel. The average for gasoline will be significantly lower than that for jet fuel but the difference will be artificial. The difference would reflect a function of the timing of the liquidity rather than indicating the real difference in value between the two refined products. This timing discrepancy could lead refiners to mistakenly prioritize jet fuel over gasoline, simply because of the way the two VWAs are composed.

Some VWA methodologies seek to address this potential discrepancy in timing by weighting towards the end-of-day period or by adjusting earlier trades. These adjustments to VWAs are, though, against the spirit of non-editorial intervention in VWAs. If the whole point of VWAs is that they are mechanical, then any adjustment reintroduces a value judgment into the whole process.

Traders sometimes refer to a 'previous settlement bias' whereby traders take their cue from where the market closed the previous day's trading rather than looking at each morning as a new price-discovery opportunity. Prices therefore tend to start close to previous levels before moving away from the previous day's settlement as the day progresses. This movement of prices is captured by VWAs but opponents would argue that VWAs simply confirm the previous settlement bias rather than reflecting activity levels once the market trend for the new day is properly established.

Another potential concern about VWAs is that the PRA may not know any special terms of a particular deal that is reported and therefore includes a deal in the VWA that may not reflect standard the market price. The price of a deal could, for example, be influenced by whether there are scheduling issues or delays with loading or unloading or by whether the deal is at the very prompt end of an assessment period. The success of the VWA methodology relies on the individual price reporter's ability to note any unusual conditions attached to each deal and to then either adjust for the impact of the conditions or else disregard the deal altogether.

One relatively common issue that PRAs operating the VWA methodology need to watch carefully is that of credit restrictions. Some parties may have to pay a premium because they are considered to be a greater risk due to their lower credit. Their deals may therefore not fully represent standard market conditions. Buyers and sellers that also cannot transact directly with each other because of credit issues also sometimes transact through a third party – a practice that is known as 'sleeving'. In a sleeve, the third party passes the commodity from seller to buyer at the level the two sides have agreed but with a small premium attached as payment for the sleeve, the costs of which may be born either by one side of the trade or by both. The price reporter will have to be alert to the sleeve in order to avoid double counting of deals – a sleeved deal may show up as two separate deals in a trade file but is actually only one genuine transaction. The reporter will also have to adjust for the cost of the sleeve in order to uncover the true value of the transaction.

Another concern that is sometimes expressed about VWAs is that traders could conclude no-risk deals with one another or with a subsidiary purely in order to dominate the VWA assessments. Although this is a legitimate concern, trading to create a false impression of market levels or market liquidity is an extremely high-risk strategy and as such is a very fringe activity. False reporting is an offense in most jurisdictions and should anyway be spotted by PRA staff reconciling deal files or by compliance departments either at the market participant or at the PRA, which are constantly looking for unusual trading patterns. Submitting "wash trades" to a PRA where the only purpose of a transaction is to create a misleading impression of price or liquidity would lead directly to the involvement of the relevant regulator, which is exactly what happened in 2002–2003 when the US Commodity Futures Trading Commission (CFTC) fined US firms millions for submitting false gas and electricity prices to Platts and other index providers.

Market-on-close

The development of the market–on–close (MOC) methodology, which is popularly known as "the Platts' window" has had such a profound impact on pricing in the commodity markets since its initial introduction in 1992 that it is discussed separately in the following chapter. But, briefly, the MOC standardized all of Platts' petroleum methodologies around a single 30-minute period ('the window') during which traders indicate their bids and offers and transact deals on a trading screen, with the last visible price setting that day's assessment.

It is no exaggeration to say that MOC has revolutionized the way PRAs operate and the way they are perceived by the wider market. Price discovery now takes place onscreen and in public and so the price reporter is principally a witness and occasional judge of the activity, rather than an active agent required to manage a panel or to call around the market order to gauge levels. The MOC was the first time that modern technology was used in the price–discovery process.

The MOC also emphasized the timing of price assessments for the first time. Previously there had been a relatively relaxed attitude to exactly when assessments were made. Under the MOC, with its emphasis on activity in the final few seconds of the window, all of Platts' petroleum assessments lined up perfectly to the second. This approach set Platts firmly at odds with proponents of all-day VWAs, such as Argus in the United States. "Platts believes that price is a function of time. An average is an artificial mathematical construction that does not reflect actual market activity", a Platts report remarked disdainfully in 2007.

PRA physical delivery

Commodity exchanges do not have a monopoly on physical delivery, at least not since the introduction by Platts of the concept of 'partials': the first time that participation in a PRA price–discovery process could lead directly to the sale or purchase of a physical commodity. Firms had previously traded cargoes of Brent or Dubai crude oil as part of the Platts' assessment process for each market, but the introduction of partials was the first time that Platts was itself responsible for matching physical bids and offers.

The partials mechanism seeks to overcome the difficulty of identifying prices in seaborne commodity markets that tend to generate infrequent but large transactions. These kind of markets had traditionally suited panel or survey methodologies and did not fit well with the new Platts MOC model, which required a greater flow of price information on a daily basis.

Platts' solution to this need for greater liquidity was to encourage the development of trade in smaller sub-divisions or 'partials' of large cargoes. These smaller deals could either be cash settled or if enough partials were transacted by the same buyer and seller, then the partials were totalled up and converted into an actual physical cargo. This cargo would then be physically delivered by the seller to the buyer.

The advantage of incorporating an element of physical delivery into a methodology is obvious. For commodity exchanges, physically settled derivatives are considered to be the absolute gold standard in terms of price discovery because the forward futures price converges directly into the spot physical market. In PRA terms, physical delivery means that there can no longer be a discrepancy between where the PRA assesses the market and where physical deals are taking place: with partials these are one and the same thing. The published price converges directly into the market price.

Critics of the Platts' partials process point to a couple of weaknesses in its design. Unlike a commodity exchange, Platts is not a regulated entity nor does it have investigative powers. This means that its ability to investigate and sanction non-performance during the delivery process is very limited. Platts' editorial management often has to adjudicate on whether material acquired through the partials mechanism was delivered within the correct timeframe and to the correct specification, which are questions of major financial significance to the two counterparties involved. The only real sanction that Platts can apply in the event that it finds against one of the parties is to suspend the firm or permanently ban it from participating in the MOC assessment process.

Second, the ability to financially settle a partials position that has not reached a full cargo size provides traders with significant optionality. In the case of traders that stop just short of a full cargo with a single counterparty, the Platts' mechanism allows them to have a major impact on pricing without actually having to take or make deliveries. In contrast, customers holding open positions to expiry in an exchange environment would have to make or take delivery, even of smaller sized parcels.

The most common criticism of the partials process is that the smaller volumes involved makes it easier and cheaper for a firm to have an outsize influence on the market. In some crude oil markets, particularly niche markets such as that for Indonesia's Minas crude oil, firms can set the Platts' price by buying or selling a 25,000 barrel partial, whereas before the introduction of the partials methodology they might have had to trade a full cargo.

Derivative based

At the other end of the spectrum from methodologies that employ physical delivery, there are also some PRA methodologies that make use of activity in the derivative markets in order to help them arrive at their assessment of the underlying physical market.

Most PRA assessments are of prices in physical commodities but PRAs will also provide assessments of where related derivative markets are trading in order to give indications of the shape of the forward curve. These assessments can also be used for mark-to-market purposes by traders. In some markets, there is a feedback loop between the underlying physical product and its related commodity in which prices in each market affect the other.

This interaction between physical prices and the derivatives market is particularly common in the refined product markets and PRAs have adapted their method-ologies accordingly. Derivative contracts will ultimately settle against the physical price as assessed by the PRA, but the PRA in many cases will make use of the nearby derivative markets in order to adjust physical prices to take into account the shape of the nearby curve. This is the case in Platts' Singapore refined products assessments as well as in Platts' major Dated Brent benchmark, in which physical trading activity is adjusted to take account of trading activity in the weekly contract for difference (CFD) market.

PRA assessments of some refined products are also produced as a differential to a regulated futures benchmark. This is the case in European gasoil, which is assessed as a discount or premium to ICE gasoil futures.

The reasons for adopting a methodology based on derivative assessments are, first, that this is the way that the underlying market itself operates and the PRA is simply adopting the convention. Second, the nearby derivative market can be a very useful source of price signals when there is little liquidity in the underlying physical market. There is also an argument that making use of derivatives, which typically would be traded or cleared in a regulated environment also could add some credibility to an assessment, although this is likely an unintended consequence rather than a reason to select this form of methodology.

The main criticism of the use of derivatives in establishing a physical benchmark is that there is a potential for "circularity" to develop. Circularity is a phenomenon in which there is a constant feedback loop from derivatives to physical prices and back again. This could lead to a situation where the derivatives trade downwards in expectation of a lower physical settlement price but therefore actually cause the physical price to fall. Essentially, this would create a self-fulfilling prophecy.

Relative value methodology

The largest PRAs publish tens of thousands of market prices every day. Obviously, not all of these prices can be the result of a specific assessment process by a price reporter, otherwise the PRAs would require much larger staffs. Some of the market assessments that the PRAs make are based instead on automated assessments of 'relative value'.

A 'relative value' methodology enables PRAs to leverage on assessments of a liquid benchmark in order to provide price indications for a less liquid market. For example, if there is a liquid bunker fuel market in Singapore but not in Malaysia, a PRA might choose to provide a price indication for Malaysia on the basis that its assessment will always be Singapore minus $1 or similar. This methodology allows PRAs to provide price indications for a much wider range of markets than they could otherwise cover, either on staffing grounds or because there is not sufficient trading activity in these markets to support a standalone assessment.

The majority of relative value assessments take a liquid market in one geographical location and then add or subtract the cost of transportation, often sea freight, to generate an assessment in another location. For example, refined products in the Middle East have traditionally been assessed on the basis of Singapore assessments minus the shipping freight between Singapore and the Middle East.

The weakness of the relative value methodology is that it provides indications of price levels rather than an actual assessment of where the market in the secondary location is really trading. When these assessments are automated, it is possible for them to diverge severely from actual levels over time. As the Middle East becomes more of a trading hub for refined products, it is notable that both Platts and Argus are considering moving away from a relative value methodology in favour of directly assessing the markets.

The relative value methodology then is a useful intermediate stage in the development of markets. It allows PRAs to expand their range more than would otherwise be possible in order to provide useful price indications for secondary locations. But the methodology cannot generate a price that is anything more than a rough indicator. As markets develop and become more liquid, PRAs will tend to turn to other methodologies to underpin their assessments.

Best offer methodology

The PRA methodologies described above comprise the overwhelming majority of independent assessments of physical prices in the commodity markets. There are some other variants that can be seen but these tend to be fairly rare. One of the more niche methodologies employed is the 'best offer' methodology in which the price assessment is based on the most competitive offers of the commodity in question.

In the uranium markets, UX Consulting (UxC) bases its important UX U3O8 Price Indicator on the most competitive offer of which UxC is aware, subject to specified form, quantity and delivery timeframe considerations. The key international cotton benchmark – the Cotlook A index – is also based on a lowest offer methodology. Cotlook's assessment is an average of the cheapest five offers of cotton from a selection of 18 quotations. Cotlook explains that its methodology identifies "those growths which are the most competitive, and which therefore are likely to be traded in most volume".

The strength of the best offer methodology is that it provides a very clear view of exactly where the most competitive sellers are offering their product. An assessment based on best offers enables other sellers to see where the competition is offering, and buyers to identify a base level around which a deal might be done. The weakness of the best offer methodology is that it does not provide much information about buying interest. In a typical market, this should not matter too much as the best offer should not be too far away from the best bid. But in a thinly traded market on the verge of a major price move, there could be substantial distance between the best bids and offers, which would not be captured under a best offer methodology.

Combining methodologies

Many PRA methodologies for individual markets do not fit neatly into the families identified above. This is generally because they combine elements of two or even three types of methodology in order to reach an approach that works well for the particular market in question. Combining methodologies generally stems from a desire to ensure special robustness in an assessment.

Methodologies are sometimes combined in order to strengthen the assessment by building in a number of checks and balances. Multiple indicators and approaches should in theory ensure that no individual price signal can get out of line or be overly influenced by individual participants. This is the theory underpinning the most important of the PRA benchmarks, Platts' Dated Brent assessment of light sweet North Sea crude oil. Dated Brent has probably the most complex methodology of any assessment: it combines physical settlement (partials) in a market-on-close environment with bids and offers for full cargoes of multiple crude oil grades, while price indicators are also adjusted by reference to derivatives (weekly contracts-for-difference or CFDs).

The combination of methodologies may also result from the desire to have a fall-back methodology in place in case of low liquidity or a significant market event. It is not uncommon to see this with VWA methodologies, where in the absence of a certain number of deals or participants, the assessment will instead default to a survey methodology.

Conclusion

Methodologies matter a great deal to PRAs, to their customers and to regulators. The methodology that a PRA adopts is a reflection of trading practices in a particular underlying commodity market, but over time the choice of methodology will itself come to affect the way that the market operates. Traders will generally want their activity to be incorporated in an assessment that they use and so they will structure their trading in order to ensure that it is reflected by the incumbent PRA. Nobody ever traded a partial before Platts introduced the concept in some of their method-ologies, for example, and no one would likely trade one again were Platts to abandon the system. Meanwhile, the adoption of market-on-close with its focus on activity at the end of the day affected the way traders managed their time and their working hours.

As we have seen, there are a large range of methodologies employed by PRAs and none of them is perfect. Any individual methodology can be critiqued, and most of them are regularly the subject of either comment or complaint by their users. The methodology that a PRA selects therefore affects its chances of becoming a benchmark and of retaining that status. As noted earlier, virtually every time an incumbent PRA has lost the benchmark to a rival, their methodology has been the cause.

Most PRAs make use of a variety of approaches across different commodity markets, although Platts is moving ever closer to greater standardization of its approach. Different methodological approaches are also combined. Some assessments can combine a survey methodology with a derivatives-related element, or adopt physical delivery that defaults to a panel or a survey in the absence of any activity.

There are no right or wrong methodologies. There are only methodologies that work or don't work, or which are accepted or not by the market and the regulators. It is nonetheless possible to identify two general developments in methodological development: first, the trend towards greater precision; second, the trend towards automation. Many modern methodologies are increasingly prescriptive and detailed compared with previous approaches that tended to be relatively vague or even consciously ambiguous in order to give individual price reporters some latitude. In general, there is a reduced dependence on editorial judgment than was the case earlier in the development of the PRA industry when the judgment of experts was more easily accepted.

The current environment with its greater emphasis on regulation and the – consequent reluctance by many counterparties to engage with PRAs has created a boom in deal-based methodologies, which are perceived to be the most easily defensible form of price assessment. But the risk for PRAs is that one of their most important characteristics is their deep understanding of the commodity markets they assess, which they demonstrate in the way that their teams engage with traders and establish assessments. Automated systems that create price assessments by simply averaging out files full of deals could be replicated relatively easily by exchanges, brokers or other platforms. If everyone sees the same data and can reach the same assessment, then it will be tough for the PRAs to differentiate themselves and hard to justify premium pricing in their subscriptions. As such, human judgment is likely to remain part of the PRA's armoury of methodologies for some time to come.

12 The market-on-close

Introduction

Perhaps the most important innovation in price reporting agency (PRA) method-ologies of recent decades was Platts' decision to move away from traditional survey methodologies in many of its key petroleum markets in favour of a new system, known as market-on-close (MOC). It is no exaggeration to say that MOC represented a revolutionary approach to pricing and its introduction made the reputation of its creator Jorge Montepeque. Yet MOC was hugely controversial: its introduction created uproar in the oil markets at the time and continues to divide opinion to this day.

MOC standardized all of Platts' petroleum methodologies around a single 30-minute period ('the window') during which traders would show bids and offers and transact deals in public. The final trade price seen in the window or the final standing bid or offer then typically set that day's assessment. MOC was eventually transitioned onto an online platform provided by the InterContinental Exchange (ICE), which became known as the eWindow.

The introduction of MOC created something of a boom for the PRA industry that is still filtering through in the recent corporate activity in the sector. Platts found that it could charge considerably more for access to screens, which made it vastly more profitable overnight. Traders that had previously rejected Platts' premium real-time offering Platts Global Alert (PGA) now found that they could not manage without it.

Platts' competitors also raised their subscription rates in response to the significantly higher fees that Platts was charging. At the same time, the rejection of MOC by the European gasoline market and later by parts of the US crude and products markets opened the door to Platts' main rival Argus, which dramatically increased its value as a result.

Summarizing MOC

Montepeque's overall concept was based on the theory of convergence. The price published by a PRA should converge with the market price, which was underpinned by the introduction of a physical partials mechanism (see the previous chapter on PRA methodologies for further details). Price assessments in every related commodity market should also be aligned and therefore their various price discovery processes should converge in terms of methodology and timing in order to enable easy comparison.

In the words of Platts,

> the MOC approach to methodology operates on the principle that price is a function of time. The MOC is a structured, highly transparent process in which bids, offers and transactions are submitted by participants to Platts' editors and published in real-time throughout the day until the market close.

This summary covers MOC nicely, although, in reality, market participants do not tend to submit any information at all to Platts' editors until the start of the 30-minute assessment window and, in fact, there is very little price discovery in most markets until the final few minutes of the window or even the final minute.

Once MOC had been brought in, prices were no longer gathered by reporters over the phone or electronically but were shown by market participants themselves to the world, or at least to Platts' subscribers. Any company showing a bid or offer had to be prepared to transact at the levels they were indicating. At a stroke this removed a lot of the bluffing from the market that had caused so many headaches to price reporters over the years.

MOC also shifted responsibility for the final assessment away from the individual price reporter. No longer could an angry trader call up and say the market was assessed way too high because a price reporter had believed something that their rival had said on the phone. Once MOC was in place a trader who saw a rival posting increasingly high bids had two choices: either sell into the bid or accept that Platts was likely to assess the market much higher. Either way, there was no reason for a trader to complain to Platts – the decision about where the market would be assessed was firmly in his or her hands.

Two key elements in the MOC methodology represented a real departure for the PRA industry: the time aspect of pricing and the use of a screen for price discovery. We will look at the impact of both below.

Time aspect of pricing

Until MOC, PRAs had not paid much attention to the precise timing of their assessments. It was not unusual for the same PRA to assess naphtha by 5pm Singapore but LPG by 5.30pm Singapore, making direct price comparisons across related markets difficult. Most PRAs did not think very precisely about time and the nature of their methodologies did not encourage it. Panel and survey methodologies are not designed to produce 'live prices' that relate to very specific timestamps. It is simply not possible for an individual price reporter to survey all of the market simultaneously so assessments tend to be more the result of information received over a longer period such as during the afternoon.

In contrast, Montepeque persuaded Platts that they should care very deeply about the timing of their assessments. This reached the point where Platts' official line became that "price is a function of time". Assessments in each of the three key trading regions – Asia, Europe and the United States – were all synchronized at the end of the trading day.

The new methodology stated that the last activity – bid, offer or deal – within the 30-minute assessment window would be the primary underpinning for the assessment, hence the name 'market-on-close'. The idea that assessments in different energy markets could be lined up to the exact few seconds represented a major conceptual shift for the industry. One of the primary virtues of MOC is precisely this clarity. There was a sense of precision about MOC that was refreshing to many, even if this precision turned out to sometimes be illusory.

Critics, and there were many, of MOC argued strongly against the window approach. Given that few commodity markets are blessed with a superabundance of spot trading activity, it might seem perverse to constrain liquidity further by artificially constructing a window outside which all price indicators are essentially ignored. This was a particular complaint of European airlines, which had previously had a strong voice in Platts' assessments of the Rotterdam barge markets but which found themselves bit-part players in the window after the introduction of MOC.

Argus' adoption of all-day volume weighted averages (VWAs) in many of the US petroleum markets was a direct riposte to Platts' decision to narrow the trading range.

Use of the screen

The other groundbreaking aspect of MOC was its structure and transparency. MOC brought the price discovery process out of the PRAs' offices and onto the screen. Suddenly the industry could see the assessments being established in front of their eyes and they could participate in the process or not as they chose. With all of the action taking place on screen, there was no more need to lobby individual price reporters or even to speak to them at all, and there would be no more surprises – the most likely final Platts' assessment was obvious to everyone watching the screen. This was the pricing equivalent of a restaurant that decides to take its cooks out of the back kitchen and set them to work behind glass walls in the dining room itself. The transparency of the process becomes a key element in the marketing of the final product.

Without technology, MOC would not have been possible. Individual price reporters could never have made enough simultaneous phone calls to get information aligned to the final few moments of a trading window. It took the introduction of a screen to deliver the level of alignment to a precise time that Montepeque was seeking. It also required significant investment from ICE in technology as the exchange had to configure its trading system in line with the requirements of Platts' editors who all wanted slightly different rules governing bids and offers in each market (see Chapter 13).

The screen also brought about a new level of transparency because for the first time company names were out in the open. Price reporters had generally spoken to their contacts on an anonymous basis and their reports were typically very light on actual company names, which were blurred into descriptions like "a Swiss-based trading house" or a "large South American oil producer". All of this went out of the window – no pun intended – when traders had to show their company names next to their bids, offers and deals on the Platts' system. Suddenly, the whole market could see who was buying and who was selling.

The initial response to the public nature of the window varied wildly. Some participants genuinely love the transparency. "Finally we can see which of our customers is trying to screw us," as one senior executive at a Middle East oil producer commented. There was certainly little regret for the previous system in which traders who might have an aggressive agenda could try to influence reporters over the phone knowing that their comments would not be directly attributed.

In contrast, others felt that the lack of anonymous trade was artificially constraining participation in the window. Many key market participants that are culturally conservative are missing from the MOC because they do not want their name to appear in public. The world's largest energy company ExxonMobil does not appear in MOC and neither do Japanese refiners or many national oil companies from the Middle East and elsewhere. In contrast, many of the firms that are not comfortable with the MOC still contribute to price discovery in other markets via survey, panel or VWA methodologies because these processes are anonymous.

The use of a trading screen, currently provided by ICE, also led to accusations that Platts is in effect running an unlicensed exchange. The Platts-ICE eWindow allows transactions initiated on the Platts' system to be automatically cleared with ICE's clearing house, which has caused some over-the-counter brokers to complain that Platts is operating a swaps execution facility (SEF) without assuming any of the administrative and regulatory burden that a broker-operated SEF would face. To date, though, there has been little appetite from any regulator to look into the exact nature of the eWindow.

Incrementability

Among its many consequences, intended and unintended, the introduction of MOC also introduced a new word into the English language: incrementability. This somewhat unwieldy coinage refers to another new concept introduced by MOC: that traders should not be able to move their bids or offers dramatically during the window, but instead should raise or lower their prices in small steps or incrementally.

Platts' focus on the last few seconds of the assessment window introduced the risk that traders could lurk in the background for 29 and a half minutes, only to jump in with an aggressive bid or offer a few seconds before the close. The solution to this risk was for Platts to introduce formal rules on how early within the window traders had to start bidding and offering and by how much and how quickly they could adjust their bids and offers during the 30 minutes. Or in Platts' own (horribly expressed) words "the purpose of time cut-offs is primarily to ensure logistical executability and standards of incrementability and repeatability in order to ensure orderly price discovery".

The guidelines on incrementability are a fixed feature of MOC, although they vary between each different market that Platts assesses. Their obvious benefit is to make market activity during the window more predictable, what Platts terms "orderly price discovery". The weakness of the concept is that it represents yet another constraint on traders' behaviour. For a firm that has benefited so greatly from free markets, there is not a lot of freedom about the MOC: the timing is restricted and even the ability to freely bid or offer is restricted.

Launch of MOC

MOC was first rolled out in Asia in the 1990s while Jorge Montepeque was running Platts' bureau in Singapore. The timing and the location of the launch was fortuitous. This was the time of the dot-com boom and Platts' parent McGraw-Hill was worried that it was being left behind in terms of technology. Senior executives were therefore supportive of Montepeque's attempts to make an innovative use of technology in the price discovery process, although some were initially concerned that Platts would fall under exchange regulations. Asia was also a good place to start a revolution. At the time, Asia was still relatively a lower priority for McGraw-Hill and for oil executives alike and so the initial introduction of MOC did not receive anything like the same scrutiny that it would later attract in Europe and the United States.

It quickly became clear that MOC was a commercial success. The use of a screen generated new subscription revenue and enabled the cross-selling of live news and market updates. There was some push back from customers in Asia who did not immediately take to MOC but the market response was relatively muted as Asian customers traditionally tended to be relatively passive in their response to methodology changes.

When Montepeque moved to London in January 2002 and looked to roll out MOC to the European petroleum markets it was a different story. One senior oil executive allegedly greeted him with "Jorge, who do you think we are? We are Europeans, not Asians, and we are not going to let you do what you want". MOC attracted intense opposition. Montepeque's reluctance to back down on the terms of the introduction set up clashes with some colleagues at Platts as well as with parts of the industry.

Montepeque's campaign benefited from the fall out of the December 2001 collapse of Enron, which shocked the global energy markets, and made his drive for greater transparency and robustness in price discovery look very prescient. The first market Platts selected for the transition to MOC was the Dated Brent market, which had experienced a number of squeezes and attempted squeezes in the early 2000s. The poor reputation of the market enabled Platts to overcome any opposition to the introduction of MOC on the grounds that Dated Brent needed radical surgery if it was to survive as a major global benchmark.

Montepeque also benefited from growing awareness at McGraw-Hill of the revenue growth that MOC had brought to Platts in Asia. This led to his position being strengthened in a quite unusual way: the McGraw-Hill Annual Report of 2002 honoured Montepeque as one of six employees across the group that had demonstrated exceptional creativity.

This award effectively insulated Montepeque from the majority of internal criticism and enabled him to push ahead with the European roll out. The results in Europe were on the whole a success for Platts, which successfully transitioned all but one of the European petroleum markets to MOC and saw huge growth in revenue as a result.

European gasoline was the one that got away from Platts. Platts' European gasoline editor Chris Judge had recently moved to Argus and was able to take advantage of industry opposition to MOC to switch the northwest European gasoline market away from Platts onto an Argus assessment based on a traditional survey methodology.

The importance of the European gasoline switch to Argus cannot be overstated. The increased revenues from being the benchmark funded much of Argus's later expansion. More significantly, though, it showed that Platts was not invulnerable and that switching benchmark was possible. It had been many years since the last energy market switch – from Platts to Argus on European and Asian LPG – and so this was an important lesson for the industry.

That lesson was learned and applied by traders in the United States, where the introduction of MOC was in places rejected. A number of key markets, including Gulf Coast sour crude oil from 2009 and some of the light refined products, decided to turn away from Platts in favour of Argus, which was offering an alternative VWA methodology. Europe's adverse reaction to MOC had more been the result of the energy industry's innate conservatism allied with a dislike for the relatively heavy-handed way that Platts had introduced the changes. In contrast, US concerns about MOC stemmed more from perceptions that it would increase their risk of government investigation and litigation.

There was a strong precedent for the industry's caution. The US Commodity Futures Trading Commission (CFTC) imposed a fine on US refiner Marathon Petroleum of $1 million in 2007 after finding Marathon guilty of pushing down the price of spot cash WTI during the Platts MOC window on 26 November 2003. The CFTC proved that Marathon had exerted downwards pressure on the Platts' assessment in order to drive down its overall cost of crude oil purchases. Aggressive behaviour by traders in the MOC window might not have raised eyebrows in other jurisdictions, but the Marathon case sent a clear message to the US energy industry that such activity would not be tolerated by the US authorities.

Under the MOC methodology, the last activity sets the day's price. This means that a single transaction between two firms will set the Platts' benchmark for, say, US gasoline, irrespective of how many other transactions between different counter-parties had taken place that day. Very few US firms were prepared to be one of just two parties responsible for setting the overall benchmark as they feared getting drawn into government investigations into energy prices or litigation from consumer groups. In contrast, Argus offered a VWA methodology that meant that in effect the entire market shared responsibility for the final assessment.

Jorge Montepeque

The most notable figure that the PRA sector has produced since Warren Platt, Jorge Montepeque created the MOC methodology while working for Platts in Singapore. He was later appointed Platts' global head of price reporting and became one of the best-known, well-respected and contro-versial figures in the global energy markets. The demands of his role overseeing Platts' pricing combined with his boundless energy and intense travel schedule ensured that he became familiar with probably more commodity markets and with more traders than anyone previously in history.

Born in Guatemala, Montepeque moved to the United States in 1976 to study economics at Hunter College, paying for his tuition with a job in a Japanese restaurant and by working at consultants PIRA Energy Group. He joined Platts in 1988 and moved with the firm to Singapore in 1991 before transitioning to London in 2002 as global head of market reporting.

During his 27-year tenure at Platts, Montepeque ushered in a revolution in energy pricing. His desire to maintain Platts' independence from the energy industry and to display leadership when the industry could not agree on a course of action sometimes led to accusations of arrogance. "Jorge's ears are painted on", one senior executive used to grumble. But even his severest critics, usually those that had their reasons for disliking MOC, acknowledged that Montepeque had an unrivalled grasp of commodity pricing issues. There were also never any accusations of favouritism or suggestions that Montepeque was motivated by anything other than a desire to improve market efficiency.

It was a tremendous shock to the industry when Montepeque finally left Platts in late 2015. Many believe that the seeds of his departure were sown as far back as June 2013 when he publicly criticized the European Commission's handling of an investigation into Platts and a number of oil companies at a major industry event in Kuala Lumpur, Malaysia (see the chapters on PRAs and regulation for further details of the investigation). Platts' owner, McGraw-Hill, still under pressure over the role Platts' sister company S&P had played in the global financial crisis, was in no mood to pick a battle with European regulators and swiftly put out a note promising full cooperation with the Commission.

Montepeque's willingness to say the unsayable, combined with a feature in the UK's *Financial Times*, describing him as "holding court" at an OPEC meeting in Vienna and wielding "great power", generated concerns within McGraw-Hill that Platts' corporate identity had become too associated with an individual employee.[1] A Bloomberg feature on Montepeque in 2013 described him as "a lightning rod for industry complaints" about Platts' dominance.[2]

At the same time Montepeque was becoming disillusioned with the direction of Platts. He was concerned about what he perceived to be commercial encroachment on editorial independence and he also came to believe that there was an increased reluctance at senior levels of McGraw-Hill to take bold decisions and to provide leadership for the commodity markets. This combination of factors finally led to his departure from Platts in late 2015.

After a brief period as a consultant, Montepeque was appointed senior vice president for origination at Italian oil giant ENI's Shipping and Trading Division in London in May 2016. He remains in high demand as an entertaining speaker at conferences and is a regular contributor to debates around energy markets and pricing.

Conclusion

The global roll out of MOC generated the greatest upheaval in the energy pricing world since the liberalization of US and European power and generation fuels markets. MOC had a profound influence on concepts of price reporting even at PRAs that did not adopt it. Lining up assessments to match specific timestamps is now standard practice, for example. MOC was also the first time that price discovery had taken place in the open outside of the commodity exchanges, but screen-based pricing is slowly taking off at other PRAs as well. Argus rolled out a screen offering in 2016.

Before MOC, Platts was used as the benchmark in virtually every petroleum market globally, with Argus, OPIS and RIM Intelligence holding smaller market shares. The rejection of MOC by the European gasoline market and by several US petroleum markets strengthened Argus immeasurably, creating a genuine, albeit much smaller, rival to Platts. But, although Platts lost control of some key markets, MOC also bolstered Platts' position as well as its revenues. In most petroleum markets outside of the United States, Platts' rivals are reduced to reporting on activity in the Platts' window, meaning that in those areas there is no real rival to Platts as a benchmark. The eWindow partnership with ICE has also proved to be extremely lucrative for Platts, which can charge significant extra fees for direct access to the platform.

There is not likely to be another methodological change comparable to the introduction of MOC any time soon. MOC was a one-off event and very much the product of its inventor. In at least the medium term, any changes to MOC are likely to be minor, such as changes to incrementability rules or changes to the timestamp. MOC can be considered a success for Platts but it was also a success for Argus as well and so as a result there is little appetite for radical methodological change at any of the incumbent PRAs. A PRA is never as vulnerable as when it is changing methodology.

Notes

1   Ajay Makan, Oil Markets: The Danger of Distortion, Financial Times, 5 August 2013.
2   Asjylyn Loder, and Lananh Nguyen, Montepeque of Platts Caught in Battle Over Oil Assessments, Bloomberg, 16 September 2013.

13 The PRAs and the exchanges

Introduction

The overwhelming majority of commodity benchmarks are either based on assessments by price reporting agencies (PRAs) or on the settlement prices of futures contracts listed on exchanges. The relationship between the two sides, PRAs and exchanges, can be very complex. PRAs and exchanges can be at the same time partners, rivals and mutual customers. The mix between these different aspects is constantly evolving as new business opportunities emerge.

Several exchanges around the world work closely with the PRAs. The largest by far are the two US-headquartered giants: CME Group, which owns the NYMEX energy platform, and the InterContinental Exchange (ICE), which acquired the International Petroleum Exchange (IPE) in London.

Other exchanges based in major commodity trading locations also have relationships in place with PRAs. These include the Dubai Mercantile Exchange (DME), Singapore Exchange (SGX), EUREX, Tokyo Commodities Exchange (TOCOM), the NASDAQ group of exchanges, the London Metals Exchange (LME) and Moscow's St Petersburg Mercantile Exchange (SPIMEX).

The traditional model of PRA-exchange relationships is that an exchange would license PRA assessments in order to use them as the settlement price for cash-settled derivatives. In new markets, the exchange would need to decide whether it wanted to attempt to develop its own physically delivered product or whether it preferred to license a price from a PRA for a cash-settled contract. A PRA might also approach an exchange to suggest a potential new product based on feedback from customers who wished to manage their physical commodity risk through derivatives. After agreeing on the business opportunity, the two sides would agree terms and conditions for a licence, and then following a product launch the PRA and exchange might cooperate on marketing the new risk management tool.

This relatively straightforward relationship is still the model for the majority of PRAs and exchanges. In some cases, though, the relationship has evolved into something more complex, where the two sides cooperate on technology or undertake specific product development projects together. One of the most widely discussed topics in exchange-PRA relationships is to what extent PRAs should be open to working with multiple exchanges or whether it makes better business sense to enter a more exclusive partnership with a specific exchange.

Exchange vs PRA benchmarks

The world's largest and most famous commodity benchmarks are all listed on exchanges. In the energy space, CME hosts WTI crude oil, Henry Hub natural gas, ULSD and RBOB gasoline, while ICE hosts Brent crude oil, European gasoil and UK natural gas. Similarly, the major benchmarks in the agriculture and metals markets are exchange listed, either again by CME and ICE or by regional exchanges or specialist exchanges such as the London Metals Exchange (LME).

These are the commodity prices that are quoted in newspapers or which tick along the bottom of business TV broadcasts. When economic commentators or academics are discussing commodity prices, they will almost certainly be discussing the two or three dozen major exchange-listed futures prices rather than the tens of thousands of commodity prices produced by PRAs every day.

The main reason why exchange prices are so widely discussed while very few non-specialists could even name a PRA lies in the differing nature of their two business models.

Exchanges want their contracts to be as accessible as possible in order to attract more hedgers and speculators to trade their products. They therefore allow their delayed data to be widely distributed for very low fees, although costs are significantly higher for up-to-the microsecond live data. In contrast, the whole business model of PRAs relies on controlling the usage of their proprietary data and ensuring that only paying customers can access it.

An exchange-listed commodity derivatives contract that only attracts ten customers will soon fail and be delisted because exchanges need high volume to compensate for the relatively low trading and data fees that they receive. In contrast, niche markets can be profitable to PRAs. Ten subscribers to a report on a specialist commodity might be very profitable if each subscriber is prepared to pay an annual subscription fee of $25,000 and the report can be prepared by a single analyst.

One other key difference between the commodity benchmarks produced by exchanges and by PRAs is that, with the notable exception of ICE's Brent crude oil contract, all of the major global commodity benchmarks listed on exchanges and cited above are physically settled.

Physical settlement means that at the end of the first-listed trading period – when the contract can no longer be traded – those customers holding long positions (buyers) receive a delivery of the actual commodity – whether it is crude oil or soybeans or copper – from those customers that are still holding a short position (sellers).

Physically settled commodity futures are considered to be the gold standard in terms of price discovery – they are regulated, openly accessible and there can be no discrepancy between the value of the financial instrument and of the underlying commodity since at expiry the futures position becomes an actual commodity when the holders of the financial instrument make or take delivery of the underlying commodity.

It is also very difficult for one exchange to 'steal' a successful physical futures contract from another exchange because the original venue is likely to have privileged access to the underlying delivery infrastructure. There are plenty of examples of exchanges losing their key contracts to a rival but it is extremely rare for these to be physical contracts. Physically delivered contracts are therefore a 'moonshot' for exchanges: difficult, costly but of huge and long-lasting value if successful. (CME Group is still profiting from the grains contract launched on one of its predecessors, the Chicago Board of Trade, way back in 1851.)

There are many advantages of physically settled commodity benchmarks but there are also drawbacks. Physical settlement is not suitable for every commodity. For example, no exchange has ever successfully listed a physically settled fuel oil contract, despite multiple attempts, largely because it would be so difficult to ensure that fuel oil deliveries meet exact specifications.

Physical delivery may also not work in locations where delivery points are restricted. Restrictions can take several forms: there could be infrastructure bottlenecks; or cases where one or two market participants dominate loading infrastructure such as grain elevators, metals warehouses or loading ports; or delivery sites could be subject to weather vagaries that make them unsuitable for all-year round deliveries, such as Russian ports that are iced in or Indian ports that are affected by the monsoon. There could also be issues with the jurisdiction itself. Exchanges will be reluctant to site a location for physical delivery in a jurisdiction where standard terms around performance and potential bankruptcies are not easily enforceable.

From an exchange perspective, it is very costly to launch a physically delivered commodities contract and the chances of success are low – industry wisdom suggests that less than one in nine futures contracts will still attract trade more than a few months after launch. Physical delivery requires exchange officials to reach agreement with market participants and infrastructure providers, most of whom will typically be extremely unwilling to change their existing business practices. Physical delivery also entails permanent and costly oversight to prevent issues developing such as non-performance on a delivery, delivery of non-standard ("off-spec") material or management of the queues at delivery facilities.

Faced with the costs of establishing physical delivery contracts as compared with the relatively low chances of success, it is little surprise that many exchanges have in recent years preferred to launch cash-settled contracts.

At the end of the prompt trading period in a cash-settled contract, participants do not hand over physical commodities but instead they hand over money depending on how their position has performed relative to an index.

Cash settlement contracts do not require any costly investment in facilities supervision. From an operational, legal and regulatory perspective, it is significantly simpler and more cost effective to launch and to maintain cash-settled contracts, even though they can also be more easily replicated by rival exchanges. But in order to launch cash-settled contracts, exchanges need to obtain a final settlement price that all of their traders will accept as the final measurement of how their positions have performed and who owes what to whom. This is where PRAs enter the picture.

Licensing PRA data

Some exchanges have created their own commodity indexes in order to settle their financially settled contracts, but the majority rely on PRA assessments. PRAs are the obvious choice to provide assessments to an exchange: assessing prices is their core job and their assessments underpin the physical trade in many commodities. By using PRA data, the exchange outsources any issues around the nature of its settlement price – the assessment methodology, etc. – to the PRA and also benefits from the positive reputation that the PRA hopefully enjoys in the specific market.

If an exchange wants its customers to use a derivative to manage the risk of their physical position, it makes sense for the exchange to select the PRA that supplies the relevant physical price assessment. This is why exchanges are always trying to pick the winners among the PRAs: there is usually no point in an exchange listing a PRA-based derivative contract unless that PRA is the benchmark for the physical market. Exchanges therefore need a relationship with multiple PRAs because no single PRA owns all the benchmarks in any commodity sector.

Assuming that the exchange has identified an opportunity for a risk management product and has correctly recognized the dominant PRA in that commodity, the next step is for the two sides to agree a licensing arrangement. This will differ from the usual subscription licence that a PRA customer would have because it will contain specific clauses allowing the exchange to use the data as the basis for a derivatives contract.

The PRA will contract with an exchange over a fixed-term period to supply it with settlement data. The duration of an exchange contract will also tend to be longer than the annual subscriptions that PRAs sell to their normal customers. A year is a relatively short period for an exchange to launch a contract and to build liquidity and so exchanges tend to license PRA data for multiple years.

PRAs provide their settlement data either in exchange for a fixed fee, for a share of the exchange's revenue, or some combination of the two. This can be a lucrative business for PRAs. A successful derivatives contract will trade a multiple of many times the underlying physical commodity. Liquid derivatives contracts also attract speculators and other purely financial players that would not otherwise have ever come into contact with a commodity PRA. By taking a cut of their exchange trading fees, PRAs indirectly gain revenue from customers who would never have become subscribers to their reports.

Licensing its physical benchmark to an exchange also strengthens a PRA's position in the underlying physical market. First, the exchange is publicly endorsing the PRA's assessments as sufficiently robust and reliable to serve as the basis for a regulated derivative contract. Second, it is a major advantage for a PRA to say that there are risk management products available based on its physical assessments, especially if its rivals cannot say the same. Third, the use of a specific PRA as a derivatives price makes its physical benchmark much more 'sticky'. A company that has hedged its price exposure to a specific PRA's assessments for the next two years will be extremely reluctant to switch from its current benchmark provider to another PRA due to the complexity of transferring its risk management position.

Licensing exchange data

Apart from the standard PRA-to-exchange licensing agreement, the reverse arrangement is also common in which PRAs license data from exchanges. PRAs can license exchange data in order to redistribute it to their subscribers through data feeds or through their published reports, although these transactions are relatively lower value than a PRA-to-exchange licence due to the more accessible nature of exchange data.

PRAs may also make use of exchange settlement prices to create their own assessments. In such cases, a physical cargo price may be derived, for example, from a front month exchange futures price plus or minus an appropriate premium or discount. This link to the exchange's settlement price may or may not be explicitly referenced by the PRA in its methodology document. Different exchanges and PRAs will also have different policies on whether an assessment derived from an exchange price requires the PRA in question to hold a special data licence from the exchange.

Beyond licensing

Most exchange and PRA relationships begin and end with these simple licensing arrangements.

Exchanges and PRAs may also cooperate on marketing efforts. Exchanges may sponsor PRA-organized conferences or the two parties may hold joint information seminars together.

Beyond licensing and marketing, the growth area for cooperation between exchanges and PRAs is in technology. Exchanges typically have substantially better technology offerings than PRAs because of the nature of the exchange business, which requires a trading screen and matching engine capable of processing trans-actions in microseconds. PRAs that are looking to add some form of price discovery screen to their offering have naturally therefore turned to exchanges as potential partners, particularly as the two sides will usually share the same customer base.

The most successful relationship in technology is ICE's provision of the software that underpins Platts' eWindow assessment process around the world. First intro-duced in 2007, Platts' analysts monitor bids, offers and trading activity in the eWindow in order to establish their assessments. Available via the WebICE trading screen, the eWindow provides a clear view of all bids, offers and transaction data communicated to Platts' editors during the Market on Close (MOC) assessment. Users can submit and confirm deal information directly to Platts and the marketplace simultaneously and can execute trades on WebICE without leaving the Platts' eWindow. The chapter on MOC provides further details of the eWindow assessment process.

The level of cooperation and technical integration required by the move to the eWindow helped to develop very strong relationships between ICE and Platts at a senior level as well as at an operational level. The two companies' operations in the energy markets, although not to date in other markets, are now so closely entwined that they would be extremely difficult to separate.

This positive relationship benefited both sides. Platts benefited from ICE's superior technology and its technical support team, while ICE was guaranteed that every energy trader would need access to its software for at least 30 minutes a day. This drove the take up of ICE's WebICE screen trading software, which then became the means by which traders also transacted much of their non-brokered derivative business.

Exchange exclusivity

One peculiarity of the commodity world relative to that of financial derivatives is that it has traditionally been very unusual for PRAs or exchanges to enter into exclusive licensing arrangements. In equity index futures, exclusivity is much more common.

The first real move towards exchange exclusivity came in the US natural gas markets. ICE entered into a purchase and leaseback agreement with Intelligence Press, Inc. (IPI) in 2007, under the terms of which the exchange acquired the natural gas indexes published by IPI in its Natural Gas Intelligence (NGI) newsletters. IPI continued to collect and aggregate prices in the wholesale natural gas market and publish its indexes, and ICE acquired the exclusive right to license the indexes for exchange settlement and clearing.

The exclusivity arrangement between ICE and IPI ensured that ICE became the dominant exchange in the US gas hubs in which NGI provided the benchmark price. ICE's competitive position in US natural gas strengthened further with the announcement in late 2016 that ICE would exclusively license several US benchmarks assessed by Platts.[1] The ICE–Platts agreement established that data from ICE's physical gas trading platform business would be incorporated into Platts' assessments of various US natural gas hubs in exchange for ICE taking exclusive rights to list derivatives based on these assessments.

This deal also included an arrangement whereby companies can report deals to Platts via ICE's eConfirm trade reporting platform. In a February 2017 subscriber note Platts suggested that "the use of eConfirm represents a more timely and efficient means of reporting trade data".[2] This was a very significant move. On the one hand, it flies in the face of the traditional desire by PRAs to control the data that underpin their benchmarks. It is also a sign of the deep trust between Platts and ICE that Platts was prepared to allow a third party to control access to data that would potentially allow ICE to recreate the benchmarks themselves, displacing Platts. And yet, this innovative move also makes it much less likely that firms will report information to Platts' competitors, solidifying Platts' pre-eminent position. If market participants are already reporting electronically via ICE, then some will likely find it more trouble than it is worth to report manually to other PRAs, especially when they do not currently use competitor PRA benchmarks.

Exchange exclusivity nonetheless remains the exception rather than the rule for those commodity benchmarks that are provided by PRAs. This state of affairs is likely to be tested in the coming years. On one hand, some exchanges and PRAs may look to follow the model of the ICE–Platts relationship, and yet on the other hand, the regulatory trend in Europe is towards an open-access model for benchmarks that may make exchange exclusivity very problematic, at least for European entities.

Exchange benchmarks

One noticeable trend in recent years has been for exchanges to consciously set out to create futures contracts that are intended first and foremost to be major commodity benchmarks. This represents a deliberate shift away from envisaging futures products primarily as products for risk management and proprietary trading.

When the DME launched its physically settled Oman crude oil futures contract in 2007, much of its launch material focused on the need for a third crude oil futures benchmark alongside Brent and WTI as well as on the perceived inadequacies of the existing Platts Oman/Dubai benchmark. Subsequent DME managements changed course, instead promoting DME Oman as a risk management and arbitrage trading tool.

A similar interest in establishing a third crude oil futures benchmark was also behind the launch of the SPIMEX Urals crude oil futures contract in late 2016 and the much discussed International Energy Exchange (INE) crude oil initiative in Shanghai, which was finally set to launch in late 2017. Both SPIMEX and INE were underpinned by strong political backing from their national governments, which viewed the establishment of an energy futures benchmark as a key tool in national economic development.

It is still too early to say whether DME Oman, SPIMEX Urals or INE will develop into major global commodity benchmarks. But it is certainly the case that the benchmark expectations attached to all of these projects at launch were not helpful. As we have discussed above, it is already difficult enough for an exchange to launch a successful and liquid physically settled futures contract without also having to pursue benchmark status in parallel. Benchmarks tend to evolve almost by accident or due to shifting industry needs, making it very difficult for exchanges to design benchmark contracts from scratch.

Exchange assessments

Given the difficulties of constructing physical benchmarks as well as the costs involved in licensing benchmarks from PRAs, some exchanges have sought to reduce their dependence on PRAs by developing their own assessments of the physical market that they can then use as a settlement price for derivatives.

Singapore Exchange (SGX) licenses PRA benchmarks from Platts, IHS McCloskey and ICIS among others but it is also perhaps the most active international exchange in developing its own physical price assessments. In some markets, this potentially brings SGX into competition with PRAs that are its partners in other areas. SGX has been particularly aggressive in the LNG space, developing its own indexes both independently and in partnership with over-the-counter brokers.

The SGX LNG Index Group (SLING) is a partnership between SGX and the Energy Market Company (EMC), which operates Singapore's wholesale electricity market. The SLING is a weekly assessment based on an adjusted panel methodology (see the chapter on methodologies for further details) in which the top and bottom 15 per cent of submissions are excluded from the average. The SLING was launched in 2015 and SGX launched derivatives based upon it in early 2016, with the first linked derivatives trade taking place shortly afterwards, although subsequent liquidity has been thin.

SGX later announced a partnership in early 2017 with interdealer broker Tullett Prebon to produce a joint spot LNG pricing index for Dubai, Kuwait and India.

SGX had already acquired significant benchmark capability with its late 2016 acquisition of the Baltic Exchange for £77.6 million. Originally an actual exchange, the Baltic has evolved into the primary source of shipping market benchmarks. Its indexes, which are generated by panels of brokers, are used to settle physical and derivative shipping contracts. The deal was portrayed as part of SGX's drive to increase its presence in the commodity markets and to build upon its strong position in iron ore derivatives.

The Tokyo Commodity Exchange (TOCOM) has also announced plans to produce its own physical assessments that it can then use to financially settle derivatives. In January 2017, TOCOM launched a physical platform for trade in gasoline, kerosene, gasoil and bunker fuels. The prices of physical trade in these commodities were intended to serve as the settlement price for derivatives scheduled for a May 2017 launch. "The Exchange expects the result to be a useful new price index and will contribute to reinvigorating the existing oil futures market", a TOCOM official said.

The importance of these initiatives was that they were perhaps the first attempt by exchanges to enter the traditional PRA space by organizing panels and price discovery windows in order to then set their own cash prices. If this became a more widespread trend among exchanges, it would potentially challenge the PRAs' position in some markets by creating alternative benchmarks. It would also have implications as regards exclusivity. The exchange that created the physical benchmark would own the intellectual property and would therefore avoid competition from other exchanges.

If this more autonomous model were to take off, it would therefore allow exchanges to list cash-settled contracts that enjoy one of the key advantages of physical settlement – exclusivity. Setting their own assessments would also allow exchanges to avoid paying fees to PRAs that could also license the same assessments to other exchanges who could launch competitive contracts.

This is still a relatively unlikely scenario, however, as exchanges do not have the staff in place to run assessment processes. SGX was obliged to adopt a panel methodology for its LNG assessment as this form of pricing requires relatively little input from staff. Exchanges do not have teams of price reporters at their disposal who can survey the market or who can check the components of a volume-weighted average.

Hiring a pricing team would be a relatively expensive investment for an exchange. PRAs can justify their staff costs because they have high levels of subscription revenue, whereas an exchange is not set up to sell subscriptions and will rely for revenue on its trading activity. It is therefore cheaper in most cases for an exchange to outsource price assessments to a PRA. This is especially true given the low rate of success of most exchange contracts – it would be potentially costly for an exchange to hire a price reporter to provide assessments for a new market when experience says that any derivative based on the assessment is more likely than not to fail.

Benchmark administration

Some exchanges may also shy away from the implications of setting their own benchmarks as the PRA industry becomes increasingly subject to regulatory scrutiny. Between the IOSCO Principles and the various items of EU legislation, in particular the Benchmarks Regulation, there is now plenty to consider before anyone enters the price assessment business.

The largest exchanges have, nonetheless, established benchmark administration businesses. CME Group has CME Benchmark Europe Ltd, while ICE has ICE Benchmark Administration. The LME also administers the London Bullion Market Association (LBMA)'s platinum and palladium pricing, although these are not regulated benchmarks.

These major commodity exchanges have therefore positioned themselves from a regulatory standpoint to provide benchmarks for cash-settled contracts themselves, without the need to license settlement prices from third parties. To date, though, none of them has moved into this space directly, perhaps because they do not wish to disturb their working relationships with their multiple PRA partners.

Conclusion

Exchanges and PRAs represent the two halves of the commodity benchmark world. Exchanges tend to offer physically settled futures in the biggest and most standardized commodities, while the PRAs cover the thousands of other smaller markets. Exchanges are important consumers of PRA data and the growth of listed commodity derivatives has generated an important new source of revenue for PRAs. PRAs have been a major beneficiary of the drive towards exchange clearing, which began after the collapse of Enron and intensified after the financial crisis. When derivatives were mostly traded bilaterally, PRAs had no visibility over them and could not derive any additional revenue from this activity. The transition from over-the-counter trade to exchanges has made activity levels more transparent and enabled PRAs to share in the additional exchange revenue.

The distinction between an exchange and a PRA is blurring more and more. Platts' eWindow mechanism is not a million miles away from the trading platform that an exchange might operate, while an initiative like SGX's SLING index or TOCOM's physical platform shows that exchanges are also working to enter the PRA space and generate their own assessments. To date, there have not been many formal corporate mergers between exchanges and benchmark providers, with the exception of the SGX-Baltic Exchange tie up, but this could well happen more frequently in the future.

Issues around exclusivity between PRAs and exchanges continue to play out. There are plenty of examples of non-commodity benchmark providers linking up with exchanges on an exclusive basis but until recently this has been fairly unusual in the commodity markets. We might expect market participants to oppose greater integration between two key parts of the trading support environment as this might tend to reduce competition. But whether increased exclusivity would be enough to attract regulatory intervention or to get customers to switch benchmark provider is unclear.

Europe's Benchmark Regulation has also reduced some of the gap in regulatory status between exchanges and PRAs. At least in Europe, the largest PRAs are now operating at a significantly higher level in terms of market supervision and compliance than was previously the case, although there is still a substantial difference between the regulatory requirements on a PRA and on an exchange. PRAs might in the future consider competing directly with the exchanges by moving to open their own regulated trading venues, just as some of the exchanges are entering the benchmark business, but to date there has been no move in this direction and two sides are likely to continue to work together as partners and occasional rivals.

Notes

1   Platts Subscriber Note: S&P Global Platts and ICE Natural Gas Agreement, 21 November 2016.
2   Platts Subscriber Note: Platts announces use of ICE eConfirm platform for gas price reporting, 9 February 2017.

14 PRAs and global regulation

Overview

Socrates would never have cut it in a modern compliance department. When asked about regulating markets, Plato quotes the philosopher as saying "there is no need to impose laws about them on good men; what regulations are necessary they will find out soon enough for themselves".

While applauding Socrates' optimism, we might perhaps question whether the commodity markets are entirely composed of "good men". Either way, Socrates' preference for laissez-faire market intervention is not shared by modern regulators, particularly in Europe. Since the global financial crisis of 2008–2009, regulators around the world have been increasing their scrutiny of the international commodity markets and therefore of the benchmark prices that these commodity markets rely upon.

It is no exaggeration to say that the drive to increase regulation of commodity markets and benchmarks from 2008–2009 onwards has revolutionized how price reporting agencies (PRAs) operate. Regulation has forced PRAs to revise their pricing methodologies, to introduce new technologies, and to change their business culture, in part by adding new teams of compliance officers. The culture of increased compliance has even led to a rash of rationalization in the PRA industry as smaller firms that are not willing to shoulder the additional cost of compliance sell out to larger firms.

International investigations into PRAs and their significance to the commodity markets and to commodity prices have principally been driven by three different bodies since the global financial crisis: the International Organization of Securities Commissions (IOSCO), a group of anti-trust regulators, and the European Union.

This chapter will examine the background to these research efforts by regulators around the world and the impact on the PRA sector of the most important of their subsequent recommendations – the IOSCO Principles.

The good/bad old days

Whenever a few veteran price reporters are gathered together, talk will turn at some point to the 'good old days'. In the mythology of UK-based PRAs, the good old days are usually dated to before Platts and Argus moved their UK headquarters to new offices in Canary Wharf and Farringdon respectively in the mid-2000s. This date range could equally well apply to almost any PRA around the world because it was clearly the global financial crisis of the late 2000s that led the PRAs to be expelled from their mythical unregulated Garden of Eden.

Before their moves, Platts' UK offices were based in Wimbledon, while the Argus global headquarters was in the unfashionable end of Islington. According to the tales, a much more relaxed environment prevailed. Long lunches with traders and brokers were common and compliance rules were limited to the relatively obvious: keep decent records and avoid conflicts of interest, whether financial or personal.

Back then, the work of a price reporter could often be closer to that of an investigating judge. In the days before recorded lines and active compliance departments, some traders often succumbed to the temptation to aggressively push their agendas to price reporters. The price reporter would have to know not only the intricacies of the market for which they were responsible but also the trading position and temperament of their contacts in order to assess where true value really lay.

This was an era where the relationship between price reporters and their customers was much closer than anything imaginable today. Meals and drinks were everyday occurrences, while romances and fights were not unknown. Nostalgic veterans will tell you that they could always speak to everyone in their market and that they always felt like they knew what was going on.

But the good old days for some were clearly the bad old days for others. In a less structured environment, there was much greater pressure on the individual judgment of the price reporter who could be subject to what amounted to bullying by more experienced traders. The personal relationships between trader and price reporter forged in bars and restaurants could also influence judgments in difficult markets. Any veteran of those days can (and with little encouragement will) tell tales of appalling and manipulative behaviour by market participants that would no longer be tolerated either by the PRA or by the participant's own firm.

Whether or not the old days were good or bad, they are now long gone. A few factors ushered in a new era for PRAs. First, their soaring profits forced a realization on PRA managements that they could no longer operate like small businesses staffed by fairly easy-going reporters but needed to add more corporate structure. This can be seen in the office moves undertaken by Platts and Argus in the mid-2000s and by periodic and usually unsuccessful attempts to impose a more formal dress code. Second, regulatory interest in the probity of benchmarks developed after the 2001 collapse of Enron, intensified after the global financial crisis of 2008–2009, and then went into hyper drive after the LIBOR scandal of 2012. Third and finally, the commodity markets themselves began to tighten up on hospitality and expense policies, while firms recorded phone calls and reviewed how their staff were interacting with PRAs. This trend towards extreme caution was exacerbated by the well-publicized European Commission raids of 2013, but can be originally traced back to the publicity around US regulatory actions: principally, the gas-price reporting prosecutions that mostly settled in 2005–2006 and the BP Products North America Inc. propane scandal, which was revealed in 2006.

False gas reporting

In 2002–2003, the US Commodity Futures Trading Commission (CFTC) pushed hard to clamp down on misbehaviour in the US gas and electricity markets following the collapse of Enron in 2001. Under the terms of the Commodity Exchange Act, the CFTC undertook a number of prosecutions of US firms for submitting false prices to Platts and other index providers, which could have affected the settlement price of NYMEX natural gas futures contracts.

In less than a year, between December 2002 and October 2003, the CFTC agreed penalty settlements with six firms: Dynergy and West Coast Power ($5 million); El Paso ($20 million); EnCana ($20 million); Williams Energy ($20 million); Duke Energy ($28 million); Enserco ($3 million). The CFTC later secured further settlements from several other firms and individuals.

In a statement typical of all of the prosecutions, the CFTC found that one of the firms, Dynergy, submitted "false or misleading or knowingly inaccurate market information concerning, among other things, trade prices and volumes, to manipulate the price of natural gas in interstate commerce". The CFTC also found deliberate attempts to conceal from Platts what they were doing. The "respondents' provision of the false reports and their collusion, which was designed to thwart the reporting firms' detection of the false information, were overt acts that furthered the attempted manipulation".

An indication of just how widespread fake price reporting had become in the US power and gas markets can be seen from the details of the complaint that the CFTC made against AEP and its subsidiary AEPES: of the 3,600 natural gas trades that AEP and AEPES submitted to Platts, according to the complaint, "approximately 78%, or about 2,800, were false or misleading or knowingly inaccurate".

Apart from the corporate fines, the CFTC also aggressively pursued the individual traders and trading managers responsible for falsely submitting reports to Platts and to other PRAs in the US gas and power space. This was a watershed moment for the industry, in which individual members of trading desks started to realize that there were risks inherent in their dealings with price reporters. From the mid-2000s onwards, individual traders and certain firms started to pull back from their usual daily conversations with PRA staff and to either replace their conversations with emailed activity files or with total silence.

Another key sidelight of the CFTC's reported enforcement actions in the gas and electricity markets in the early and mid-2000s was the agency's growing frustration with what it perceived to be a lack of cooperation from Platts, which ultimately ended with the CFTC taking Platts to court on four separate occasions. On each occasion, federal courts over-ruled Platts" claim of "journalistic privilege" for its records and handling of pricing data on the grounds that the CFTC was entitled to full cooperation in its investigations into potential market manipulation.

BP propane scandal

The CFTC's next major prosecution in the commodity space was its June 2006 complaint that accused traders at BP in Houston of attempting to corner the market for propane in 2003–2004, driving up the price of the fuel, which is used for cooking and heating, for millions of US residential customers. The traders had acquired the vast majority of the capacity of the key TEPPCO pipeline system, enabling them to drive spot prices higher by artificially withholding propane supplies from the market.

BP later admitted the charges and agreed to pay a total of $303 million in damages: the largest manipulation settlement in CFTC history. The size of the penalty sent a loud and clear message to the market that the CFTC was prepared to investigate any allegations of malpractice in the commodity markets very aggressively and to impose severe penalties. The release of the BP traders' phone calls containing a frank and open discussion of their tactics was also a wake-up call to the markets. The publicity provoked a widespread review of internal and external communication policies by many commodity trading firms, which led in part to a greater awareness of the risks of too open communication with external agents such as PRAs.

IOSCO investigates

One of the many issues that were worrying the recession-hit Group of 20 (G20) nations when they met in Seoul, South Korea on 12 November 2010 was oil price volatility. After all, international oil prices had been exceptionally volatile in 2007–2008, with WTI trading from highs of almost $140 down to lows of below $40. By the time of the Seoul summit, WTI was trading at around $80/bl and the leaders of the G20 wanted to understand just what was going on in the energy markets.

Under the umbrella title of 'Fossil Fuel Price Volatility', the G20 leaders made a number of requests to such entities as the International Energy Forum (IEF), International Energy Agency (IEA) and the Organization of the Petroleum Exporting Countries (OPEC) to provide advice on improving data on oil stocks, production, refining and consumption as well as information on long-range forecasts. The G20 also asked the International Organization of Securities Commissions (IOSCO) to further monitor developments in the over-the-counter oil markets and to recommend measures to make the markets more transparent.

The Seoul Summit Document also contained a bombshell for PRAs:

> [T]he IEF, IEA, OPEC and IOSCO to produce a joint report, by the April 2011 Finance Ministers' meeting, on how the oil spot market prices are assessed by oil price reporting agencies and how this affects the transparency and functioning of oil markets.

This was the first time that PRAs had ever been directly spotlighted and by the heads of government of the G20 countries no less. This was also the first time that most PRA officials had ever heard the acronym IOSCO but IOSCO quickly become the focal point for global discussions about the role and regulation of PRAs. It is important to note that this initial enquiry by the G20 came out of an interest in understanding the causes of volatility in the energy markets, unlike later European attempts to regulate PRAs, which stemmed from post-LIBOR suspicions about the integrity of benchmarks.

Following the Seoul summit, the IEF–IEA–OPEC–IOSCO agreed to appoint two well-known consultants Elizabeth (Liz) Bossley and John Gault to prepare an initial report on the activities of PRAs in the oil market, which was submitted to the G20 Finance Ministers in October 2011.

The consultants' report was based on interviews with the PRAs and stakeholders such as oil companies, brokers, banks and exchanges. The report was widely considered to be fair to all sides of the PRA debate and to provide a very clear overview of the current state of PRA activities.

The report highlighted that PRA customers felt that they were generally very professional but that the handling of complaints was not always clear, while the process around making changes to assessment methodologies could be opaque and frustrating. The authors pointed out the lack of an independent formal complaints procedure at the PRAs that they reviewed and the lack of any "external, independent audit of the price assessment process".

One specific issue that was raised was the dominance of Platts with Bossley & Gault noting that "even some of Platts' most vehement detractors do not feel able to cease using Platts" because of a combination of legacy term deals and the basis risk involved in using a different benchmark when the available derivative risk management tools reference Platts. There was also a question about whether Platts' eWindow system should be defined as an information-gathering tool or as an actual trading system.

In terms of regulation, the report's authors noted the essential paradox that would come to dominate discussions of PRA regulation: most interviewed respondents wanted to see the PRAs regulated, but there was no agreement on by whom, nor any confidence that a regulator would understand the highly specialized work of PRAs. "Many respondents expressed the view that bad regulation is worse than no regulation at all", Bossley & Gault observed.

The IEF–IEA–OPEC–IOSCO report prepared by Bossley & Gault was presented to the G20 Leaders Cannes Summit in November 2011. The Cannes Summit Final declaration included the following statement:

> Recognizing the role of Price Reporting Agencies for the proper functioning of oil markets, we ask IOSCO, in collaboration with the IEF, the IEA and OPEC, to prepare recommendations to improve their functioning and oversight to our Finance Ministers by mid-2012.

The debate about regulating PRAs had clearly moved on at Cannes. The recognition that PRAs are key to the "proper functioning of oil markets" assigned the PRAs the kind of systemic importance that meant that the G20 was now asking for specific recommendations on improving "functioning and oversight" of PRAs. Notably, IOSCO – the regulatory body – was now charged with taking the lead, while the IEF, IEA and OPEC were asked to collaborate rather than treated as equal partners.

IOSCO's Technical Committee Task Force on Commodity Futures Markets, which had been transformed into the Standing Committee on Commodity Futures Markets in 2011, put out a Consultation Report in March 2012 to ask for feedback on questions arising from the report prepared by Bossley & Gault. The focus of the questions was the accountability and governance of PRAs, such as the potential need for third-party oversight of PRA processes, particularly complaints and formulation of methodology.

The attention of the IOSCO Committee was largely focused on four PRAs at this point: Platts, Argus, ICIS and OPIS. The IOSCO Committee deemed that these four PRAs covered most of the scope of world oil price reporting. The issue about the relevance of involving other PRAs was discussed on several occasions internally and in external meetings, but resulted in no addition to the selected PRA list for review.

Russian initiative

At the same time as IOSCO was receiving its initial report into PRAs, the Federal Antimonopoly Service (FAS) of the Russian Federation created, in partnership with the Austrian Federal Competition Authority (AFCA), an 'International Working Group on Investigating Issues on Pricing at the Oil Product Markets and Methods of Their Functioning'.

The Working Group was founded in October 2011 to promote the development "of price indicators setting out a fair price for oil and oil products, formed on market conditions; providing competitive pricing in the frame of oil and oil product trading". The Working Group aimed to investigate pricing issues and to share experiences and approaches among its members in terms of applying anti-trust legislation to the oil markets.

As well as the Russian and Austrian regulators, the Working Group included representatives from Portugal, Kazakhstan, the USA, Ukraine and Germany among others. The Working Group held five different meetings in 2012–2014 and reported on the contents of its discussions to international bodies such as the Interstate Council for Antimonopoly Policy (ICAP), at its meetings in Minsk and Irkutsk, the OECD Competition Committee at its meeting in Paris, and to the Intergovernmental Group of Experts on Competition Law and Policy (UNCTAD) at its July 2013 meeting in Geneva.

The Working Group published its final report in 2014 entitled "The International Working Group on Investigating Issues on Pricing in the Oil and Oil Product Markets and Methods of their Functioning: results, tasks and development strategy".

The report laid great emphasis on the development and maintenance of an "Oil Information Platform" that would enable competition authorities to exchange fundamental information concerning national crude oil and oil product markets. The main focus of the Platform was to enhance interaction between competition authorities in order to enable investigations into potential competition law infringements.

The IPRO Code

Sniffing which way the regulatory wind was blowing, the three largest PRAs – Platts, Argus and ICIS – got together and in April 2012 they presented their own Independent Price Reporting Organization (IPRO) Code.

The concept behind the Code was to present best practice for PRAs and to commit any organization that signed up to the voluntary standards to annually certify its own compliance with the Code and to periodically employ an outside auditor to provide an external review its compliance. A summarized version of the seven clauses of the IPRO Code are as follows:

1   Robust governance, management structure and clear reporting lines.
2   Avoidance of potential conflicts of interest and management of any that arise.
3   Published price methodologies; adherence to same; consultation about any potential changes.
4   Non-discriminatory participation in and integrity of data collection processes.
5   Maintenance of policies and procedures for the prompt and fair handling of complaints.
6   Upholding of confidentiality and proper record-keeping.
7   Compliance with all appropriate laws and regulatory requirements.

The IPRO Code never really took off in terms of PRAs around the world all signing up for it because it was quickly superseded by official guidelines provided by IOSCO. Membership remains at the time of writing limited to the 'Big Three' of Platts, Argus and ICIS. But the IPRO Code definitely served its purpose, in that it framed the debate during the IOSCO deliberations. IOSCO insiders believe that the IPRO did have an influence on IOSCO going for a voluntary, rather than directly regulatory, compliance approach. The PRAs continued to cite the IPRO Code during the later discussions about potential European Benchmark Regulation.

The IPRO Code also marked a change of sentiment from the larger PRAs by marking their acceptance that some form of additional scrutiny of their activities was inevitable. The IPRO Code was effectively an acknowledgment by the largest PRAs that they are providers of key benchmark data to the commodity and financial industries rather than simple publishers that could claim journalistic privilege. Platts had unsuccessfully employed a 'journalistic argument' citing the freedom of press when faced with CFTC enquiries in the early 2000s, and PRAs continued to use this argument for some time after the IPRO Code, both in private and in public, although IOSCO never really took it seriously as an argument. But after the publication of the IPRO Code, the PRAs' claims were made with increasingly less conviction.

The impact of LIBOR

While IOSCO was in the midst of seeking feedback from PRAs and their stakeholders, UK weekly *The Economist* published an aggressive critique of Platts' Urals crude oil pricing and the role played by Swiss trading house Gunvor in establishing the assessment (Riddles, Mysteries and Enigmas; *The Economist*, 5 May 2012). *The Economist's* report drew a strong response from Platts, which was nettled by the accusations that its market-on-close process might be susceptible to the influence of a single trading firm.

This adverse publicity was particularly unhelpful for the PRAs in terms of its timing during the IOSCO consultation process. The report was, however, a storm in a teacup compared to the explosion of fresh revelations in the long-running LIBOR scandal, which totally changed the nature of the PRA debate.

After mutterings for years, it became very clear in 2012 that all was not well with the London Interbank Offered Rate (LIBOR), perhaps the world's most significant interest rate benchmark. Individuals at certain financial institutions were later found guilty of manipulating their LIBOR submissions in order to benefit their trading position. The adverse publicity around the charges exacerbated already high levels of public suspicion of the financial sector in the wake of the financial crisis.

The tone and content of some of the communications that were revealed between participants in the LIBOR mechanism would have looked rather familiar to anyone involved in commodity price reporting in its pre-compliance era. But if some of the attitudes were the same, the punishments were definitely of a different order.

When the CFTC discovered widespread false reporting in the US gas market, the largest fine it handed out during its 2002–2003 enforcement campaign was $20 million, while BP's record propane-related fine was $303 million. In contrast, LIBOR manipulation attracted fines of a whole different magnitude. Deutsche Bank paid out $2.5 billion to US and UK regulators for its role in the LIBOR scandal, while UBS paid $1.5 billion and Barclays $450 million. The liabilities for individual traders were also of a different order to those seen in commodity market enforcement actions. When Tom Hayes was found guilty of manipulating LIBOR, a UK court sentenced him to 11 years in prison and was ordered to make financial restitution of almost £900,000.

The vastly increased severity of the consequences of manipulating LIBOR in part relate to the much greater significance of LIBOR to the global economy compared with regional commodity benchmarks such as US gas, electricity or propane. But, in another way, the more extreme penalties also reflected a change in the public mood following the global financial crisis. The greater awareness of the damage that manipulation of a benchmark could do to the real economy led politicians to push for tougher penalties in financial cases and cases involving benchmarks. A generalized sense of public outrage fed into a greater appetite for regulation and for enforcement, kicking off what has been called 'the era of compliance'. This drive for greater regulatory scrutiny started with financial benchmarks but was swiftly expanded to cover commodity benchmarks as well.

The IOSCO Principles

IOSCO's long-awaited recommendations – the Principles for Oil Price Reporting Agencies – were finally published in October 2012. The four largest PRAs – Platts, Argus, ICIS and OPIS – had been consulted throughout the drafting of the Principles.

The impact of LIBOR in the minds of its drafters can be seen in statements such as "the recent LIBOR settlements illustrate the vulnerability of benchmark setting processes to potential manipulation in order to benefit positions on derivatives markets".

Notwithstanding the unflattering comparisons to LIBOR, the final IOSCO report was considered as a success for PRAs, which successfully avoided the imposition of any direct regulation on their activities.

The focus of the Principles was less on the activities of PRAs in assessing prices in the physical markets and more on the use of PRA prices in settling derivative contracts. Although IOSCO had taken the lead in drafting the report, there were three other international organizations involved (IEA, IEF and OPEC). Officials from these three did not want to see regulation of the underlying physical market. This view was shared by certain IOSCO Committee members, particularly from states with oil production interests. IOSCO is an organization composed of securities regulators and it was therefore not within IOSCO's remit to focus on physical energy regulation. There were a number of attempts to expand the role within the IOSCO Committee to take a larger interpretation of the remit, but every time these were rejected. The name of the responsible Standing Committee – the Standing Committee on Commodity Futures Markets – explicitly set the focus on commodity derivatives.

The adoption and implementation of the IOSCO Principles was made voluntary, although national regulators were recommended to consider prohibiting derivatives trading in contracts based on assessments from PRAs that were not compliant with the Principles. The Principles therefore were chiefly relevant to the larger PRAs with licensing agreements in place with derivatives exchanges.

The following is a brief summary of the IOSCO Principles, which were grouped into two main headings: one relating to methodologies and the other to price assessments:

Quality and integrity of PRA methodologies

- *Methodology*: A PRA should formalize, document and make public detailed methodologies, which should be designed to generate reliable indicators of oil market values, free from distortion and representative of the particular market to which they relate. PRAs should also explain their rationale for adopting a particular methodology and their procedures for internal and external review and approval of the methodology.
- *Changes to a Methodology*: PRAs should also make public explicit procedures and rationale of any proposed material change in their methodology as well as providing sufficient time for and attention to stakeholders' comments. A PRA should routinely examine its methodologies to ensure that they reliably reflect the physical market.

Quality and integrity of price assessments

- *Market data used in price assessments*: PRA should ensure the quality and integrity of the price assessment process by providing detailed specifics of the physical commodity being assessed as well as the priority ranking afforded to price information such as deals, bids and offers, and other market information. PRAs should aim to ensure submitters provide all of their relevant data and that any outlying data is noted and recorded. PRAs should publish a concise explanation of how they reached their assessments.

- *Integrity of the reporting process*: PRAs should define who can submit data to them; they should verify their identity, and they should investigate any discrepancies in data submitted.
- *Assessors*: PRAs should have guidelines in place to ensure their staff are sufficiently trained and have back-up cover.
- *Supervision of assessors*: Internal controls should be in place, including sign off to assessments by a supervisor.
- *Audit trails*: data and judgments regarding assessments should be documented with names attached and information should be retained for at least five years.
- *Conflicts of interest*: PRAs should document, implement and enforce comprehensive policies and procedures for the identification, disclosure, management and avoidance of conflicts of interest and the protection of integrity and independence of assessments. The policies and procedures should be kept up to date. In the case of any identified conflicts, there should be appropriate segregation of functions within the PRA in terms of supervision, compensation, systems access and information flows.
- *Complaints*: A PRA should have in place and publish written procedures for receiving, investigating and retaining records concerning complaints made about a PRA's assessment process.
- *Cooperation with regulatory authorities*: Audit trails, other documentation required by these principles and all other relevant information shall be readily available to market authorities in carrying out their regulatory duties and handed over without delay in accordance with applicable law.
- *External auditing*: A PRA should appoint an independent, external auditor with appropriate experience and capability to review and report annually on the PRA's adherence to its stated methodology criteria and with the requirements of the Principles.

IOSCO consequences

The relatively straightforward content of the IOSCO Principles, which differed in only a few details from the voluntary IPRO Code, ensured that the larger PRAs had very few issues with IOSCO's proposals, which were subsequently ratified by the G20 in November 2012. At the time, the PRAs saw the Principles very much as the lesser of two evils, given the scope of impending EU regulations.

The IOSCO Principles were criticized in some quarters as 'neither fish nor fowl'. The Principles imposed a significant compliance burden on PRAs in terms of documentation and external audits but shied away from direct regulation. It was also not clear whether the introduction of the Principles would have any genuine impact on the price assessment process or the process by which price methodologies are devised and revised.

Rather than any major change in their approach or quality of their work, perhaps the major consequence of the introduction of the IOSCO Principles was a surge in the cost of doing business for PRAs. Firms now had to invest in data management systems that tracked the origins and development of their assessments and assigned a responsible person at each step. Firms also had to enhance their compliance departments to review their internal processes as well as hiring costly external auditors to review their compliance with their own internal procedures as well as with the IOSCO Principles.

The larger PRAs took these costs in their stride and some felt that by strengthening their businesses, the Principles had actually improved their commercial results. Pushback by the larger PRAs was limited to some grumbling about the implementation of the second external audit under the Reasonable Assurance standard.

The compliance burden fell heavier on smaller firms and one unintended consequence of the Principles was that they encouraged smaller privately-owned PRAs to sell up to larger firms rather than invest heavily in new systems and staff. It appeared that increased regulatory costs would reduce competition in the sector, particularly from small challenger start-ups that lacked a wealthy backer.

The larger PRAs were quick to publicize their acceptance of the IOSCO Principles and most issued regular press releases about successful external audits of their compliance. One unintended consequence of the IOSCO Principles was that a confusion developed in the market as to whether or not PRAs were actually regulated. As a securities regulator IOSCO could not regulate the PRAs, only the commodity derivative markets that used their assessments, but nonetheless some market participants developed a misconception of what the Principles meant for the markets.

The four separate audits of the four largest PRAs that were under review – Platts, Argus, ICIS and OPIS – were all completed within just over a year after the publication of the IOSCO Principles. The review of Argus was dated 11 October 2013, ICIS 17 October 2013, OPIS 23 October 2013 and Platts 1 November 2013.

The first benchmarks outside these four to be audited by a third-party were CRU Indices' US Midwest hot-rolled coil, cold-rolled coil, hot-dipped galvanized coil and plate price indices – the most widely used carbon steel indices in the world. The CRU audit was completed in mid-October 2013 and was announced by CRU chief operating officer Fraser Murdoch, as coming "at a time when some price reporting agencies (PRAs) have been under attack and some are still under investigation". This audit of a group of benchmarks was swiftly followed by external reviews by audit firms of the energy assessments generated by Platts, Argus and ICIS, and later by reviews of other PRAs and of the bigger firms' non-energy businesses.

The IOSCO Committee undertook lengthy discussions with the Institute of Chartered Accountants in England and Wales (ICAEW) about audit standards and agreed to Limited Assurance standards for the first set of audits in 2013 and Reasonable Assurance standards for the second set in 2014, though the Platts 2013 audit was largely drafted according to Reasonable Assurance norms.

To those critical of the PRAs, these external audits, which operated under the umbrella principles set out by IOSCO, allowed the pricing firms to appear to be directly regulated and on a par with stakeholders such as banks or exchanges, which were subject to very different and more exacting regulatory regimes. Critics tended to describe the IOSCO Principles as a confirmation of the status quo, pointing out that IOSCO is an umbrella body of regulators rather than a direct regulating entity, while its Principles remain essentially voluntary and have no legal status.

Despite these criticisms, it was generally felt in the commodity industry that the IOSCO Principles represented a step forward for the PRA industry. After more than a century since Warren Platt founded the first modern assessment service, there was at last a clear official definition of best practice for a PRA. The IOSCO Principles would play a key part in framing the later debate around the EU Benchmark Regulation and they were widely adopted, not just in the oil markets, which were their original target, but also in sectors such as generation fuels, metals and agricultural markets.

The publication and adoption of the IOSCO Principles represented perhaps the most important milestone in regulatory discussions of the PRA sector, but their adoption did not end the regulatory pressure that the PRAs had experienced since the global financial crisis: within a year of the publication of the IOSCO Principles, there was a whistleblower incident at ICIS in London, a European Commission raid on Platts and the announcement that the European Union was drafting specific Benchmark Regulation.

The ICIS whistleblower

In November 2012, Seth Freedman, who had been working at ICIS Heren assessing prices in the UK gas market since the start of the year, reported his concerns about unusual trading patterns to the UK Financial Services Authority (FSA). Freedman had previously raised his concerns with senior ICIS editorial staff, who subsequently reported them to the UK energy regulator, the Office of Gas and Electricity Markets (Ofgem).

Freedman's allegations, which he detailed in the UK's *Guardian* newspaper, received some publicity in the post-LIBOR environment and the UK government was swift to promise severe punishment for any entities found to be manipulating the gas market. The story was embarrassing for ICIS, particularly after Freedman revealed recordings he had covertly made of his colleagues and managers discussing the trades in question in a very frank manner, which also revealed their concerns about how regulators might handle any potential alerts.

Despite some lurid coverage of Freedman's allegations and intense scrutiny of ICIS's internal processes, no LIBOR-esque smoking gun was ever discovered. A joint investigation by the FSA and Ofgem failed to discover any evidence of manipulation after a 12-month enquiry.

There were nonetheless consequences of the ICIS whistleblower case. The first was doubtless unintended: Freedman's decision to reveal covert recordings and transcripts of email and instant messages with colleagues and customers in the UK media spooked some very key gas companies, like Norway's Statoil, that had previously been contributing information to PRAs. Some London-based banks also decided to cease speaking to the three main UK gas reporting agencies: ICIS, Argus and Platts. This tended to ensure that UK gas benchmarks became less robust than they had been before concerns about their robustness were raised.

The second consequence was that when ICIS held a consultation process to gain feedback on its gas benchmarks in April 2013, a large number of customers said that they favoured indices based on all-day averages of actual transactions rather than indices that involved editorial judgment. At least in the UK gas market, regulatory pressure and the weaknesses publicly revealed by Freedman combined to reduce interactions between PRAs and the market they served. With reduced trust between the markets and PRAs, more mechanistic methods of determining price benchmarks began to look safer to both sides.

"LIBOR in a barrel"

With the LIBOR scandal and the ICIS whistleblower still fresh in the mind, it was inevitable that there would be huge publicity when on 14 May 2013 officials from the European Commission made unannounced appearances at the offices of Shell, BP and Norway's Statoil as well at visiting Platts' London office where they took away files, laptops and phones.

The Commission stated that it had "concerns that the companies may have colluded in reporting distorted prices to a Price Reporting Agency to manipulate the published prices for a number of oil and biofuel products. Furthermore, the Commission has concerns that the companies may have prevented others from participating in the price assessment process, with a view to distorting published prices. Any such behaviour, if established, may amount to violations of European anti-trust rules that prohibit cartels and restrictive business practices and abuses of a dominant market position".

The visits, which became quickly known as "the raids", sent shockwaves across the commodities and PRA industries. The potential implications were beautifully summed up by *The Economist* of 18 May 2013 as "LIBOR in a barrel". Media reports calculated how many billions the oil majors might have to repay if they were found guilty of manipulating the oil price, while many thought that a successful enforcement action might even spell the end of the Platts' eWindow mechanism.

The blaze of publicity quickly died away and it became clear that either the Commission officials had bitten off more than they could chew or else they could find nothing. The focus of the investigation narrowed to the ethanol market and Commission officials carried out further visits to ethanol producers in October 2014 and March 2015. In December 2015, the Commission announced that it had ended its investigations into BP, Shell and Statoil, although it would open a formal anti-trust investigation into three smaller biofuels producers: Spain's Abengoa, Belgium's Alcogroup and Sweden's Lantmannen.

The Commission confirmed that it was no longer investigating crude oil or refined products, but was focusing all of its attention on whether ethanol producers had colluded to drive Platts' assessments higher. There was no suggestion that Platts itself would be part of the investigation. The raids of 2013, which had seemed set to trigger a full-scale investigation of behaviours in the Platts' pricing windows, had finally fizzled out into a much less ambitious anti-trust investigation into potential manipulation of Platts' European ethanol benchmark.

Table 14.1 Selected chronology of recent PRA regulatory developments

Dec-06	CFTC accuses Platts of lack of cooperation in its investigations
Jun-07	CFTC settles last false gas price reporting cases
Aug-07	US Court orders Platts to assist the CFTC
Oct-07	BP pays $303mn to settle US propane suit
Apr-08	First media reports on issues with LIBOR
Nov-10	G20 Leaders' Seoul Summit asks for a preliminary report on PRAs
Mar-11	Birth of Europe's Agency for the Cooperation of Energy Regulators (ACER)
Oct-11	Russia's FAS launches working group on oil pricing
Nov-11	G20 Leaders' Cannes Summit requests a fuller report on PRAs
Dec-11	EU Remit legislation comes into force
Mar-12	IOSCO publishes consultation paper on PRA activities
Apr-12	Platts, Argus, ICIS publish voluntary code of conduct
May-12	*The Economist* publishes a critique of Platts' Russian oil pricing
Jul-12	UK criminal investigation launches into LIBOR manipulation
Oct-12	IOSCO publishes principles for Oil Price Reporting Agencies
Nov-12	G20 endorses IOSCO principles
Nov-12	Allegations of UK gas price manipulation by ICIS whistleblower
Apr-13	UK FCA publishes MAR 8 on benchmarks
May-13	European Commission raids Platts and oil/biofuels companies
Jul-13	IOSCO publishes principles for financial benchmarks
Sep-13	European Commission proposes new benchmark regulations
Oct-13	CRU US carbon steel prices pass an external review
Oct-13	External auditors conclude first external review of a PRA
Nov-13	OFGEM & FCA conclude UK gas prices were not rigged
Jul-14	OFGEM supports extending IOSCO principles to UK gas and power
Sep-14	IOSCO publishes report on implementation of PRA principles
Oct-14	European Commission raids a number of ethanol companies
Mar-15	European Commission raids a Spanish ethanol firm
Sep-15	IOSCO publishes 2nd report on implementation of PRA principles
Dec-15	European Commission opens ethanol antitrust case
Jun-16	EU Benchmark Regulation published
Aug-16	EURIBOR becomes first benchmark on EU regulated list
2018	EU Benchmark Regulation comes into force

Conclusion

Despite the embarrassment of the Commission's failed investigation into Platts and the oil majors, it was Europe that increasingly made the running in terms of PRA regulation from 2012 onwards. Regulators in the other key commodity trading regions such as the US and Asia appeared relatively satisfied with the work done by IOSCO and most viewed the publication of the IOSCO Principles as the final word on the PRA sector, given that issues of market manipulation and false reporting were generally already well covered in the criminal codes of individual jurisdictions. European regulators continued nonetheless to push hard on issues surrounding benchmarks to the dismay of some of the PRAs. We will explore the array of regulations introduced by Brussels in the next chapter.

15 PRAs and European regulation

Overview

So far only the European Union has shown any interest in regulating the price reporting agencies (PRAs). An array of legislation has redrawn the landscape in Europe for PRAs and for their customers in the commodity markets. Other key regulatory jurisdictions in North America and Asia have not shown any appetite to date to intervene in market pricing issues, but the new rules drawn up in Europe will inevitably have an effect on PRA operations around the world, given the interconnected nature of their coverage of the international commodity markets.

European Union officials felt that the IOSCO Principles did not go far enough and their primary aim was to take the work on price reporting carried out by IOSCO and to formalize it within a legal and regulatory framework. This has drawn support from those who criticized the IOSCO Principles for not introducing penalties for failure to adhere to its standards.

Officials also expressed concern that, given the "flexibility as to their exact scope and means of implementation, Member States are likely to adopt rules at national level which would implement such principles in a divergent manner". There was concern that this could lead to the fragmentation of the single market, given that different standards could be applied across Member States.

Opponents to the European approach are easier to find than enthusiasts. Critics say that the European regulations are overly prescriptive and do not make sufficient allowance for the distinctive nature of the commodities markets. Some have even described the rules as a solution in search of a problem, given that very few cases of manipulation of PRAs have ever been proven. Perhaps the most telling criticism is that by increasing regulation, the European authorities have deterred companies from communicating with PRAs, thereby reducing the information flow that helps to generate accurate price assessments.

There is also a suggestion that the European rules are easy for globally mobile businesses to avoid. In the absence of a worldwide approach to regulation it is possible for entities such as PRAs to avoid European rules simply by moving their operations outside the region. The concern is that Europe could risk losing its role in commodity market oversight to other regulators who may lack either the political will or the technical knowledge to provide effective supervision. To date there has, however, been no indication that a wholesale move out of Europe is under serious consideration at any of the major PRAs.

Introducing MAR 8

The official review of the LIBOR process detailed a number of failures that had ultimately led to the LIBOR scandal. In its final report of September 2012, it noted weaknesses in controls at the firms submitting information, weaknesses in the governance of the benchmark and lack of credible oversight. The review recommended that LIBOR activities should be subject to statutory regulation.

The UK government decided to follow this advice and it incorporated the ability to regulate benchmarks into the Financial Services Act of 2012. Under the umbrella of this legislation, the UK's Financial Conduct Authority (FCA) published its Market Conduct Chapter 8 on Benchmarks, known as MAR 8, which was implemented in April 2013.[1]

The purpose of the FCA's rules was to set out the requirements applying to firms that are either benchmark submitters or benchmark administrators. The obligations were fairly straightforward for both sides. Benchmark administrators were required to corroborate submissions and monitor for any suspicious activity, while submitters were required to implement and maintain a clear conflict of interest policy and appropriate systems and controls.

At first, LIBOR was the only benchmark specified in the rules. But in 2015 a number of other UK-based benchmarks were added to the regulated list. The majority were financial but the list also included the London Bullion Market Association's gold and silver benchmarks and the ICE Brent Index. The UK legislation introduced direct regulation of benchmarks for the first time but the requirements were directed towards benchmarks that were perceived to be of systemic importance to the broader economy and the activity of PRAs was not affected.

European Benchmark Regulation

Shortly after the implementation of MAR 8, the European Commission carried out unannounced visits to various oil companies and Platts in May 2013 as part of an investigation into concerns that firms may have reporting false prices or deliberately prevented others from participating in the price assessment process.

It was against this backdrop that the European Commission first published its "Proposal for a Regulation on Indices Used as Benchmarks in Financial Instruments and Financial Contracts" in September 2013. The Commission noted in its initial statement that "any risk of manipulation of benchmarks may undermine market confidence, cause significant losses to investors and distort the real economy".

This initial proposal, which later became the European Union's Benchmark Regulation (EU 2016/1011), appeared to be a straight reaction to the LIBOR scandal of 2012 (see the previous chapter for further details). The Commission's first press release in July 2012 was virtually entirely focused on financial benchmarks, although it also included a reference to commodities in its definition of a benchmark:

> A benchmark is any commercial index or published figure calculated by the application of a formula to the value of one or more underlying assets or prices, including estimated prices, interest rates or other values, or surveys by reference to which the amount payable under a financial instrument is determined. Underlying assets or prices referenced in benchmarks can include interest rates, or commodities such as oil, provided that these determine the amount payable under a financial instrument, such as a derivative.
>
> (European Commission press release, 25 July 2012)

This almost throwaway reference to "commodities such as oil" effectively opened the door for the direct regulation of PRA benchmarks for the first time.

Many European Commission officials felt that IOSCO's Principles for PRAs had been watered down too far and relied too much on self-regulation. Some observers suggested that the difference in approach between IOSCO and the European Union was also a reflection of tension between the traditionally more laissez-faire northern European governments and their oil champions Shell and BP, both of whom had strongly advised against direct regulation in their IOSCO submissions, and between France and the Mediterranean countries, which had a greater interventionist tradition. This latter approach was reflected in the submission from French oil major Total to IOSCO, which broke ranks with its fellow European oil majors by recommending direct supervision of PRAs by a regulator such as the European Securities and Markets Authority (ESMA).

Building on REMIT

The European Union had already shown an appetite for intervention in the energy markets and for increased supervision of their price benchmarks, although its previous focus had been on the European gas and power markets. Regulation (EU) No 1227/2011 of the European Parliament and of the Council on Wholesale Energy Market Integrity and Transparency, known to its friends as REMIT, had been adopted back in October 2011.

REMIT was designed to crack down on potential market abuse in the European gas and power markets, in part by introducing pan-European standards and cooperation among regulators in order to provide a continent-wide oversight of markets that were increasingly pan-European rather than single jurisdiction. REMIT also recognized that the physical gas and power markets were inextricably linked with their respective derivative markets and so attempted to ensure that regulators looked at both together.

One of the forms of market manipulation specified in the REMIT legislation was "deliberately providing false information to undertakings which provide price assessments or market reports with the effect of misleading market participants acting on the basis of those price assessments or market reports". This was a nod towards the issue of false reporting of gas and power trades to PRAs that had been uncovered in the United States (see previous chapter for details). Europe's Agency for the Cooperation of Energy Regulators (ACER) was designated as the key entity overseeing REMIT's provisions.

The revolutionary aspect of REMIT was that it required firms trading in the European gas and power markets to register and then to report their wholesale market transactions, including orders to trade, to ACER either directly or through a third party. This reporting requirement applied to both physical and derivative transactions. As the UK gas and power regulator Ofgem noted, REMIT thereby improved regulators' "visibility of the market and in turn the activities of the PRAs" as ACER and its constituent entities could now access full details of all of the activity in the underlying markets, which they could then compare to the assessments of price published by PRAs.

ACER's first chairman Lord Mogg noted that Ofgem would have been able to conclude its investigation into the ICIS whistle blower case much more rapidly if it had had access to the data that was reportable to ACER under REMIT. Although with several thousand entities reporting an enormous range of transactions and other data to ACER through multiple channels, it is hard to imagine how ACER's very limited staff could quickly sift through millions upon millions of data points in order to resolve investigations rapidly. Concerns were also expressed that the reporting burden of REMIT could deter smaller participants from trading in the European power and gas markets, potentially reducing liquidity and as a consequence damaging the price formation process.

Benchmark Regulation consequences

The European Benchmark Regulation was scheduled to come into effect in 2018 but in August 2016 the European Commission adopted an "Implementing Regulation" ahead of time that designated EURIBOR (the Euro Interbank Offered Rate) as the first index to be formally recognized as a benchmark under the terms of the regulation.

Under the terms of the Benchmark Regulation, European PRAs have to decide whether or not to register individual pricing benchmarks with the regulator or not by adding their indices alongside EURIBOR on the snappily titled "List of Critical Benchmarks Pursuant to Article 20(1) of Regulation (EU) 2016/1011".

The Benchmark Regulation does not oblige PRAs to register their benchmarks, but no European exchange will be allowed to list a product that refers to a benchmark unless that benchmark is registered. The PRA therefore has a choice. If it wishes to avoid direct regulation of its benchmarks, it can keep them off the list of critical benchmarks. But by doing so, it could risk the health of its benchmarks as any derivatives based on a non-registered PRA price would no longer be suitable for trading or clearing in European exchange venues such as ICE Europe or Germany's EEX.

The principal entities disadvantaged by the Benchmark Regulation are therefore Europe's exchanges rather than its PRAs. The PRAs retain the freedom to bypass the regulations by only licensing their benchmarks to non-European players, such as the CME Group, the Singapore Exchange (SGX), the Tokyo Commodity Exchange

(TOCOM) or the Dubai Mercantile Exchange (DME). In contrast, the only way around the legislation for European exchanges is to relocate outside of the European Union.

A further complexity relates to whether the UK will apply the European Benchmark Legislation in its current form after its departure from the European Union. The majority of PRA and exchange business in Europe is, after all, based in London.

Reporting obligations

During the public consultation period for the Benchmark Regulation, one of the biggest concerns for the PRAs was the impact that increased regulation might have on their information flow. There was a clear risk that some customers would simply cease communication with PRAs if Europe imposed too much of a burden. Argus summed up the PRAs' concerns in its response to the European Commission's Consultation Document on the Regulation of Indices:

> market sources, as well as their compliance and legal departments, are likely to decide that, rather than accepting and having to comply with a new level of regulation, it would be safer and simpler to discontinue voluntarily supplying information to journalists.

The drafters of the European legislation were aware of this concern and sought to address it directly in the Benchmark Regulation: "Contributing to a benchmark is a voluntary activity. If any initiative requires contributors to significantly change their business models, they could cease to contribute." But officials still felt that "requiring good governance and control systems is not expected to lead to substantial costs or disproportionate administrative burden. Therefore this Regulation imposes certain obligations on supervised contributors."

Under the terms of the benchmark regulation, European PRAs are expected to check that their contributors conform to certain standards in order to make use of their information: "the administrator shall not use input data from a contributor if the administrator has any indication that the contributor does not adhere to the code of conduct referred to in Article 15". Benchmark providers are also required to "ensure that contributors have in place adequate internal oversight and verification procedures". Article 15 obliges the administrators of critical benchmarks to publish a code of conduct stating policies towards data submission, record keeping and management of conflicts of interest, among others.

This is likely to prove a challenge for PRAs who rely entirely on voluntary submissions. The data that PRAs need to do their job is provided on a purely voluntary basis by commodity market participants. The day that PRAs start questioning these firms about their internal compliance processes and requiring them to sign declarations will likely be the last day that the PRA receives information from them.

This concern was one of the drivers behind Argus following Platts onto the screen and creating its Argus Open Markets price discovery platform. Some of the largest energy companies had announced that they will only communicate to PRAs electronically since this method provides them with an electronic record of all communications.

Energy consultant and commentator Peter Stewart has expressed concern that European policymakers do not understand the difference between what he terms "vertical" and "horizontal" transparency.[2] For Stewart, horizontal transparency "requires the disclosure of trade data, such as happens in the Platts' window and on futures exchanges". In contrast, vertical transparency "is more subtle, requiring a dialogue about why the market is moving and what the consequences are – such a dialogue may include market participants and market observers". Vertical transparency has been generally provided by price reporters and by the newswire services. This is now in jeopardy, at least within the European Union.

A two-tier communication market has already begun to open up. Many of the largest firms have decided to share their bids, offers and transactions with PRAs purely through electronic channels. In contrast, many smaller firms, particularly those who are based outside Europe, still have no issue in speaking to PRAs. These firms do not feel the same legal constraints and they do not have the huge compliance framework of large firms like the oil majors.

This two-tier market is one of the unintended consequences of the European regulation. PRAs are no longer getting their market insights and explanations from firms like BP and Shell, which are instead just providing hard, factual information electronically. The background information about the market – its fundamentals, direction and developments – is coming instead from firms in non-EU jurisdictions like Switzerland and Dubai.

There is a certain degree of irony in the fact that the drive to greater regulation in Europe has ensured that a European PRA that is not wholly using screen-based methodologies is now more reliant than before on information from less regulated entities.

Mind the gap

Underpinning the Benchmark Regulation, is a conceptual gap between how European officials and PRAs look at benchmarks. This is evident from the assertion in the Benchmark Regulation that "any discretion that can be exercised in providing input data creates an opportunity to manipulate a benchmark. Where the input data is transaction-based data, there is less discretion and therefore the opportunity to manipulate the data is reduced". This spells out that in the eyes of the Commission only one of the 13 PRA methodologies described elsewhere – the volume-weighted average (VWA) – has a reduced susceptibility to manipulation. In reality, the vast majority of PRA commodity benchmarks are based on other methodologies and have proved very successful in capturing activity in the commodity markets. There are legitimate drawbacks to the VWA methodology and it is not suitable for low volume, opaque markets, for example.

MIFID II, EMIR and MAR

The Benchmarks Regulation is the main piece of European law that affects PRAs. For the commodity markets, however, the most important new regulations are the Markets in Financial Instruments Directive, known as MIFID II, and the European Market Infrastructure Regulation on Derivatives, Central Counterparties and Trade Repositories (EMIR).

MIFID II is a package of rules set to take effect across the EU in January 2018 and which grew out of the principles for financial regulation that were agreed in 2009 by the Group of 20 nations (G20) in order to reduce the risk of another global financial crisis. MIFID II expanded the G20 principles in scope significantly. Addressing the concern to the commodity sector, the European legislation introduced new position limits on commodity derivatives trading, among other changes.

EMIR imposes requirements to improve transparency and reduce the risks associated with the derivatives market. Under the terms of EMIR, certain users of derivatives must report their activity to a trade repository, which then passes it to a competent national authority that analyses it for evidence of systemic risk. Larger users are also required to make use of clearing facilities in order to mitigate their risks.

The costs for European commodity market participants of compliance with these new pieces of legislation are enormous, with MIFID II drawing particular ire. The chief executive of ICE, Jeff Sprecher, has described MIFID II as "a terrible piece of legislation that imposes tremendous costs on the industry".

The EU agreed in 2016 to delay the implementation of MIFID II by one year to 2018 amid industry concerns over the complexity of the legislation. UK financial regulators have said they still plan to implement MIFID II despite the country's decision to exit the EU.

The other piece of recent European legislation that affects the commodity markets is the Market Abuse Regulation (MAR). Of all the recent European market-related directives, the MAR is perhaps the one that has come in most under the radar. Laws to prevent market abuse are nothing new and the MAR has not really changed much in terms of its definition of abuse. The new rules do, however, contain some significant changes. The biggest change is that national regulators, such as the UK Financial Conduct Authority (FCA) will for the first time have oversight of the physical markets which underpin derivatives.

National regulators have never previously paid much attention to the physical markets that underpin the derivatives that they regulate. But for the first time, assuming that MAR is fully implemented in the UK, the FCA will be responsible for overseeing the Platts-based physical Brent market, rather than just the Brent futures market listed on ICE.

This opens up some interesting questions. Does a UK regulator have jurisdiction over physical benchmarks based in the UK or over all physical benchmarks that underpin derivatives that are cleared in the UK? If the latter, how would the FCA investigate international markets like those in Dubai or Singapore, where the derivatives are cleared in a London-based clearing house? The FCA does not currently have the staff or the technical knowledge to investigate accusations of malpractice in physical markets around the world.

Conclusion

The full impact of the European regulatory onslaught has yet to be felt in the commodity markets. The Benchmarks Regulation and MIFID are not due to come into effect until 2018. But already the prospect of these directives is changing market behaviour. The European Benchmark Regulation will likely have the effect of promoting screen-based price discovery and a greater reliance on volume-weighted averages rather than panels and surveys as a methodological approach.

The new regulations are also likely to usher in, at least in Europe, a new era of arms-length dealings between PRAs and the markets that they cover. With compliance issues to the forefront, much of the market colour – Peter Stewart's "vertical transparency" – could disappear or be sharply curtailed. This would be a shame. Being challenged by traders and getting the direct views of market practitioners keeps price reporters on their game and ultimately leads to better price assessments. A price discovery mechanism that involves fewer interactions and a reduced number of participants risks being more open to abuse and manipulation that the current systems that have been tried and tested over many decades.

Notes

1   www.handbook.fca.org.uk/handbook/MAR/8/
2   Peter Stewart (2013) Hard Truths about Market Transparency, Oxford Energy Forum, Issue 94, 4.

16 Academic research into PRAs

Introduction

Academic coverage of the price reporting agencies (PRAs) and the benchmarks that they provide has been limited, with a few honourable exceptions. This relative lack of academic attention is a surprise when one considers how embedded the PRAs are within modern commodity trading and risk management systems.

The majority of research in the sector has been devoted to the price of commodities rather than their pricing. Substantial work has been done on the factors that influence commodity prices and the impact of fluctuating commodity prices on consumer and producer economies. This is obviously the area of greatest public concern as the outright price of commodities affects every consumer and dramatic moves in commodity prices have the ability to reshape entire societies.

Nonetheless, the way in which commodities are priced deserves greater study. In most studies of commodities, academics have taken exchange-listed futures prices as a proxy for the entire commodity suite and have based their research accordingly, rather than looking at the benchmarks provided by PRAs or at the methodologies underpinning those assessments.

This greater focus on exchange data is likely to be partly a consequence of the dominance of future benchmarks in some commodity classes, particularly in agriculture. But it is also likely due to the greater ease of accessing futures data compared with PRA data. PRAs tend to be very jealous guardians of their data sets, which are after all their commercial life blood, and so are less inclined than futures exchanges to make their data freely available to academic researchers. Given the cost of PRA subscriptions, few academics have the budget to subscribe to PRA data feeds or to pay for historical downloads. This is a shame, given that substantially more price data on global commodities is generated by PRAs than by any other source.

Research interest in PRAs is nonetheless growing, particularly since the LIBOR scandal helped to ensure greater awareness of the power of benchmarks. A growing number of academic papers have been published in recent years that address PRAs, although most still tend to look at the relationship between PRA benchmarks and the futures markets, rather than concentrating on PRA benchmarks themselves and the methodologies that underpin them.

Role of the OIES

Given the much greater importance of PRAs to the energy sector than to agriculture and metals, it is not surprising that most of the academic work on PRAs has come from researchers with a focus on energy.

Much of the research work on oil pricing builds on research done in the 1970s–1990s by Robert Mabro (1934–2016) who became fascinated by energy after researching the economies of the Middle East at Oxford University in the early 1970s. Mabro was involved in many of the first studies on energy prices. He published the first guide to the Brent market – *The Market for North Sea Crude Oil* – in 1986 in collaboration with Robert Bacon, Margaret Chadwick, Mark Halliwell and David Long, and in 1993 he and Paul Horsnell published perhaps the first in-depth study of price discovery in the oil markets: *Oil Markets and Prices, The Brent Market and the Formation of World Oil Prices.*

Mabro founded the Oxford Institute for Energy Studies (OIES) in 1982, which has gone on to become an important focal point for the discussion of pricing issues. Many of the most significant contributions on benchmarks and pricing have been published by the OIES, either as monographs and papers, as part of its Energy Comments series, or as part of the quarterly *Oxford Energy Forum* publication. David Long and Margaret Chadwick, who are closely associated with the Institute, went on to found Oxford Petroleum Research Associates and have published a number of important contributions to the discussion of pricing issues.

OIES' current director Bassam Fattouh is currently one of the pre-eminent academics working on energy pricing issues and his 2011 study, *An Anatomy of the Crude Pricing System*, remains the most cited academic paper on how PRAs assess the crude oil markets. OIES has published a series of notable papers on PRA benchmarks, dedicating the February 2012 and November 2013 editions of the *Oxford Energy Forum* to issues surrounding oil benchmarks.

PRAs and Brent futures

A recurring theme in OIES studies has been the relationship between PRA assessments of the physical North Sea market and the Brent crude oil futures market. Key contributions have come from Elizabeth (Liz) Bossley, who is a leading consultant with Consilience Energy Advisory Group (CEAG) and specializes in the Brent market. Christophe Barret, then of Credit Agricole and currently with Total, also published an important paper in March 2012 ("Brent Prices: Impact of PRA Methodology on Price Formation") in the Oxford Energy Comment looking at how changes in PRA methodologies in the Brent market have succeeded in keeping Brent futures anchored into the physical market.

The link between Platts' assessment of Dated Brent and the Brent futures market was further explored in September 2016 by four academics – Alex Frino, Gbenga Ibikunle, Vito Mollica and Tom Steffen – who produced a report sponsored by the Capital Markets Cooperative Research Centre (CMCRC) entitled "Do Unregulated Spot Oil Benchmarks Drive Directional Trading in Brent Futures?" The report found that physical oil market participants who were watching the Platts' window assessment process for Dated Brent had a significant informational advantage over other traders in Brent futures who were unaware of the activity on Platts. The physical traders were able to realize significant gains as a result.

US research

The central role played by the OIES in acting as a central hub for pricing research has ensured that the UK has tended to lead the way in terms of the academic study of pricing issues and PRAs. There has been significantly less research published into PRAs in the United States so far, which is surprising given that many of the largest and best established PRAs are American in origin.

Columbia University's Center on Global Energy Policy is the primary institution driving energy research in the United States, but to date it has focused most of its attention on geopolitical issues rather than pricing debates.

Perhaps the best known US authority on pricing issues is Vincent Kaminski of Rice University in Houston, who has authored books on the US power market, on energy derivatives and on managing energy price risk. Kaminski has a very strong background as a practitioner: he was head of quantitative modelling at Enron and also worked for Citigroup, Sempra, Reliant Energy and Citadel. The fourth edition of *Managing Energy Price Risk*, which is edited by Kaminski, includes a chapter on PRAs written by Dan Massey of Argus.

Price discovery

There has been a relatively large body of academic work relating to the nature and theory of price discovery, although virtually all of it relates to the stock markets and in particular how price discovery functions when securities are listed on multiple stock exchanges.

Wai-Man Liu, Emma Schultz and John Swieringa looked into the issue of the primary location for price discovery in the crude oil markets in their 2014 article for *The Journal of Futures Markets*, which was entitled "Price Dynamics in Global Crude Oil Markets". The Canberra-based academics argued that ICE Brent rather than the over-the-counter market was the primary location for price discovery in the North Sea crude oil markets, but that on days when Brent and WTI are correlated, it is WTI that provides the primary price discovery function.

Official studies

Much of the most useful research carried out into the PRAs has been undertaken by various official bodies and regulatory organizations rather than by professional academics. The IOSCO studies and papers that have been cited throughout this book are perhaps the most thorough review of how PRAs operate in the energy markets and their methodologies.

The International Energy Agency and the UK's Financial Conduct Authority, previously the Financial Services Authority, have also separately touched upon pricing issues in their position papers, as has the research arm of the Organization of Petroleum Exporting Countries (OPEC).

Ratings agencies

Academic researchers have paid significantly more attention to the PRAs' cousins, the ratings agencies. Ratings agencies gather financial and economic data, which they then analyse in order to provide independent assessments of the credit-worthiness of securities and the entities that issue them. This provides investors with a convenient way of judging the credit quality of various different investment opportunities.

Just as in the PRA space, there are a handful of large global ratings agencies – Standard & Poor's (S&P), Moody's and Fitch – and a large number of smaller niche or regional players. S&P is actually a sister company to Platts as both are part of the McGraw-Hill stable, with Platts now formally known as S&P Global Platts.

Credit ratings agencies have many similarities with the PRAs but also some important differences. They developed in a similar way to PRAs, first emerging in their modern form in the United States in the twentieth century before coming to global prominence from the 1970s onwards. Ratings agencies also apply a methodology to the data they gather in order to provide a final assessment that then may or may not be used as a benchmark. So far this all sounds very familiar to those familiar with PRAs.

The business model of ratings agencies and PRAs contains, however, a very notable difference: ratings agencies are paid directly by the issuers of the security for providing their ratings, although they also derive substantial revenue from selling subscription access to all of their ratings. The ratings agencies strongly deny that this compensation model compromises their independence on the grounds that analysts' compensation is not linked to the payments made by issuers.

Academic research into ratings agencies have tended to focus on the method-ologies that they employ, why their assessments might differ and the accuracy of their results. Since the financial crisis, this work has taken on greater urgency. Much of this work has a limited relevance to the PRAs, although the theoretical approaches may be useful. PRAs do not have the same compensation structure and it is also impossible to back test PRA assessments in the same way. Researchers into ratings agencies can check their assessments of financial health against actual default rates. In contrast, it is impossible to check whether a PRA's spot gasoline or iron ore benchmark was actually correct or not as there is no definitive event that can prove or disprove the assessment.

Conclusion

Academics would find fertile ground for study in the PRAs whose assessments are equally as important to modern economic life as those of the ratings agencies. The relationship between PRA assessments and the futures markets is beginning to attract more interest and much good work has already been done. The next step is for greater research into the PRA assessments themselves and the design of benchmarks.

The impact of different methodological approaches on assessments by different PRAs; the impact of the move towards more automated price discovery processes such as the Platts' eWindow and volume-weighted averages; and comparisons of the snapshot approach of the market-on-close compared with all-day assessments would all be worthy of greater study.

The general lack of interest in the PRAs from an academic standpoint partly reflects the generally low profile that PRAs maintain as well as the difficulty of accessing their data. But there may also be a perception of 'guilt by association'. The generally poor reputation of commodity producers and traders among the general public, which assume that firms are profiting unreasonably from basic human needs, may be reflected unconsciously in the academic community. Senior academics report that research students are queuing up to work on projects related to renewable energy but few show interest in fossil fuels, for example. With hydrocarbons still the core strength of PRAs, it may be that younger researchers will only start to show greater interest once the PRAs develop significant benchmarks in bio-energy and renewables.

17 Conclusion

The future of PRAs

Introduction

In many senses, price reporting agencies (PRAs) have come a long way since the creation of the first modern PRAs over a century ago. A few are now billion-dollar businesses, while some PRAs increasingly resemble financial services firms more than they do the traditional news media. Once a western phenomenon, there are also PRAs all over the world operating in multiple languages and covering commodity markets that did not even exist a couple of decades ago.

In another sense, though, the industry has been remarkably stable. PRAs have followed more or less the same business model since their creation – generate news and pricing from interactions with market participants and then sell this aggregated information back to the industry in the form of an annual subscription.

There has been plenty of innovation along the way, particularly with the Platts-led move to market on close and screen-based pricing, but Warren Platt would broadly still recognize the company he founded in 1909 and their current competitors in the benchmark industry. It remains to be seen how transformative the next few decades will be. New pricing providers are challenging the ways that the traditional PRAs do business, either in terms of methodologies, accessibility or subscription price. Technology and direct regulation also represent two potential game changers for the status quo, while the recent moves towards greater consolidation in the sector are likely to continue.

PRAs in 2050

Will there still be PRAs in 2050? It would be foolish to bet against it. Many PRAs have already lasted for decades, while some have been around for centuries. But what will the PRA of 2050 look like? Borrowing a crystal ball, there are a few observations that we could make.

First, it seems likely that more and more price discovery will take place on a screen. Assuming that regulation is not wound back dramatically, the greater transparency and the easier auditing of a screen-based methodology will likely come to displace assessments by traditional price reporters, especially as phone calls, emails and face-to-face meetings with traders become increasingly discouraged by commodity firms' compliance departments.

Although PRAs will still be active in 2050, by then the actual price reporter may be an endangered species. When the activity on a screen spits out an index price, either as the last price traded or as a volume-weighted average, the price reporter's role is largely reduced to watching the activity and ensuring that there are no errors or compliance issues in the assessment process.

Algorithms are likely to get smarter and to be able to make assessments with increasingly little human intervention. There will therefore be fewer price reporters and the ones that still exist will likely be focused on the more opaque and niche markets. In more liquid markets, price reporters will give way to technical staff whose primary role will be to ensure the smooth running of the price-discovery platform and the algorithms that generate the final price assessments. These employees will be watching multiple markets and will not necessarily have ever met a trader in their lives.

If we assume that screen activity will generate more and more benchmarks, then by 2050 it seems a fair assumption that most PRA staff will no longer be situated in the major capitals. PRA management will be reluctant to pay for expensive office space in central London, Singapore or Houston when most of their, by now much smaller, staff have zero customer contact. PRAs will always need experienced staff that can go out and meet customers, answer their questions and promote their indexes, but these will be a limited number of experienced business development staff. These employees will still be located in small offices near their customers. The rest of the support staff will have moved out to cheaper locations.

Unlike today when many PRA business development staff are experienced former reporters or editors, this career path will be likely closed off with the disappearance of traditional price reporters. The business development teams of 2050 will instead be recruited directly from the commodity industry – former brokers or traders.

With costs so dramatically reduced – much fewer staff, cheaper office space, better use of technology – profit margins are likely to remain intact for most PRAs, even though they will likely have come under pressure from the industry to limit their annual hikes in subscription revenues. Income may have been reduced but overall profit margins are likely to be similar or better due to the increased efficiency of their operations.

Corporate activity

The 'Big Three' of Platts, Argus and ICIS could become a 'Big Four' in the future if IHS Markit were to combine all of its disparate pricing assets – CMAI, OPIS, McCloskey Coal and PRIMA Markets – into a single global benchmark business, potentially under a single brand name and leveraging the technological strength of the broader IHS Markit business.

It is hard to imagine that more than 100 benchmark providers will still be active in 2050. Consolidation has already been a feature of recent years and this is likely to continue, particularly as regulatory pressures are only likely to increase for PRAs. The higher cost of compliance with multiple regulatory regimes around the world is likely to drive PRAs to merge in search of economies of scale. The period from

2020 onwards will also likely see the retirement of many of the founders of smaller PRAs that established their businesses in the 1980s and 1990s.

The energy sector is already mature in terms of PRA benchmarks and it is hard to see much more consolidation there, given how concentrated the ownership of benchmarks already is. But other parts of the business are ripe for more consolidation – the fertilizers, petrochemical and Chinese metals sectors are all home to a large number of relatively small players that could merge or be taken over.

If we can imagine that there might only be a reduced number of global PRAs left in business by 2050, it seems likely that at least one of them will be headquartered in Asia. The continued growth of commodity consumption in the east and its relative decline in the west is likely to push at least one Asian PRA into the global major league. If the Chinese government could support the development of domestic non-futures benchmarks and avoid the temptation to intervene whenever officials dislike the direction of prices, then there would be a high probability that one of the leading services will be of Chinese origin. A Chinese acquisition of a major western pricing service would send a very interesting message to the global commodity markets.

By 2050, it is also not outlandish to imagine more mergers between exchanges and PRAs. SGX has already paved the way with its 2016 acquisition of the Baltic Exchange and that is unlikely to be the last deal as exchanges look to lock down more exclusive intellectual property. Or perhaps a PRA will move upstream by acquiring an exchange or at the very least opening up a fully regulated trading venue. The Chinese metals PRAs have already pioneered moves in this direction.

Speeding up

Another change over the next couple of decades may be in the frequency of assessment. The typical model has been for PRAs to provide assessments of prices once a day or, in less active markets, once a week or once a month. In the future, it is possible, however, that PRAs will generate real-time price assessments of the markets they cover. After all, traders buy and sell commodities throughout the day.

Sweden's Marine Bunker Exchange (MABUX) has already moved in this direction. MABUX calculates its assessments of marine bunker fuel in real time by using a non-linear formula that adjusts the port prices that it has observed most recently to take into account minute-by-minute changes in related energy futures contracts such as ICE Brent or CME WTI.[1] The MABUX initiative still relies on infrequently assessed port prices to generate part of its live indexes so it has not yet achieved genuine live pricing but it represents a step in this direction.

The concept of live price engines that update dynamically as bids, offers and trades are heard in the market or inputted onto a screen is still a work in progress. The difficulty will lie in persuading traders that so much transparency is in their interests as well as encouraging them to report market information to PRAs more frequently than once a day or less. This is a challenge when so many are already reluctant to engage with existing price-formation processes.

Technology developments

The development of live pricing engines or algorithms that generate benchmarks without significant human intervention will require greater investment in technology than the PRAs have made to date. Platts has access to world-class technology through its partnership with ICE but its own capabilities are as a result limited. Argus, Metal Bulletin and some of the Chinese metals PRAs have made some investments in developing their own technology but it is fair to say that none of the PRAs has truly explored the full potential of applying advanced technology to their businesses.

Data analytics has been a focus of the large western PRAs in recent years and has led to a number of acquisitions. But most PRAs are still playing catch up to services like Bloomberg and Thomson Reuters and many consumers of PRA data take it through some form of data management system such as the wire services or specialist vendors rather than direct from the PRA itself. The firm in the pricing sector with the deepest expertise in data analytics and delivery systems is IHS Markit but the giant firm has yet to really leverage the complementary nature of the PRAs it owns, let alone apply its advanced technology to enhance their offerings.

Revenue trends

The cost of subscriptions to the data services of the largest PRAs has tended to rise at above the rate of inflation in recent years, despite the relatively tough trading conditions that many commodity market participants have experienced since the financial crisis. Traders have always moaned about the cost of PRA subscriptions but complaints have been more vocal in recent years. It still remains to be seen, though, at what point rising PRA subscription costs will become a determinant in benchmark usage. To date costs have not been relevant.

Some pricing providers already see dissatisfaction with rising subscription costs as an opportunity to challenge traditional market incumbents. Bunkerspot, which provides price assessments for ship fuels around the world, specifically markets itself as a "cost-effective" alternative to other data providers, while Indian plastics service PolymerMIS promotes itself as the "economical" alternative to what its marketing material terms "extremely expensive USA-based company" and "very expensive UK-based company".

Competition on cost grounds has generally not proved very successful in the world of benchmarks, where reputation and acceptability tend to count for more, given the scale of traders' exposure to the benchmarks relative to their subscription fees. But for customers that primarily take a PRA subscription for informational purposes rather than for benchmark usage, then cheaper solutions are likely to be more appealing. The OPEC Secretariat switched its oil market subscriptions from Platts to Argus in January 2016 on cost grounds, for example.

The most likely impact of subscription fee inflation is that it acts as a deterrent for market participants to adopt PRA pricing in new areas. This impact has already been felt to some extent in the agricultural sector, which is less accustomed to the PRA model, and where some firms have pushed back against fee increases by PRAs that have established a position in agricultural markets. Firms are less likely to embrace indexation if they sense that they are thereby committing themselves to significant subscription spends forever.

The next few decades are likely to see a further divergence in PRA charging policies. Some PRAs will continue to raise subscription rates every year until they are close to the levels that the major energy consultants charge for their more limited-circulation reports. These high rates will open the door for cheaper pricing providers to emerge and to find a niche that is still profitable among the more cost-sensitive customers. Whether cheaper services will be able to attract benchmark usage is more doubtful but economic theory tells us that outsized profit margins rarely persist indefinitely and so some rebalancing can be expected. The larger PRAs may, however, be able to leverage technology to reduce their costs, enabling them to either maintain their margins or compete more aggressively on subscription rates with their smaller rivals. Increased consolidation in the sector is also likely to help keep subscription prices relatively firm.

Regulatory changes

There is little chance that recent moves towards increased scrutiny of PRAs will be rolled back in the near term. Indeed, it would likely only take one well-publicized scandal related to a major PRA benchmark for further direct regulation to be imposed.

The United States has until now focused on punishing attempts to manipulate benchmarks after the fact, while the European model retains the punitive aspect but also aims to create an environment that deters manipulation before it happens. At some point it seems likely that their two approaches will become more closely aligned, likely with the United States potentially moving more towards the European model.

Another big question is how other regulators outside Europe and the United States will approach benchmarks over the coming years. The IOSCO Principles established a broad consensus on best practices for how PRAs should operate, but a global agreement on benchmark management was beyond the IOSCO Committee's remit.

Without some form of global agreement, or at least a global consensus, there is a concern that companies operating in some jurisdictions will be disadvantaged. This regulatory arbitrage could lead firms to move their pricing activities offshore, weakening the oversight that new rules were supposed to strengthen. Pricing centres such as Singapore, which has experienced a number of commodity trading scandals, will need to apply the same rules as Europe and the United States if global oversight is to function smoothly.

PRA benchmarks do not necessarily need more regulation; they need better and smarter regulation. PRAs are not equipped to carry out a regulatory role themselves. Apart from their commercial need to retain their benchmarks and not annoy their key customers, they cannot cross-reference physical positions against offsetting derivative positions because they lack jurisdiction over the exchange-traded markets. PRAs also have no real tools to punish perceived or real misbehaviour beyond potentially banning the firm in question from their price-discovery process (a double-edged sword given that PRAs need information flow) or reporting their suspicions to a regulator who may or may not be equipped to investigate.

If regulators are serious about overseeing commodity benchmarks, then they will need to increase their staffing levels and technical expertise over the next few years. Improved cooperation will also be required. At present, the regulatory entity overseeing a particular benchmark is often different from the one overseeing the related derivatives market and as a result there is virtually no 'joined-up' scrutiny. For example, if there were suspicions that a company was influencing the Platts Dubai crude oil markets in order to make money from a large related derivatives position, this would be very difficult to investigate. Platts' assessments of the Dubai market are produced in Singapore, although Platts is headquartered in London and part of a US corporation. The Singaporean authorities could investigate the price-discovery process. But any Dubai derivatives positions are shared between CME Group, ICE, DME and TOCOM so the Singapore authorities would require the cooperation of four separate regulators to look into the related derivatives positions. It is small wonder that few international investigations have ever taken place into PRA benchmarks.

Compliance within PRAs is also likely to intensify. We could expect more and more PRAs to adopt the oversight systems already used by MySteel and Metal Bulletin, which track all of the calls made by reporters and record whether anyone answers and, if so, how long the discussion lasts. These systems allow editors and management to check that their price reporters are calling a good spread of market participants and provide a highly auditable trail of the source of the information that underpins their assessments.

Conclusion

Price reporting has not traditionally been a glamorous or well understood business, although the high valuations of PRAs in recent years have raised the sector's profile. Price reporting is, however, quietly essential to the smooth operations of markets and by improving transparency price reporters improve market efficiency and price discovery.

When the UN's Food and Agricultural Organization (FAO) was looking for projects to improve the earnings of small farmers in Africa, it turned to a price information service, Esoko (previously TradeNet), which had been founded by Mark Davies. By improving the flow of market information, Esoko is credited with boosting farmers' incomes by around 10–15 per cent. Esoko shows that accurate price information really does make a difference to the efficient operation of markets.

The speed of market development often depends on the presence of independent benchmarks. Independent benchmarks make banks more comfortable about providing finance to buyers and sellers as well as drawing new participants into markets, improving liquidity and contributing to better price discovery and sharper pricing.

One of the reasons that it is hard to imagine PRAs ever disappearing is the speed with which pricing services enter new markets that lack benchmarks. When some of the US states began to decriminalize the use of cannabis from 2012 onwards, a specialist PRA was quick to emerge. Cannabis Benchmarks was founded in 2015 by a group including former Platts employees. The firm produces spot and implied forward assessments of standardized wholesale cannabis products, such as indoor flower and greenhouse flower.

PRAs are likely to continue to play the central role in commodity pricing that they have done in recent years but their business model will inevitably change with time. They will derive more revenue from non-core activities like data management as they continue to diversify. PRAs will also make greater use of technology in the price-discovery process and we could see the development of live pricing engines that generate up-to-the-minute assessments. Corporate activity is likely to be intense: PRAs will merge and be taken over, but new PRAs will inevitably emerge, especially in new markets. Seven new PRAs were founded between 2013 and 2016 alone.

Amid all the potential changes that the next few years will bring, the challenge for PRAs is not to lose sight of their core function: reporting commodity benchmarks. We started with a definition of PRAs as "firms that assess the fair price of commodities and report these values to a wider audience that then uses those assessments of price either for information purposes or else as the basis for physical or financial transactions". Amid their quest for diversification and for corporate activity, PRA managements need to remain focused on establishing and protecting benchmarks, which is what differentiates their businesses from other media and analytics firms.

Note

1   Chris Thorpe, Price Point, Bunkerspot Magazine, October/November 2016.

18 Further reading

Overview

Relatively little has been written to date that deals directly with the background, methodologies and role of price reporting agencies (PRAs).

Coverage of PRAs has tended to come in the context of trading manuals or in general discussions of energy prices. As we have seen, PRAs have also been the subject of relatively little academic research, at least compared with their cousins, the rating agencies.

The most comprehensive discussion of PRAs in recent years has in fact been the research carried out by various regulatory authorities, among which the work of IOSCO stands out, and in the various submissions made to regulatory bodies by the PRAs themselves and by other stakeholders such as energy companies, consultants and exchanges.

The Oxford Institute for Energy Studies (OIES) also regularly covers issues around energy pricing and benchmarks in its quarterly *Oxford Energy Forum* publication, which is edited by Bassam Fattouh and Peter Stewart. Another interesting source is the Oil Voice website, which has hosted articles on PRA benchmarks authored by Consilience Energy Advisory Group Ltd (CEAG).

The business press, such as *The Economist, Financial Times* and *Wall Street Journal,* have also all covered the various regulatory initiatives relating to PRAs in depth as well as running news stories about their corporate activity such as the various acquisitions and buyouts seen in recent years.

IOSCO reports

The following represent the key documents issued either singly by the International Organization of Securities Commissions (IOSCO) or by IOSCO in partnership with the International Energy Forum (IEF), International Energy Agency (IEA) and the Organization of the Petroleum Exporting Countries (OPEC). All of these documents are freely available online at www.iosco.org, which also hosts the various responses submitted by relevant stakeholders.

- Bossley, E. and Gault, J. (2011) Oil Price Reporting Agencies, Report by IEA, IEF, OPEC and IOSCO to G20 Finance Ministers.

- Technical Committee of IOSCO (2012) Functioning and Oversight of Oil Price Reporting Agencies – Consultation Report.
- The Board of IOSCO (2012) Principles for Oil Price Reporting Agencies – Final Report.
- The Board of IOSCO (2014) Implementation of the Principles for Oil Price Reporting Agencies – Report.
- The Board of IOSCO (2015) Implementation of the Principles for Oil Price Reporting Agencies – Report

Further reading on the commodity markets

The following do not necessarily deal directly with PRAs but are an excellent source of background and of further reading for those interested in exploring the commodity markets in which PRAs play such a crucial role.

- Bain, C. (2013) *The Economist Guide to Commodities – Producers, Players and Prices, Markets, Consumers and Trends*, London: Profile Books
- Bossley, E. (2013) *Trading Crude Oil: The Consilience Guide*, London: Consilience Energy Advisory Group Ltd.
- Bossley, E. (2013) *Trading Refined Oil Products: The Consilience Guide*, Consilience Energy Advisory Group Ltd.
- Chevallier, J. and Ielpo, F. (2013) *The Economics of Commodity Markets*, Hoboken, NJ: Wiley Finance.
- Clewlow, L. and Strickland, C. (2000) *Energy Derivatives: Pricing and Risk Management*, London: Lacima Publications.
- Horsnell, P. and Mabro, R. (1993) *Oil Markets and Prices, The Brent Market and the Formation of World Oil Prices*, Oxford: Oxford University Press.
- Kaminski, V. (2012) *Energy Markets*, London: Risk Books.
- Kaminski, V. (2016) *Managing Energy Price Risk*, 4th edn, London: Incisive Media.
- Labuszewski, J., Nyhoff, J., Co. R. and Peterson, P. (2010) *The CME Group Risk Management Handbook: Products and Applications*, Hoboken, NJ: John Wiley & Sons.
- Roncoroni, A., Fusai, G. and Cummins M. eds. (2015) *Handbook of Multi-Commodity Markets and Products: Structuring, Trading and Risk Management*, Chichester: John Wiley & Sons.
- Schofield, N. (2007) *Commodity Derivatives: Markets and Applications*, Hoboken, NJ: John Wiley & Sons.
- Simkins, B. and Simkins, R. eds. (2013) *Energy Finance and Economics: Analysis and Valuation, Risk Management, and the Future of Energy*, Hoboken, NJ: John Wiley & Sons.
- Swindle, G. (2014) *Valuation and Risk Management in Energy Markets*, New York: Cambridge University Press.
- Tamvakis, M. (2015) *Commodity Trade and Finance*, 2nd edn, London: Informa Law from Routledge.
- Valiante, D. and Egenhofer, C. eds. (2013) *Price Formation in Commodities Markets: Financialisation and Beyond*, Brussels: Centre for European Policy Studies (CEPS).

Lighter reading on the commodity markets

The following are highly recommended for any reader looking to get more of a flavour of the commodity markets and their pricing, the development of commodity exchanges, and insights into the culture and development of commodity trading. The following is a brief personal selection chosen not just for their insights but also because they are highly entertaining.

- Ammann, D. (2011) *The King of Oil: The Secret Lives of Marc Rich*, New York: St Martin's Press. The stranger-than-fiction tale of how Marc Rich virtually invented modern oil trading.
- Bower, T. (2009) *The Squeeze: Oil, Money and Greed in the 21st Century*, London: HarperPress. A compelling romp through the oil industry in the first decade of the new century, featuring a chapter on the introduction of market-on-close.
- Liss, D. (2003) *The Coffee Trader*, London: Random House. Excellent novel set in 1659 among the traders of the first European commodities exchange in Amsterdam.
- McGrath Goodman, L. (2011) *The Asylum: The Renegades who Hijacked the World's Oil Market*, London: William Morrow. Fun tales of how the NYMEX developed into the world's leading oil exchange, often despite itself.
- Morgan, D. (1979) *Merchants of Grain*, New York: Viking Press. The classic account of the development of the modern agricultural markets and the trading houses that dominate them.
- Newman, K. (2013) *The Secret Financial Life of Food: From Commodities Markets to Supermarkets*, New York: Columbia University Press. Very readable guide to the development of individual agricultural commodities and their related derivatives.
- Rubino, A. (2009) *Queen of the Oil Club: The Intrepid Wanda Jablonski and the Power of Information*, Boston, MA: Beacon Press. Biography of one of the great energy reporters who founded news and analytics service *Petroleum Intelligence Weekly*.
- Yergin, D. (2009) *The Prize: The Epic Quest for Oil, Money and Power*, London: Simon & Schuster. A masterpiece that is the undisputed classic account of the development of the modern energy industry.
- Yergin, D. (2011) *The Quest: Energy, Security, and the Remaking of the Modern World*, London: Penguin. The forward-looking follow up to *The Prize*.

Index